LNWR CARRIAGES

A CONCISE HISTORY

DAVID JENKINSON

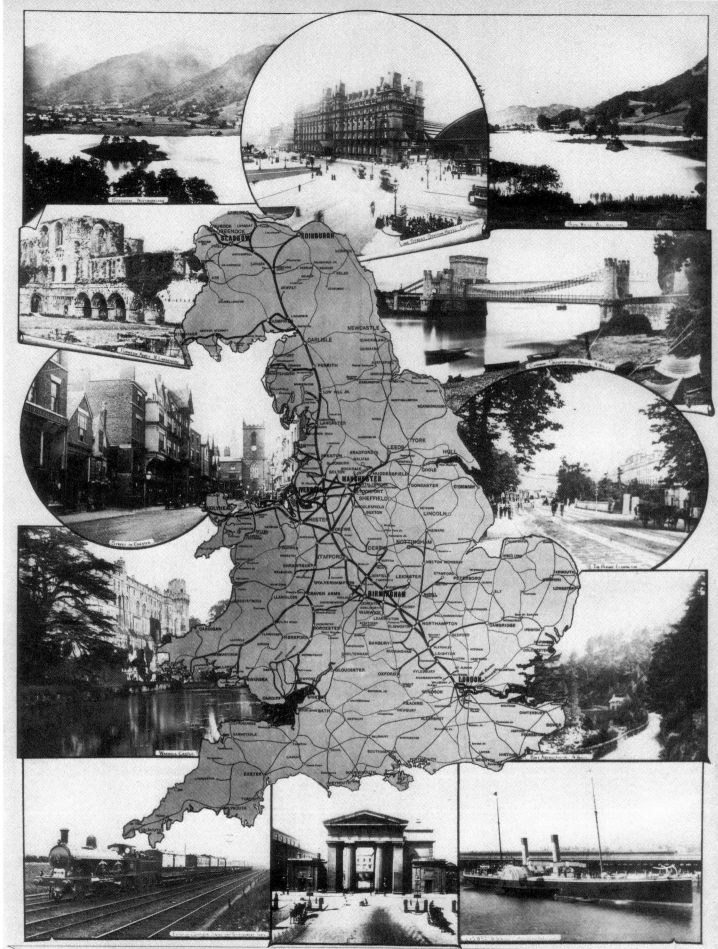

LONDON & NORTH WESTERN RAILWAY.

The LNWR system, 1895, from an official LNWR Poster.

LNWR CARRIAGES

A CONCISE HISTORY

(including West Coast Joint Stock)

DAVID JENKINSON

PENDRAGON

*This book is dedicated to the memory of the Premier Line
and to the craftsmen of Wolverton Carriage Works, past and present*

This book was first issued by Oxford Publishing Co. in 1978 as 'An Illustrated History of LNWR Coaches'. The present publisher would like to thank OPC for its courtesy in releasing its rights in the title to enable this new version to be published.

This edition © David Jenkinson and The Pendragon Partnership 1995

Published by The Pendragon Partnership, PO Box No. 3, Easingwold, York, YO6 3YS.
All rights reserved.

Jacket Design by Barry C. Lane, Sutton-in-Craven.

Printed by The Amadeus Press Ltd., Huddersfield, West Yorkshire

British Cataloguing-in-Publication Data: a catalogue reference for this book is held by the British Library.

ISBN No. 1 899816 01 1

Note: Unacknowledged pictures in this book are from official negatives, many of which have now been transferred to the National Railway Museum. Other pictures are individually credited and the publisher regrets that copies of photographs and drawings appearing in this book cannot be made available to readers.

Contents

LIST OF FIGURE DRAWINGS AND TABLE REFERENCES

Foreword

It is hard to realise that is some 30 years since I began my researches into the singularly distinctive carriages built at Wolverton for the LNWR and West Coast Joint Stock (WCJS) and almost twenty years since the first draft of this book was completed. At that time, there were many books which made reference to the famous 'white' trains (sic!) built there, but no-one had ever attempted to give some form of systematic treatment to the pre-group products of Wolverton taken as a whole. Therefore, aided and encouraged by several friends, I took upon myself this somewhat impudent task.

Much to my surprise, although a number of detailed studies of some of the more specialised aspects of Wolverton's carriages have appeared during the years which followed, my first effort is still the only published general overview. Since many continue to ask me where they can obtain a copy, while second hand versions of the original seemingly change hands at exorbitant prices(!), I have ventured to risk what is essentially a reprint of my original work.

As with the original edition, it is necessary to repeat, if only for the ultra pedantic, that this book never pretended to be more than a general survey. Space and cost limitations made it impossible to include all which could be said and even in 1978, when petrol was less than 50p per gallon and full length LP records could often be obtained for not much more than £1.00, it was still rather expensive at £9.90. Thus, the only way it can be made available again at a cost (relative to other prices) actually cheaper than the original, is to go for a straight reprint as far as possible. Happily, because the original version was written at some distance from the events portrayed therein and the essential facts have not changed, there has been no need to make any basic changes, save to augment the bibliography and add some amplifying notes by way of tidying up loose ends which reviewers noted in the first version. I would like to thank all those who have helped this process by corresponding with me on the subject.

From the above, it will be clear why I have had to make arbitrary decisions regarding items either to be omitted or dealt with but briefly and can only offer apologies to any whose views diverge from mine in this respect. Essentially, I feel that for most people, the railway carriage is essentially something in which to travel and this is where I have chosen to lay emphasis. Thus, readers should not expect to find an overtly specialised account within these covers, much less a complete record of every single passenger rated vehicle built at Wolverton for that matter. In fact, I have concentrated on carriages built during the last thirty years or so of the pre-group period and in particular on vehicles which survived mostly to the LMS and (in some fair measure) into BR days as well.

However, I believe there to be some logic to this restricted approach. One has, of course, to start somewhere; but it was in 1893 that the first corridor train was built for the West Coast Anglo-Scottish services – a momentous event (corridor trains were rare anywhere in Britain at this time) which marked a very significant watershed in passenger coach development at Wolverton. And I am more than mindful that since I first wrote this account, a number of more specialised sub-themes have been explored elsewhere – see bibliography; to add them to my book would not only increase costs but also seem to be a form of plagiarism. This work is based on my own research into a period which I find particularly fascinating and I alone am responsible for the details contained therein.

Concerning deliberate omissions (caused by considerations of space), I have excluded detailed treatment of most non-passenger coaching stock (NPCS) rather than give short measure to the passenger carrying vehicles. But I have included the passenger brake vans in Chapter 4 and offered a short summary of other NPCS at Chapter 8. I have also excluded self-propelled electric stock which is well written up elsewhere.

The prime sources for this book were the three 1915 diagram books, many official works drawings and the large quantity of official photographs first made available to me by BR(LMR) back in the 1960s. In this context it should be stated that the 1915 books are known to contain a few minor errors, some of which may have crept into the book in spite of my best endeavours – although I have to say that since the book was first published in 1978, no specific examples have been notified to me! However, the 1915 books list only capital stock and since a great number of additional vehicles existed in the duplicate stock list, it should be mentioned that where I state or infer 'sole survivor' (or some such), this should be taken to mean 'in capital stock'. Likewise, where I state 'not known' it is more correctly interpreted as 'not known to me'! Fortunately, this is mostly peripheral information of no great significance.

Having come to the subject partly by way of wanting to make more accurate models, I have tried to bear in mind the interest of modelmakers in these pages. It is to these people that future generations will often turn to discover how our early railways really looked, given that museums can only house a fraction of what was built – assuming it has survived anyway. However, I need to make two small points in this respect. Firstly, space does not permit me to offer full pre-group numbering details, especially prior to 1910, partly because I do not have all the information but also because the random nature of much of the numbering would occupy an uneconomic amount of space were it printed in full. Instead, I have offered an extended (albeit simplified) general note overleaf. Fortunately, the more systematic LMS numbers lend themselves (for the most part) to a form of summary and I have therefore been able to quote most of the LMS series.

Secondly, with regard to carriage dimensions, I have tended to 'round out' some of them, ignoring minor fractions. Many LNWR carriages (especially the six-wheelers) were nominally one inch longer than the exact length quoted but since this was often explained by end beading (assuming it had not either come off or been replaced by a metal patch!), it seems only of pedantic significance. I have actually observed wooden carriages being repaired and it is clear that with the expansion, contraction, warping, rotting and shrinking with which regularly take place in service, not to mention many layers of paint, that anyone who thinks that a carriage length can be specified down to the last inch is fooling themselves – as also are those who think that a locomotive driving wheel diameter can be quoted to the last quarter inch. The LNWR was not so foolish: even its works drawings are often annotated with dimensions quoted either as 'full' or 'bare' – ie a bit longer or shorter than stated – if such was necessary to make everything fit!

Finally, although this survey is mostly confined to the last 30 years of the LNWR as reflected by the 1915 situation, I have felt it desirable in Chapter 1 to allude briefly to the pre-1890 period by way of background. For this information, I am indebted to the efforts made on my behalf by the late Richard Cole of Tring whose widow sent me his completed notes just after his untimely death. Likewise, my thanks go to Jim Richards and the late Geoffrey Platt for encouraging me in the early days, offering a multiplicity of good advice and supporting material in the process, not to mention persuading me to write it in the first place.

To all who have in any way helped both in the preparation of this work and/or written to me with supplementary information, may I offer my warmest thanks? I hope their encouragement was justified and that the end product is not too unworthy of the subject which provided its inspiration.

DJ
Raskelf, North Yorkshire
May 1995

Explanatory Note – Carriage Diagrams and Carriage Numbering

Note: Carriage numbering principles are given in outline only for more general understanding of the book. In particular, the 1910 LNWR renumbering was modified in 1912 as a result of the abolition of second class. Also, where neat blocks of numbers are quoted (ie LNWR – 1910; LMS – 1933), it should not be assumed that all available numbers were taken up.

To simplify the understanding of the text and pictures in this book, it seems appropriate to place the explanation of carriage diagrams and carriage numbering at the beginning of the work. All other explanatory notes will be found before the Appendices at page 168.

Carriage Diagrams

The basic document relating to railway coaching stock is the Carriage Diagram Book and without this source, it is difficult to obtain an accurate or balanced picture of the situation. The diagram book is used to enable operating staff to work out train loadings, weights, seating accommodation and so forth. It also indicates whether or not a particular vehicle will clear a specific loading gauge or whether the mechanical specification of a coach is appropriate for the service in question – for example, the correct braking system in relation to the locomotive(s) to be used.

The Wolverton diagram books gave the interior plans, seating capacity, tare weight, overall dimensions, method of lighting and braking and the running numbers of all LNWR and WCJS coaching stock. Unlike the MR and LMS diagram books, the Wolverton documents did not give an exterior elevation of the vehicle. For the historian this is a pity but from the company standpoint it was logical enough since outside styling has little or nothing to do with the suitability of the vehicle from the traffic viewpoint.

Several editions of the diagram books were issued as coaching stock developed over the years and although none of them gave precise dates of building for the vehicles contained within, nor were the books themselves dated, it is known that the final editions were issued at about the time of the first world war, probably circa 1915-16. It is these versions which have been used as the basis for the analysis of LNWR/WCJS vehicles contained in this volume. Three books were involved, viz: LNWR (conventional locomotive hauled); LNWR (motor fitted); WCJS (conventional locomotive hauled).

The diagrams themselves were always referred to by the page number on which they appeared. Thus, D14 refers to the diagram which was found on page 14 of the book and in order to understand this page numbering, it is necessary to appreciate the method by which the diagram books were prepared.

Each class of coach (Saloons, Sleeping Cars, corridor coaches etc) was allocated a block of pages in the book, generally with blank pages both within and separating the individual sections in order to provide space for designs emerging after the book was issued. The order of page numbering was to give the largest coaches first, proceeding through to the smallest of any generic type. Since coaches tended to become larger over the years, this generally caused the page numbering within each block to be in reverse order to the date of introduction of the coaches into service. The blank pages, if available and in correct sequence, were used both for new designs and for rebuilds of older coaches which were allocated new diagram numbers. If no blank page was available, the coaches concerned received 'A' or 'B' diagram page numbers (sometimes as far as E, F and G) in order to maintain the general pattern

of a diminishing coach size through the book. Thus, for example, D264A was a coach design larger than D265 and equal in size or smaller than D264.

A summary of the basic diagram page allocations for locomotive hauled stock is given below:

WCJS Page(s)	LNWR Pages(s)	Basic Category
–	1-12	Royal and Special Saloons
1-5	14-22	Sleeping Saloons
9-10	27-48	Dining, Kitchen and Tea Cars
13	52-86	Day, Invalid, Family, Club and Picnic Saloons
14-15	91-122	First Class coaches
18-19	125-7	First Class brakes
22-31	128-201	Composite coaches
41-4	204-51	Composite brakes
49-56	261-305	Third Class coaches
62-71	306-67	Third Class brakes
79-82	370-90	Passenger full brakes
77-8 83-103	391-429	Postal, Parcels and Newspaper vans
106-8	430-68	Other non-passenger carrying coaching stock

Within the ordinary passenger carrying series, the sequence of diagrams was in the following order: corridor; lavatory non-corridor; suburban. At the time of issue of the final diagram books, all WCJS passenger carrying vehicles were of corridor type. Finally, the reader should assume that, unless otherwise indicated, diagram numbers quoted in the text of this volume refer to LNWR locomotive hauled coaches.

Carriage Numbering

Carriage numbering is not, perhaps, the most exciting subject one can write about but an appreciation of the basic principles can frequently resolve many problems or even aid the discovery of missing vehicles in an otherwise logical sequence. This is especially useful where other evidence is incomplete and the numbering system is as informative as was the final LMS series.

At the time of the grouping, the LNWR was using a somewhat unsophisticated system of carriage numbering which allocated a block of numbers to each class of coach thus:

1-2500	Third Class (all types)
2501-4500	Composite (all types)
4501-4999	First Class (all types)
5000-5500	Saloons (all types, including sleeping and dining cars)
5501-5600	Mostly empty but with a few self-propelled vehicles
5601-5700	First Class brakes (all types)
5701-6400	Composite brakes (all types)
6501-8000	Third Class brakes (all types)
8001-9500	Full brakes
9501-9600	Post Office coaching stock
9601 upwards	Other non-passenger coaching stock

Within each block, numbers were taken up on what appears to have been a 'lowest available vacant number' basis, generally as coaches were placed in service and without regard to precise diagram type. This meant that as coaches were scrapped, their numbers were used again for new vehicles, often of markedly different character. In general it was rare for more than a few consecutive numbers to be allocated to one specific design of coach and for this reason, all LNWR and WCJS diagrams incorporated a full list of running numbers which was kept up to date by those departments which needed to know the information.

The WCJS coaches were numbered in a separate series from the LNWR vehicles, starting again from No. 1; but in the WCJS lists, no attempt was made to rationalise the numbering even on the simple LNWR pattern. Nevertheless, it was much more common for WCJS coaches of any one design to receive a fairly continuous number series than their LNWR contemporaries.

The LNWR system dated from about 1910. Previous to that date, an even more haphazard scheme was in use which adds very little to the understanding of Wolverton coaches. At the 1910 renumbering, some coaches received totally new numbers, others retained their original ones and further vehicles had whole thousands added to their original numbers. If any number series became completely full, the oldest coaches in the series usually had their running numbers 'cyphered' by the addition of an 'O' prefix (occasionally an 'A' suffix) in order to release the original number for a new coach.

When the LMS was formed in 1923 ex-Midland Railway coaches mostly kept their old numbers and the LNWR and WCJS coaches were placed together immediately following them, being renumbered into the following simple series:

4301-6415	Third Class
6461-7984	Third Class brake
7985-9543	Composite
9544-9940	Composite brake
9941-10020	Electric stock
10021-10317	First Class (including brakes)
10321-10686	Saloons (including sleeping and dining vehicles)
10694-10700	Steam railmotors

This list also included ex-North London Railway stock which is not the subject of this book. In fact, the series 6416-60 was wholly given over to ex-NLR second class coaches. Finally, it should be noted that non-passenger coaching stock, including full brakes, was numbered into a separate series ranging between 2000 and (at least) 5384.

The new LMS numbers were allocated in ascending diagram page order and the coaches on any particular diagram were usually renumbered in pre-group number order. This meant that the largest and, therefore, generally the newest of the coaches were given the lowest LMS numbers in any series. Although this system was not particularly refined, it did, at least in most cases, collect all the coaches of any particular type and diagram into one consecutive series. The basic fault was that inadequate provision was made for the numbering of newly built LMS standard coaches. The general principle was to use appropriate gaps in the pre-group lists but this did not work too well since the blocks of numbers selected in 1923 were frequently too small to absorb all the new LMS coaches, even allowing for withdrawals of older stock. In consequence, by the later 1920s, the LMS itself had to resort to the old LNWR principle of cyphering the running numbers of some of the older pre-group coaches by the addition of an 'O' prefix.

In 1932/3, the situation was so confusing that the LMS introduced a completely new and systematic numbering scheme. The principle of a block allocation by generic vehicle type was retained but to a much more refined degree:

1-299	Dining Cars
300-799	Sleeping Cars
800-999	Other saloons (except departmental coaches)
1000-4999	Side corridor coaches
5000-7399	Side corridor brakes
7400-9799	Gangwayed open coaches
9800-9999	Gangwayed open brakes (all third class in fact)
10000-17999	Non-corridor coaches
18000-19999	Non-corridor lavatory coaches
20000-24999	Non-corridor brakes
25000-25999	Non-corridor lavatory brakes
26000-27999	Four and Six wheel passenger carrying coaches
28000-29999	Self propelled passenger carrying stock
30000-30199	Kitchen only cars
30200-30399	Post Office coaches
30400-33499	Passenger full brakes
33500-44999	Other non-passenger coaching stock
45000 upwards	Departmental saloons

Each of the main passenger carrying blocks was further subdivided into first, third and composite categories in that order and within each category, new LMS coaches were numbered *upwards* from the lowest number in the series and the pre-group coaches were renumbered *downwards* by company from the highest number in the series, the oldest pre-group coaches usually receiving the lowest numbers in the respective pre-group company allocations.

This system left a gap in the middle of each category for the new construction of LMS standard types. However, because the lowest numbers in the pre-group part of any series were now carried by the oldest coaches, there was a tendency for the gap in numbers between the LMS and the pre-group types to be maintained as scrapping took place. On some occasions, of course, LMS construction occupied more than the available blank numbers and, in consequence, further renumbering of a few residual older coaches took place to clear complete blocks for the new LMS vehicles. However, this was not a serious or widespread problem.

The second LMS series generally had the effect of reversing the order of LNWR/WCJS coach numbering compared with the 1923 allocations. However, it was not a straightforward block for block renumbering. In 1923, coaches were generally renumbered in pre-group number order but in 1933 opportunity was taken to reorganise them into the order of first building. This was often further refined by putting all coaches of the same length and width into one consecutive series (by age) before proceeding to another dimension. Many of the original LNWR numbers had been in order of first building but because of the Wolverton policy of re-using older numbers, this was not always the case. This fact, together with coach withdrawals and the odd mistakes which inevitably followed such a comprehensive reorganisation, meant that the second LMS number series did not always exactly correlate with the first LMS or the LNWR/WCJS series, even though the number of coaches involved was the same in most cases. However, the second LMS series is the most useful from the analytical point of view since it helps to confirm building dates and immediately draws attention to any anomalous features.

In view of the fact that most coaches carried at least three numbers during their period of life in revenue service, it will not be the general policy to refer to coach running numbers in the text of this volume. However, full numbering data is incorporated in the summary tables at Appendices I–III.

Vintage London and North Western — a typically mixed array of LNWR stock seen at Rugby forming the "Sunny South" special and hauled by a "Prince of Wales" Class 4-6-0.

Chapter 1   Preliminary Survey

Early Days

The London and North Western Railway enjoyed 76 years of independent existence before it became the major constituent company of the LMS at the 1923 grouping; yet this survey of coaching stock is mainly concerned with developments during the last thirty or so of those years with but limited reference to the pre-1890 era. It is true that records of mid-nineteenth century carriages are not very comprehensive, but it is not for this reason that the first forty or more years of LNWR carriages · will receive but short measure in this work. For one thing, Mr·C. Hamilton Ellis in his book *'Railway Carriages in the British Isles from 1830 to 1914'* includes much relevant detail of early LNWR carriages in the broad context of coach development generally. Secondly, the inescapable fact emerges, when examining the situation in more detail, that carriage evolution at Wolverton was laboriously slow during mid-Victorian times; so much so in fact that the vehicles built in the 1880s were, in many cases, little improved in type or style over those which had carried passengers at the middle of the century. However, during its final phase, the LNWR amply compensated for its earlier sluggishness, almost as if it was ashamed of its previous record — and it cannot be denied that by comparison with other lines, especially its arch-rival the Midland Railway, there was more than a little catching up needed as rail travel entered the last decade of the nineteenth century.

Plate 1 A train of very early LNWR four-wheelers behind a Ramsbottom 0-4-2T at Sutton Coldfield.

(Author's Collection)

Plate 2 A miscellaneous assortment of LNWR carriages of the 1870s and 1880s at Crewe.

It is hard to say, with certainty, just why LNWR coaching stock had fallen behind the standards achieved elsewhere. For a railway company of its size and distinction, remarkably little, in readily accessible form, remains on record of its early carriages, so one can only speculate. What does seem fairly clear is that the company management cannot escape some share of responsibility — for this was the era of Richard Moon and F. W. Webb. By all accounts, the carriage department was very much subsidiary to the needs of the shareholder and the incidence of practices which, in our present day, we would make respectable by calling 'cost-effective', was by no means infrequent. Other factors too cannot be ruled out. Hamilton Ellis remarks on the relative lack of imagination of the carriage superintendent, Richard Bore, while Webb himself had a vested interest in such matters as radial underframes and chain brakes as opposed to the more efficient bogies and automatic brakes. The short traverser installed at Euston as late as 1870 is often advanced as a reason for restriction in coach length to 34ft until 1882 — and so it may have been. But one cannot seriously believe that this would have been an insurmountable problem had management really wanted to make major changes and improvements.

Nor, in spite of some published suggestions to the contrary, does the emancipation of the third class passenger by the rival Midland Railway in the 1870s, or the opening of the Midland route to Scotland, appear to have had much effect on coach development at Wolverton. It almost seems as though the LNWR was imbued with a self-satisfied arrogance which would brook no changes. It has even been cynically suggested that Euston probably weighed the cost of carriage improvements against the likely cost of compensation in the case of injury to passengers.

Wolverton records show that the four and six wheel stock built earlier than the 1870s was very diverse, with many variations of dimension and design. Some standardisation must have existed because there were classes of 21ft 6in four wheelers, 26ft full brakes (four and six wheel) and the very numerous 27ft 6in coaches, mostly 7ft 9in wide and 7ft 2in high. But even in these classes there were variations of height, width, wheelbase and so forth, which makes their study very confusing; and their external lines were still very reminiscent of the pioneer railway age.

At the same time, it is only fair to state that the LNWR was probably little different from many other companies during this period. It was not until the 1870s and 1880s that matters began to stagnate, when nothing larger than 34ft long could be built until 1882 and even then, bogie coaches were still another ten years or so away. The Midland, by contrast, had introduced bogie coaches on quite a number of services in the 1870s.

2

Plate 3 An early 30ft first class coach, damaged after an accident and minus its centre pair of wheels. This was an example of the 7ft 9in wide stock and built c. 1887.

(the late R. P. Cole's collection)

From 1874 until 1890, about 1500 coaches and vans 32ft long were built at Wolverton to some 36 different designs. Commonest of these were about 350 five compartment thirds, over 300 composites with a centre luggage compartment, nearly 200 full brakes and some 140 centre luggage thirds. Most compartment coaches were 7ft 9in wide and 7ft 4in high, representing a much higher degree of standardisation than hitherto. All coaches ran on chassis with a 20ft wheelbase and the square cornered window frame with an inner rebate made what was probably its first appearance in these vehicles. Many of these 32ft coaches were without torpedo ventilators when first built but later were given roof ventilation. Some of them may also have been built with individual upper steps outside each compartment — again reminiscent of earlier practice. All coaches had side chains and most were fitted with the chain brake (see page 4). Of the 36 types, the following list indicates some of the more numerous or interesting types:

Design	Dimensions		Date Built	Approx No. left in 1894
	Width	Height		
Sleeping Saloon	8' 00"	7' 8"	1875/1879	2
Family Saloon	"	"	1874/1882	30
Third Picnic Saloon	"	"	1887	6
First Picnic Saloon	"	"	1882	8
Lavatory Compo Brake (3/G+Lu/Lav/1/2)	"	"	1890	20
Lavatory Composite (3/1/Lav/1/2)	8' 0"	7' 4"	1880-1	39
Bow-ended composite (½F/1/2/3/½F)	8' 0"	7' 4"	1876/1879	17
Parcel Sorting (1 door)	"	"	1834	12
Parcel Sorting (2 door)	"	"	1888	18
Post Office	8' 0"	?	?	31
First Class (4 compartment)	7' 9"	7' 4" & 7' 8"	1877/1884	44
Lavatory Composite (3/2/Lu/Lav/1/3)	7' 9"	7' 8"	1890	61
Composite (3/2/1/3)	7' 9"	various	1883/1887	29
Parcels Van	7' 9"	7' 4"	1882/1890	28
Dog Carriage	7' 9"	?	?	6
Second Brake (2/2/2/G+Lu)	7' 6"	7' 4"	1878-9	11
Third Brake (3/3/G+Lu/3)	"	"	1878/1881	75

(some had end compartment for the guard)

Approximately contemporary with these 32ft coaches were some slightly shorter brake vans with somewhat smaller body dimensions. In 1874 a batch of 30ft brakes, twelve in all, had bodies only 6ft 10in wide and 7ft 2in high while their immediate successors to a 30ft 6in length were but two inches taller. There were variations in the number and position of roof skylights and some early vans had the old type squared off tops to the guard's lookout. Clearly, full standardisation had not yet arrived.

Little else calls for comment until the appearance of 33ft and 34ft coaches from 1881 onwards. There was only one type of 33ft coach, a lavatory composite, of which 65 were built between 1882 and 1884. These coaches were 8ft wide and ran on chassis with a 21ft wheelbase. One residual survivor reached the final LNWR diagram book as D168 and survived until 1927.

The 34ft length was somewhat more interesting. It was used for about 90 coaches built between 1881 and 1890 to eight different types. These coaches were the longest six-wheelers built by the LNWR and it is somewhat surprising that although the celebrated Euston traverser was removed by 1882, these 34ft vehicles continued to be built for several years after the much quoted cause of restricted coach lengths was no longer a relevant issue. The 34ft designs are summarised below and, as can be seen, the more numerous designs were merely extensions of the 32ft types. The coaches represent an interesting phase in LNWR history with, perhaps, the twin saloons being the most interesting *(see Plate 4 and 5)*.

Design	Dimensions		Date Built	Approx No. left in 1894
	Width	Height		
Twin Sleepers (Irish Mail)	8' 0"	?	1881	2
Twin Dining Saloons	8' 0"	7' 10"	1882-3	10
Third Picnic Saloon	8' 0"	7' 8"	1881	2
Third (5 compartments plus luggage)	8' 0"	?	?	6
Parcel Sorting coach	8' 0"	7' 8"	1890	10
Composite Brake (3/1/G+Lu/2/3)	7' 9"	7' 4"	1883/1885	17
Third (six compartments)	"	"	1883/1886	22
Third Brake (3/3/G+Lu/3/3)	"	"	1884-5	20

Many of the above mentioned 32, 33 and 34ft six-wheelers made use of Webb's patent radial truck at one end. Two axles were rigid in the normal way while the third axle was fixed to a separate movable frame, controlled by guideblocks and springs, which allowed limited side-play (about 2½in.) either side of the centre line. Subsequent LNWR six-wheelers of the 1890s reverted to conventional chassis construction and became highly standardised on a

Plates 4 & 5 Twin Ladies' and Gentlemen's 34ft clerestory saloons Nos 104, 103 as built in 1882. They were later (1889) converted to dining cars and fitted with bogies – see *Plate 56*. Note the offset gangway in the original condition. The enlarged view shows the Ladies' saloon, 104.

30ft chassis. However, Webb did not confine his radial axle to six-wheel coaches. During the 1880s, increasing use was made of eight-wheel vehicles to a new 42ft length. These coaches had two radial trucks with the centre pair of axles rigid in the frames.

Naturally enough, Webb claimed that these radial underframes were superior to bogies because they prevented rolling. However, they were prone instead to alarming lurches unless, by good fortune, they were negotiating curves whose radius was exactly compatible with the geometry of the underframe at the speed in question. Combined with the extraordinary Clark and Webb chain braking system, these coaches made the LNWR train a somewhat archaic phenomenon, even by the standards of the day.

The Clark and Webb braking system has been well described elsewhere but a word or two here will not be out of place. Essentially, it was a somewhat primitive mechanical arrangement whereby the guard could apply the train brakes, by means of chains and drums, to several vehicles at once. Unfortunately, the necessary physical effort to operate these brakes, coupled with the 'slack' which had to be taken up in the chains, rendered it impossible to control the brakes in more than about five coaches from any one brake van. Thus, a long train had to have several brake vans, whose individual guards had to synchronise their activities to produce an effective stop. Needless to say, the incidence

of chain breakage was high and the system did not show up too well at the Newark brake trials of 1875 even when all conditions were in its favour. Webb, however, remained adamant that the system was satisfactory; but it is not surprising that LNWR engine drivers developed the habit of stopping and starting their trains very gently indeed, thus helping to establish a tradition of non-jerky starting and stopping which has remained, in some measure, to this day.

Within these early coaches, space was often cramped and neither the lighting (usually by oil lamp) nor the upholstery was much more than spartan for the ordinary traveller. Some coaches were fitted with lavatories (usually for first class passengers only) and there were a few attempts made to build more specialised vehicles like sleeping cars and saloons, but to be truthful, little emerged from Wolverton to rival the better products of Derby, Doncaster, Swindon and many other establishments.

In two respects, however, these coaches of the 1880s did have a familiar look. Firstly, they wore the famous two colour livery and secondly, they exhibited, externally, the distinctive form of body panelling which remained characteristic of Wolverton until 1912. Furthermore, the coaches mostly carried a plain radiused roof (or arc roof) which remained the characteristic LNWR profile until after the turn of the century.

(Text continues on page 8)

Plates 6 & 7 Two views of Birmingham New Street, taken in September 1885 with early LNWR coaching stock well represented. Note the extremely well rounded corners of the windows and lower panels of the four-wheelers to the left in the upper view, also the non-continuous upper footsteps located outside the doors only. Judging from the Midland coaches on the right of the upper picture, the much vaunted carriage superiority of the MR at this period in history is not greatly in evidence.

Plates 8-11 The four pictures in this spread show the luxury stock built on 42ft radial chassis in 1884 for prestige services. Above *(Plate 10)* is shown one of four similar sets marshalled:— Brake third, Ladies' Saloon, Gentlemen's Saloon, 2nd/3rd class brake composite. Opposite *(Plate 8 — upper)* is the interior of Gentlemen's Saloon No 126 and *Plate 9 (below)* shows Ladies' Saloon No 122. At a later stage, these saloons were given cove roofs, bogies and other alterations and in this later form can be seen at *Plate 182*, page 138. The final picture *(Plate 11 — below)* shows one of the brakes (unidentified) converted to corridor form at the head of a train of arc roof stock. No diagram appears in the final diagram book for this conversion and the vehicles appear on D352 (see Appendix I) along with the non-converted equivalents.

Plate 12 The basic 42ft radial coach — a seven compartment suburban third class vehicle to D292. This picture of LNWR No 112 shows the coach as built but some of them were later given bogies. A variation of this design (possibly even a conversion) had a luggage compartment in the centre — see also Chapter 5.

It is hard to say exactly when the first tentative moves were made towards improved standards, but they spanned the period 1887-93. In 1887, Richard Bore retired as carriage superintendent and was succeeded by C. A. Park — a much more imaginative designer. Park was clearly not as enamoured of chain brakes and radial underframes as was his predecessor. On the first count, successful replacement of brakes was not too difficult, for Webb had been conducting experiments with the non-automatic vacuum brake since 1881 and in 1887 standardised the automatic vacuum brake for the company. As for the radial under-frames, these continued for a few more years; but one suspects that competition from other railways, together with prompting from Park, eventually caused Webb to change his mind. Furthermore, the autocratic Richard Moon retired in 1891 which removed another barrier to change. Whatever the reasons, radial underframe con-struction ceased at about the same time as the conversion of all coaches to automatic vacuum brake was completed (1892).

It is worth mentioning that this period also coincided with improvements in carriage lighting. Until the 1870s, lighting had been by oil lamps, frequently neither effective in illumination nor safe in use. From the 1870s onwards, oil lights were generally replaced by the Pintsch system of compressed oil gas, carried in cylinders, usually below the carriage. These were not without their incendiary problems either — as witness the accident on the Midland Railway at Haws Junction as late as 1910 — but most companies used them extensively, the LNWR being no exception. However, during the 1880s, experiments were being conducted into electric lighting by many railways, the main problem being to achieve effective generating capability within the train. The LNWR, as was its wont, tended to take a rather jaundiced view of these experiments and did very little work on its own account. It only began to take a real interest when a genuine breakthrough came in the 1890s with the development of the Stone's patent battery system in which a dynamo was driven by pulley and belt off one of the axles of the coach. This, combined with storage batteries, gave a highly efficient illumination system with none of the disadvantages of oil or gas.

Thus, although gaslit coaches continued to be built to some extent well into the twentieth century, the scene was set in the early 1890s for the radical developments which were to commence at Wolverton with the building of the first corridor train in 1893. For the next thirty or so years, improvement was to be as rapid as it had hitherto been slow — and it was to result in some of the finest and most beautiful carriages ever to run in Europe, let alone Britain. By 1923, although there were still some bone-shakers to be seen, the LNWR had little cause to feel ashamed of its coaches by comparison with anyone.

Coaching Stock Revolution 1893-1902

By the 1890s, many of the features which eventually became familiar during the subsequent decade had been established, at least in embryo. Perhaps the most obvious of these was the outward appearance of the carriages.

With but a few exceptions, mainly sleeping and special saloons, coaches exhibited an almost exclusively low-roofed style with the roof profile taking the form of an arc of a circle. Body width was generally 8ft 0in over panelling, although quite a number of 8ft 6in wide coaches were put into service — generally for the West Coast Joint Stock. Most brake compartments had projecting lookouts which increased the width to 9ft (8ft coaches) or 9ft 2in (8ft 6in coaches). However, some later WCJS brakes were built without lookouts. At the start of the period, body lengths had become largely standardised at 28ft for four-wheel coaches, 30ft for six-wheelers and 42ft for eight-wheeled vehicles. This latter dimension dated, of course, from the radial period but by 1893, 42ft coaches were being built on bogie underframes with 8ft wheelbase bogies. In numerical terms, six-wheel coaches were by far the most common.

During the 1890s, bogie coach length gradually increased through a short lived 45ft phase to a standard 50ft coach length, first employed in 1897. This latter dimension became adopted for most bogie coaches, corridor or non-corridor and was widely multiplied. Four- and six-wheel coaches, probably by virtue of their simplicity and cheapness, continued to be built until c.1900 but were confined mainly to suburban types and full brakes.

Exterior body panelling was very characteristically styled in what has become known as the traditional Wolverton pattern. As with most British companies at this time, the exterior body convering was made from wood sheets with the joints between panels covered by raised capping strips (or beading). Whereas most railways made use of small horizontal panels both above and below the windows (eaves and waist panels), the LNWR did not normally use these features, except on outside doors. Thus, there was only one main horizontal waist line beading strip on a Wolverton coach and this was at quite a low level. Coupled with the absence of a continuous eaves panel and accentuated by the two colour livery (page 22), this exterior styling possessed a distinctive appearance. Its essential characteristics can be appreciated by perusing this page. It should, of course, be mentioned that some other railways also adopted this style of panelling — possibly imitating the LNWR.

Coach ventilation was by traditional droplights in the doors (and sometimes in the fixed windows) supplemented by louvred bonnets at the tops of the doors and, usually, above the long windows of gangwayed stock and saloons. Torpedo ventilators of quite imposing size were placed on the roof. Lighting was almost exclusively by oil gas until the late 1890s when electrically lit coaches began to emerge from the works. During later years, many gas lit coaches were converted to electric lighting but some vehicles remained gas lit for their whole lives. Coach heating was on the steam heating principle from the locomotive of the train, but a few early specialised vehicles had their own self-contained heating systems fed from a stove within the coach.

In terms of vehicle types, there was quite a noteworthy change in emphasis during this ten year period. In 1893, the typical best express trains were composed of 42ft non-corridor stock incorporating lavatories. Quite a considerable number of these coaches had been built between 1887 and 1892 and were therefore quite modern. In consequence, many were fitted with replacement bogies, to continue in

Plates 13-15 The paper boy, chocolate seller and Guard at the turn of the century. All three pictures give good details of arc roof stock.

use for many years. However, the first corridor train, utilising 42ft bogie stock, appeared in 1893 and was clearly a harbinger of things to come. A few 45ft corridors were built in the 1895-6 period and after these, corridor coach construction to the new standard 50ft length started in earnest in 1897. These new 50ft coaches supplemented and eventually replaced the bulk of the lavatory non-corridor stock on express trains and, as a result, little need was felt for much further construction of this latter type of vehicle. In consequence, the arc roof lavatory coaches still represented some three quarters of the total LNWR examples of the genre as late as the time of grouping.

The new corridor coaches were, by modern standards, quite small vehicles but, in relation to their size, were moderately heavy. This feature, coupled with Park's newly designed bogies, gave the coaches superlative riding qualities by contemporary standards and their survival rate into LMS days was further testimony to their essential fitness. The fact that their low arc roof gave them somewhat old fashioned appearance should not be allowed to obscure the quite remarkable advance which they represented over all that had gone before. Even the Midland Railway (generally considered by most writers to have had the best coaches of the LMS constituents) produced no better general service stock in the late 1890s than did the LNWR — and was far less lavish in its provision of gangwayed vehicles.

By contrast with the change from lavatory to corridor stock for main line use, LNWR suburban coaches changed but little. Four-, six- and eight-wheeled coaches all continued to be built and, length apart, the 50ft bogie coaches of 1900 were little different from their 1890 predecessors.

Throughout the whole of the arc roof period, LNWR coaches had to make provision for three classes of passenger. First class compartments were quite luxurious and, indeed, in the later WCJS corridor coaches became extremely spacious and elaborate. The compartments varied in size from 7ft to 7ft 6in between partitions and the common standard for first class seating was three per side in non-corridor coaches with two per side in corridor stock. Of course, in non-corridor lavatory coaches, one seat had to be omitted from the layout to give access to the lavatory door — it being no longer deemed proper to screen the door with a seat as had once been the case. Presumably a visible door was preferable to asking a fellow passenger to vacate the seat in order to gain access to the camouflaged lavatory behind.

Second and third class compartments were identically dimensioned but smaller than the firsts — in general about six feet between partitions or a little less. In non-corridor seconds there was often a centre armrest dividing the seat into two twin-seat portions, thus giving four seats per side as opposed to five per side in the third class. Second class seating was softer than third class. In side corridor coaches, both second and third class compartments seated three per side without armrests. When the second class was abolished on the LNWR in 1912, the compartments were generally downgraded to third class, but it is not known whether they were always or necessarily re-upholstered.

Plate 16 Although the locomotive has obviously been 'faked' onto the picture at a later date, this photograph gives a very good impression of the West Coast corridor trains of the 1890s. From the engine backwards, the first eight coaches can be identified as the following diagrams (see Appendix I):— WCJS D71; WCJS D55; LNWR D31A; LNWR D41; WCJS D53; WCJS D68; WCJS D54; WCJS D10.

Plates 17-18 Two views of Riverside station, Liverpool at about the turn of the century. Both pictures feature arc roof corridor stock. In the upper picture can also be seen a pair of 8ft 6in wide clerestory dining cars while in the lower picture can be seen a pair of special saloons — third and fourth vehicles from the camera.

Plates 19 & 20 The classic Wolverton twelve wheelers, both WCJS dining cars. The shorter vehicle (WCJS 483) is one of the pioneer 50ft 6in cars built in 1892 while WCJS 561 is to the more familiar 65ft 6in length and was built in 1897 – WCJS D10 – see also Chapter 3.

Possibly because of the need to provide two and sometimes three classes of accommodation within one coach, the use of half (or coupé) compartments was quite common in the days when carriage dimensions were relatively small. Many LNWR and WCJS vehicles displayed this feature which, understandably, some authorities have referred to as a 'honeymoon' compartment. In the non-corridor lavatory type of coach, the half-compartment was often located at the extreme end of the vehicle and the seats sometimes arranged in such a way that end as well as side windows could be provided.

The arc roof period was also noteworthy for the introduction, on a large scale, of sleeping and dining cars. Although these specialised vehicles had been in use for some years prior to 1893 and, indeed, several sets of new dining cars had actually been built during 1892-3 for the pioneer corridor trains, it was not until the later 1890s that the really characteristic West Coast twelve-wheelers began to come into service in quantity.

These celebrated coaches have become almost legendary and are considered in detail in later chapters. Suffice to say at this point that their styling was totally different from the traditional Wolverton pattern and was based on that which had been introduced on the bulk of the 1892-3 dining cars. The coaches had a genuine row of waist panels with the upper edge heavily accentuated by an additional waist rail. Above this waist rail, the side panels between the windows were of vertically orientated shape with markedly rounded upper corners, which shaping was imitated by the window openings. Above the windows and upper panelling was a deep eaves moulding which was frequently used to carry the legend 'Sleeping Saloon', 'Dining Saloon' etc. In later cars, the descriptive wording was placed in the waist panels.

Entrance to the cars was gained by end vestibules considerably narrower than the 8ft 6in wide main body; and access to these vestibules was by means of outside steps guarded by the most elaborate wrought iron handrails, into whose supports was worked a quite delicate ironwork filigree. The whole coach was surmounted by an elegant clerestory roof, domed at the ends.

Unlike the early British Pullman cars, which were American both in concept and in outline, the profile of the Wolverton dining and sleeping cars was essentially British. Nevertheless, the coaches did possess some features clearly inspired by transatlantic practice and some of the exterior detail work, particularly around the entrances, would have looked equally well at home on a Milwaukee Road Pullman Palace Car. Towards the end of the arc roof period, the entrance vestibules were widened slightly for new construction and some of the elaboration disappeared. Two examples of this later period can be seen in the preserved LNWR dining cars, one at the National Railway Museum, York, and the other in private ownership.

This distinctive form of carriage 'architecture' remained the LNWR/WCJS standard for twelve-wheel stock until the grouping — and was perpetuated, only slightly changed, by the LMS until 1928 — but was never used on general service ordinary coaches. The nearest approach was to be seen on a few 45ft Family Saloons of 1894 vintage which were given waist and upper panelling of 'twelve-wheel' style but without clerestories or elaborate end vestibules.

It can thus be seen that the changes wrought at Wolverton during the 1893-1903 decade were little short of revolutionary, if one compares travelling conditions at the start and finish of the period. In 1893, with a few noteworthy exceptions, travel was distinctly mid-Victorian on the West Coast route — and not very good mid-Victorian either. Only ten years later, the facilities available rivalled and, in some cases, outmatched those provided in our present day. Certainly a modern British Rail first class compartment shows little advantage in comfort and none at all in spaciousness compared with those delightful four seat compartments provided in the 50ft corridor coaches — and one suspects that the meal in the West Coast diner may have been better too!

Plates 21 & 22 End views of typical Wolverton twelve-wheel coaches. Above is the non-gangwayed end of WCJS 483 *(opposite)*, showing the ornate scrollwork at the entrances of the early cars. Below is an unidentified 9ft wide clerestory car showing the much wider entrance lobby of the later series coaches and the suppression of the ornate handrails.

Plates 23 & 24 Family saloons to D62 also carried the 'twelve-wheel' style of panelling. *Plate 23 (above)* shows one of them, virtually 'as built' at the end of a World War I ambulance train. The second vehicle in the train is a 42ft diner — see page 44. *Plate 24 (left)* shows LMS saloon 909 (ex-LNWR 5081) after conversion to picnic saloons. *(Plate 24 — Author's collection)*

Of course, a price had to be paid and this was in the matter of train weight. The newer gangwayed trains, quite apart from having more facilities and giving more spacious accommodation, tared considerably more per seat than their non-corridor predecessors and this had considerable ramifications in the locomotive department. It is no coincidence that George Whale instituted an urgent programme of locomotive construction just after the turn of the century; and it was not simply a question of the

reliability or otherwise of the Webb compounds. The fact is that, compound or not, the LNWR engines simply did not have enough power to pull, heat and brake the newer and heavier trains which Wolverton was now producing. In a very real sense, the 'Precursors' and 'Experiments' were as much a response to progress at Wolverton as they were to the demands of the locomotive department for replacement of the compounds with something more reliable.

Plates 25 & 26 The LNWR was also mindful of passengers who were unable to make use of its sleeping and dining cars. The pictures are self explanatory. Note the non-passenger coaching stock livery on the coaches behind the refreshment trolley.

Plate 27 This five coach set of cove roof corridors, clearly shows the sleek lines of this period of LNWR coach evolution. The leading coach, a brake first to D127, is additionally interesting in having twin springs to the bogie bolsters. Two of these brake firsts were later given clerestories and allocated to the Royal Train — see pages 82-3.

Towards Maturity 1903-7

In ten short years, Wolverton had pushed itself into the forefront of British railway carriage building and, when studying the diagram books, one feels that by the start of the Edwardian period most of the catching up had been completed. The 'Premier Line', equipped with hundreds of new bogie coaches, dozens of new dining and sleeping cars and with an ample supply of modern locomotives coming into service, was at last living up to its name. The effect at Wolverton seems to have been the institution of a more experimental phase in coach construction where sheer volume of production could take second place to innovation and experiment.

The main visible signs of this change were a further increase in carriage size and, at long last, a change in roof profile from the by now very old fashioned looking arc roof to a beautiful low elliptical form, not much higher overall, but with a very delicate curved section between the cantrail and the main roof arch. The visual effect was absolutely right, especially when this low elliptical roof (or 'cove' roof as it is often called) was combined as it usually was, with a new wider cross-section of 9ft over body panels and a new length of 57ft over headstocks. The overall effect was very stylish and surprisingly modern. These new enlarged dimensions were, with but a few exceptions, almost universal on new corridor coaches but non-corridors continued to be built to 50ft and sometimes 54ft lengths, the latter being confined to lavatory stock. Furthermore, a few non-corridor designs continued to retain the older 8ft body width with the new roof shape — an aesthetically much less pleasing arrangement.

Exterior bodyside panelling retained the traditional Wolverton stylistic features although increasing use was made of steel sheeting in place of wood. The joins, however, were still concealed by raised wooden beading strips and it is doubtful if the casual observer realised that there had been any change. Nevertheless, it caused carriage weight to continue to rise.

It was probably this increase in weight, together with the new 57ft length, which was responsible for the third major change to the design of coaches. The new 57ft underframes were now made exclusively of steel sections where previously there had often been a mixture of timber and steel. A new 9ft wheelbase bogie was also introduced early in the cove roof period and this combination of 57ft underframe with 9ft bogie was to prove prophetic. Towards the end of the pre-group period, the Midland and Caledonian Railways adopted similar standards and it became the norm for LMS coach construction, albeit using the MR-derived angle iron trussing rather than the LNWR round bar, turnbuckle and queenpost arrangement.

The cove roof itself had its origins in the old 42ft sleeping saloons, the lower roof section of the clerestory twelve-wheelers and the roof profile of some of the more specialised saloons. One can only wonder why a roof style dating back in some cases to the late 1880s did not come into more widespread use until the early 1900s, but thus it was.

As in the late 1890s, so too in the early 1900s, the bulk of interior innovation was made in the long distance coaching stock. The typical cove roof corridor coach was a very spacious vehicle. First class compartments were rarely less than 7ft 6in between partitions and yet still seated but four passengers although the compartment width had now risen to around six feet. A typical corridor first, weighing 32 tons, carried but 24 passengers in superlative comfort. Non-corridor firsts, however, seated four per side but there was still plenty of room.

The second and third class passengers too had a much better allocation of space. Many compartments went up to 6ft 6in between partitions and although the extra coach width did permit four per side seating in corridor coaches at crowded periods (six per side in non-corridors), for most of the time the lower orders could stretch out a little more than before.

Non-corridor stock continued to be somewhat uninspired. There was little need for new lavatory stock, although that which was built incorporated most of the innovations found in the corridor coaches. As for suburban coaches, all construction was now of bogie style but the basic principle still remained of obtaining maximum seating capacity within minimum compartment length. In fairness, it is hard to see how it could have been otherwise and at least, except in conditions of extreme crowding, there was a little more room in the compartment.

Regarding twelve-wheel stock, the cove roof period was one of consolidation rather than innovation. Further dining and sleeping saloons were built and the familiar clerestory was retained, but with the doming at the end of the roof now confined solely to the clerestory itself. This slight change went with an increase of body width to the new standard 9ft dimension and a further widening of the end vestibules, though still not to the full width of the coach. This left no room for the elaborate wrought iron handrails as on the 8ft 6in twelve-wheelers but this apart, the 9ft clerestories probably represented Wolverton's finest achievement in purely visual terms. It is singularly appropriate that it was during this period and in this style that the magnificent Royal Train vehicles were constructed for King Edward VII and Queen Alexandra (see page 117).

(Text continues on page 19)

Plates 28-31 Four interior views of cove roof brake tri-composite No 1833. An exterior view and drawings can be found at pages 80-1.

Plate 32 The final LNWR clerestory style. The coach is an emergency messroom vehicle, converted in 1942 from WCJS composite dining car to WCJS D9 – see also page 58. Apart from the addition of an extra centre door, little change is visible from its original form.

Plate 33 LNWR carriage reservation labels.

Plate 34 LNWR carriage rug as used in first class compartments.

Plate 35 (above) A posed picture of newly shopped Wolverton coaches c. 1905-10. From left to right the types are: Cove roof brake composite D214, 8ft 6in wide first class diner D29, 8ft 6in wide first class diner D30 (as built), three more diners to D29 (the nearest one having the intermediate width entrances), three semi royal saloons to D1, brake composite D214.

Plate 36 (below) A complete set of 'American Special' stock – see page 135, *Fig. 41* for details. The first class coaches are at the far end.

The cove roof period was a short one, but within it were produced some of the most elegant and comfortable railway carriages ever built in Britain for non-supplementary fare paying passengers. Although there were still better things to come in terms of interior amenity, all the essential ingredients of Wolverton's final flowering were evolved during the cove roof period and, if the author is allowed a personal opinion in what is a very subjective area, no better looking carriages ever took to the rails than those which the LNWR built during 1903-7.

The Final Phase 1907-22
The start of the final phase of LNWR and WCJS coach building represented less of a break with previous tradition than that which had taken place at the close of the arc roof period; for the only immediate visible change was the adoption of a full elliptical roof profile on all coaches, including twelve-wheelers. In fact, the first elliptical roof coaches were ordered (and shown on works drawings) with the cove roof. Indeed, many cove roof designs continued in production with no change save for the new roof profile. Nevertheless, several changes did appear at the start of the elliptical roof period which were of more than passing interest.

The most spectacular innovation was the adoption, in 1907, of the elaborate twelve-wheel styling for complete trains rather than for dining and sleeping cars only. The chosen services were the American Special boat trains between Euston and Liverpool (obviously for prestige reasons) and the even more famous and celebrated 2 pm 'Corridor' from Euston to Scotland — the direct lineal descendant of the pioneer West Coast corridor train. The coaches for both these services are described at pages 130 to 137 but one can only get matters in perspective when one realises that these sumptuous vehicles appeared only fifteen years or so after the first ever West Coast corridor service utilising 42ft arc roof stock.

This innovation was not to be more widely adopted — it was fearfully extravagant in terms of train weight in relation to passenger numbers — but at least we can be grateful that cost-effectiveness was not the motive in these particular instances.

The other changes during the elliptical roof period were more mundane, but much more widespread and significant in the long term. Mention has been made of the lavish and, perhaps, too extravagant use of space in the cove roof corridor coaches. Once the pioneer elliptical examples had been built — in general, those which were largely identical to the cove roof types — the LNWR generally tended to adopt somewhat smaller compartment dimensions again. The firsts came down to seven feet or so between partitions and were given three seats per side as standard, while the seconds and thirds reverted to the old 6ft dimension (give or take an inch or two). This must have reflected some sort of concern about increasing train weight or, possibly, additional train length which may have been embarrassing at certain stations. There was also a considerable number of corridor coaches built to a narrower 8ft 6in width — presumably for working over lines with restricted clearances. It is also worth mentioning that there was some proliferation in the number of differing designs put into service during the elliptical roof period and there was a certain amount of fluctuation in coach length. Many sources suggest that the 57ft length, first introduced in the

Plate 37 The early elliptical roof stock is well exemplified by this view of the twin Club Saloons to D71, built in 1908 — see also page 143 and Appendix II. An interior view is given overleaf.

Plate 38 The sumptuous first class compartment of the D71
Club Saloon — see previous page.

cove roof period, became the LNWR standard, but this is an
oversimplification. Quite a number of corridor coaches
were built to the old 50ft length, not to mention a new
52ft 6in dimension during the elliptical roof period. These
variations in design and dimension are all considered in
detail in Chapter 4.

In terms of non-corridor stock, the basic change was the
final adoption of 57ft as the length for all coaches, albeit
after a few batches of intermediate length (see Chapter 5).
The basic trend was for suburban type vehicles to be
favoured and lavatory stock was only built in small
quantities, generally for inter-district working.

Perhaps the most noteworthy change in elliptical roof
general service stock, apart from the considerable variety
of lengths and types represented, was the final abandonment
of the traditional Wolverton panelling style in 1912.
Mr H. D. Earl had recently taken over from Park as carriage
superintendent and, perhaps, felt it desirable to make some
changes — as was sometimes expected of a new chief.
Park had supervised the basic updating of LNWR coaches
so it was mostly the ephemeral features that were altered.

From 1912 onwards, LNWR coaches were built with
waist and eaves panelling in the orthodox British fashion.
Even so, the detail treatment was peculiarly Wolverton.
Waist panels had completely semi-circular ends and, above
the waistline, the lower corners of the upper panelling were
square rather than rounded for a year or two. The most
characteristic feature, however, was on the corridor side of
gangwayed coaches where, in place of the eaves panel, the
fixed windows were surmounted by long toplights. Toplights
had often been fitted just below roof level in the brake
compartments of passenger coaches before this time, but

this was the first occasion when they were employed in the
actual passenger carrying part of the coach.

Although this new toplight feature was generally
confined to the corridor side of gangwayed coaches, it is
convenient to refer to all elliptical roof stock built during
this period as 'toplight' stock — to distinguish it from the
earlier elliptical roof coach designs built with traditional
panelling — and this practice will be adopted in this book.

Twelve-wheel dining and sleeping car construction
continued at a lower rate during the elliptical roof period.
World War I caused some of the slowing down but basically,
there was already a sufficient number of clerestories in
service for it to be unnecessary to continue new
construction at such a frantic pace. At the same time,
several interesting developments took place. Firstly was an
increase in length to 68ft for the final batches of sleeping
cars, which set the pattern for LMS stock after the grouping,
and secondly was a final increase in vestibule size to almost
the full width of the coach thus causing a final abandonment
of any pretentions to fancy handrails at the entrance doors.

Like most of this chapter, this section has concerned
itself with the basic generalities of LNWR coaching stock.
No real mention has been made of several other very
important groups of coaches which the LNWR put into
service. These included Motor Fitted (or Push-Pull) vehicles,
passenger full brakes, travelling post offices and the like.
Before summing up, it should just be mentioned that there
is no real need to isolate these groups in a general survey
since, for the most part, the coaches concerned tended to
follow the basic trends already outlined. Where there were
significant departures from the norm, these are covered in
the appropriate specialist chapters.

Plate 39 (above) A typical Toplight corridor coach – WCJS brake third No 299 to Diagram W65. It became LMS 6499, later 6316.

Plate 40 (right) Taken to illustrate the method of connecting slip coaches, this picture also gives a clear comparison between the traditional Wolverton panelling (on the right) and the post-1911 style of treatment.

Plate 41 Panel and lining detail on a 'Toplight' corridor composite of World War I vintage.

In summing up progress at Wolverton before the grouping, it seems fair to conclude that the end of the first world war probably marks the close of purely independent carriage design on the LNWR. By this time, the company had virtually standardised 57ft ordinary and 68ft twelve-wheel coaches and these traditions were carried into LMS days. The basic change at Wolverton after 1922 was the gradual introduction of Midland style panelling and detail fittings as standard for most new LMS coaches. However, tradition died hard and the LMS management was persuaded not only to adopt LNWR carriage dimensions and interior arrangements for general service but also to build its early sleeping and dining cars to a basically LNWR inspired style. So perhaps, in the event, honours were even.

Carriage Livery

No general survey of Wolverton built carriages could be considered complete without mention of the famous two-colour carriage livery sported for so many years by the vehicles built there. Its exact date of introduction is not certain, but, contrary to popular opinion, it did not exist from the dawn of time.

By all accounts the earliest LNWR coaches were finished in an 'all-over' dark shade — probably dark brown — and a favourite explanation states that with this livery, the sunshine caused the upper panels to fade and the paint to peel. The company therefore adopted white painted upper panels in the belief that this would give longer life to the paintwork. If true, this explanation is entirely in the best Richard Moon/F.W. Webb tradition. Be that as it may, the familiar later livery dates well back into the nineteenth century (probably as early as 1850) and was certainly in use by the 1860s. When most of the coaches considered in detail in this book were built, a reasonably standard specification had been evolved, along with clearly prescribed painting methods.

Before painting, coach bodies were primed with white lead, blemishes to the surface being stopped and filled up. The coach was then rubbed down with composition blocks before being primed all over again with white lead. At this point, preparation for the final coats was made. The lower panels were primed with lead colour and then painted with a chocolate colour mixed from Indian Red and Drop Black (exact proportions not specified). Mouldings were similarly treated and then both panels and mouldings were painted 'Carmine Lake'. Louvred ventilators were usually lake.

The upper panels were treated first with Tub Lead to which a touch of Ultramarine Blue was added. The finishing coat was of dry White Lead, ground in raw linseed oil with ' . . . just sufficient Ultramarine Blue added to conteract the yellowing of the varnish in the finishing coats.' Underframes were painted with Black Japan and the ends were painted Chocolate (*not* lake). Roofs were supposed to be grey but many were finished, when new, in white. Certain non-passenger coaching stock, usually of the less exalted kind, was finished all over chocolate. Full brakes, post office coaches and many varieties of parcels and similar vans were given the full two-colour style.

Lining on the rounds of the raised mouldings consisted of a ½in gold coloured line edged with ⅛in white. This white edging appeared on both sides of the gold line when applied to lake panels but on one side only when the mouldings were adjacent to white panels *(see Plate 13)*. The gold colour itself was made from Yellow Ochre, Lemon Chrome and Orange Chrome in unspecified proportions. Lettering and numbering was also in this gold colour, sans-serif in style and edged in black for LNWR stock. West Coast Joint Stock carried the same lining but lettering was shaded green to the left and below. Transfer crests (LNWR or WCJS) were applied to lower panels, usually one or two per coach side, and monogrammed initials were often used as well. Edges of doors carried a fine ⅛in white line.

Class designation and other descriptive wording was applied within the waist panel of the doors and running numbers were located just above the waist rail (traditional stock) and in the waist panel of toplight styled coaches. Window frames, bolection mouldings and droplight frames were usually varnished wood, but some pictures indicate that bolection mouldings — especially on toplight coaches — were sometimes picked out in white. It should also be mentioned that the lower edges of the louvred side ventilators were almost invariably given the gold lining treatment. Double doors to brake vans, or the van portion of passenger carrying brake coaches, were given slate waist panels in order that destinations could be chalked on the doors. These were usually genuine pieces of slate and not slate painted. Descriptive wording and running numbers on Dining and Sleeping Saloons were, at first, executed in rather large florid characters above the windows. However shortly after the turn of the century, smaller sans-serif insignia, gold coloured and attractively backshaded, was placed in the waist panelling.

The classic LNWR livery is often referred to as 'plum and spilt milk' and this probably gives an approximation to its overall effect. The lake shade was extremely dark — much deeper than the Midland colour — and probably the nearest approach, outside museum exhibits, is the so-called 'Claret' colour of the present day Royal Train. The upper panels are less certain. It was clearly intended that they should be seen as white but the addition of the small amount of blue, the yellowing effect of varnishing, the consequences of exposure to weather and the vagaries of carriage cleaning would probably impart a subtle variety of hues to a typical LNWR carriage ensemble. Colour perception varies notoriously between individuals, colour awareness deteriorates with age and our memory of colour is normally very bad (whatever we might like to think) so the most that can safely be said is that the upper panels of LNWR coaches probably seemed 'off-white' to most observers. The overtones would almost certainly be in the yellow-green-blue part of the spectrum.

Whatever the precise shade, all contemporary observers are agreed that the overall effect was a magnificent livery, whether behind a shiny black LNWR engine or, in the case of the WCJS, teamed with Caledonian Blue. In fact, it has been said that the Caledonian Railway itself adopted a similar livery because the directors were attracted by the appearance of the WCJS coaches.

Footnotes: 1. Since the above livery information was written a very fine book has been published by the HMRS (in collaboration with Pendragon) entitled 'LNWR Liveries'. This gives very comprehensive information and readers are advised to refer to this title for specific details.

2. The word 'Chocolate' in the above description of carriage ends &c is more properly described as 'quick brown', a purple-brown paint shade of somewhat lower quality designed to give a close approximation to the more expensive carmine lake.

3. After the first edition of this book was issued, the author was privileged to supervise the restoration of the preserved Royal Train vehicles at the NRM to their original livery. In so doing, accurate colour matches for both the carmine lake and off-white were made but even the reputedly much more colour-stable nature of modern paint and varnish technology has not prevented the varnish over the white colour changing the overall hue to a sort of bluish-green in some areas with the passage of time.

Chapter 2   Sleeping Cars

The Evolutionary Phase

The British sleeping car was almost born at Wolverton — almost, but not quite; for the honour of introducing the first sleeping car onto the railways of this country went, rather improbably, to the North British Railway in April 1873. However, Wolverton was not very far behind and in October 1873, the first West Coast sleeping coach was placed in service. History tells us very little about this pioneer vehicle, but it is believed to have been a somewhat spartan 33ft six-wheeler (some sources quote 30ft) and is thought to have accommodated four ladies and eight gentlemen in transverse berths in three compartments. The design is generally attributed to Richard Bore and was something of a fore-runner of the Family Saloon type of vehicle.

The developments which took place during the twenty years or so between the introduction of the first Wolverton built sleeping car and the starting point of this story are somewhat shrouded in the mists of antiquity. What can safely be said is that progress in passenger travel was nothing like as rapid as it was later to become. However, the early Wolverton sleeping saloons, few in number and relatively short in overall length, did tend to develop a fairly characteristic arrangement. A fairly typical example is depicted at *Plate 42*. Regrettably, no contemporary pictures of these coaches have been located. The 42ft version is shown at *Fig. 1* and at *Plate 167* is illustrated a saloon conversion, believed to have originated from a similar 42ft sleeping coach.

Within these early sleeping saloons, a longitudinal arrangement of berths was preferred. Contemporary descriptions of the 42ft coaches which superseded the six-wheel type, portray a well equipped and comfortable vehicle incorporating sprung mattresses (with pillows, sheets and rugs), carpets, sound-deadening floor material, lavatories, a self-contained heating system and, of course, liberal and elaborate use of lincrusta and various wood finishes such as American walnut, bird's-eye maple, oak, sycamore and satinwood. Each berth could be individually enclosed by longitudinal curtains and in some of the cars, fold-away upper berths were provided in the two wide end compartments thus providing space for a dozen passengers if need be. It would appear that these upper berths were for peak periods only and were not too popular. A contemporary account states that the public 'prefer the bedsteads.'

This style of sleeping car was quite popular and several substantially similar batches were built both with radial and bogie underframes. In fact, the final examples did not emerge until 1895. At the advent of the twelve-wheel era, many of the 42ft cars were fairly new and although gradually withdrawn from overnight services, some of them went into further use as saloons for day and departmental use. Unfortunately, their ultimate disposal is not always known.

These early coaches were, of course, quite small vehicles by contrast with those used on the Midland Railway which had adopted the American type of Pullman sleeping car in July 1874. It needs very little imagination to envisage Moon and Webb viewing these massive MR bogie cars with the greatest of suspicion — at all events, as far as their company was concerned, 42ft was to remain the standard for many more years, However, like it or not, the larger bogie coach was here to stay and in order to understand why the changes did eventually take place, it may help to digress for a short space to consider the advantages of heavier and larger cars.

(Text continues on page 26)

Plate 42 Departmental saloon No DM284672 at Rugby. Although very similar to many other contemporary saloons, the slightly elevated roof above the cantrail indicates probable sleeping car origin for this vehicle.

(Author's collection)

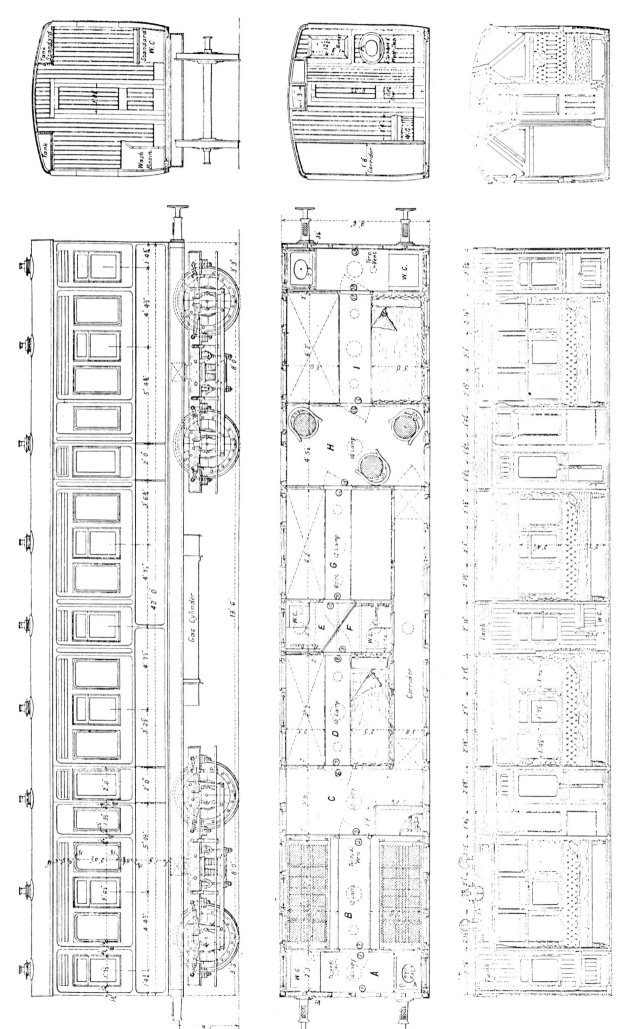

Figure 1 This drawing shows the body and underframe of one of the later pattern 42ft sleeping cars built in 1893/4 with bogie chassis. In general, however, the body style is fairly representative of most of the cars built during the 42ft period as can be seen by comparison with the photograph which depicts one of the earlier 42ft radial chassis cars built in 1884. *(Drawing from 'Engineering', courtesy National Railway Museum)*

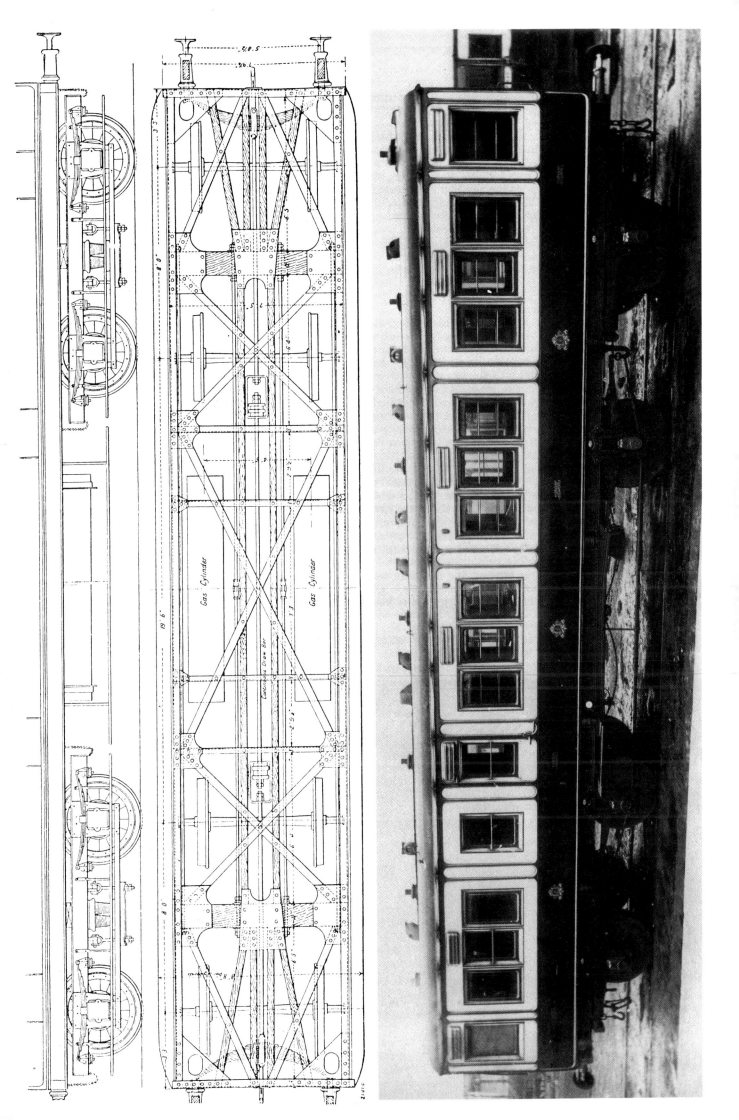

In the pioneer Midland Pullman sleepers, the convertible berths were arranged longitudinally in two tiers on either side of the central gangway. Since the coaches themselves were in the form of large open saloons and the sexes were mixed, all the necessary disrobing operations had, perforce, to take place behind the green rep curtains with which the berths were screened. In spite of this disadvantage, the comfort of the Pullmans overcame any Victorian reticence on the part of the public. The massive construction of the cars made them, by the standards of the 1880s, superlatively smooth riding vehicles and they were very popular.

None of these advantages, nor, indeed the popularity of the coaches, seemed to make much impression on the LNWR management and it was probably only when the question of safety came into the reckoning that matters began to change. Late in the nineteenth century, collisions at Northallerton and Thirsk revealed the considerable shock-resistant quality of heavy bogie coaches and the agitation following these events seems to have been instrumental in the general adoption throughout Britain of much heavier rolling stock from about the close of the Victorian period.

At Wolverton, this eventually led to the adoption of a twelve-wheel style of coach which, as it was progressively refined, became as characteristic of the West Coast route as did the locomotives which hauled it. It is with the story of the sleeping car versions of the twelve-wheel style that this chapter is basically concerned.

Although LNWR sleeping coaches had a longer history than refreshment vehicles, it must be recorded that the classic twelve-wheel coach had its origins in the latter field. These vehicles are considered in detail in the next chapter but the styling characteristics which they pioneered were adopted for sleeping cars too, remaining substantially unchanged for almost thirty years and only slightly modified during the first five or six years of the LMS age.

At this stage it should be pointed out that until well after the grouping, sleeping cars in Britain were the exclusive preserve of the first class passenger. There must

have been a great demand for such vehicles on the West Coast route for, in the 24 years before the grouping, well over sixty of these massive sleeping cars were placed in service. In toto they represented no fewer than thirteen variations on the theme first established with the pioneer design of 1897 and this multiplicity of types merits further comment.

Sleeping cars were never built in very large batches and such was the progress in amenity and styling that almost every order for additional coaches resulted in some new feature being added to the design. However, the position was not as complicated as a bald reference to thirteen types might infer. Firstly, it should be remembered that coaches built for the WCJS were listed in a separate diagram book and regarded as different types from the contemporary examples in LNWR ownership. There were differences between the two, but these were usually of quite minor character.

The second aid to rationalisation was in the external shaping of the coaches where only three principal variations existed. The earliest cars employed the 8ft 6in body width and had the clerestory roof of the first style. The second variation saw an increase in width to 9ft 0in and the abandonment of doming on the main roof ends although retained on the clerestory; while the final stylistic expression was with the full elliptical roof and, later, an increase in length to 68ft. Plans of all the types are given at *Fig. 2*.

The Clerestory Era
The building of 8ft 6in clerestory coaches was confined to the few years straddling the turn of the century. Two basic interior layouts were adopted and examples of both layouts are found in both diagram books thus giving four variants. Marginally the earliest to appear were the coaches to LNWR D20 and WCJS D5 in 1897. These were 11 berth cars with five single and three double berths. The five single berths were arranged transversely across the coach with a narrow side corridor alongside. Separating the single from the double berths was a fairly large open area fitted out

Plate 43 This WD coach of World War I vintage started life as a 42ft sleeping car, other details unknown. Its general configuration is similar to that shown at *Fig. 1*.

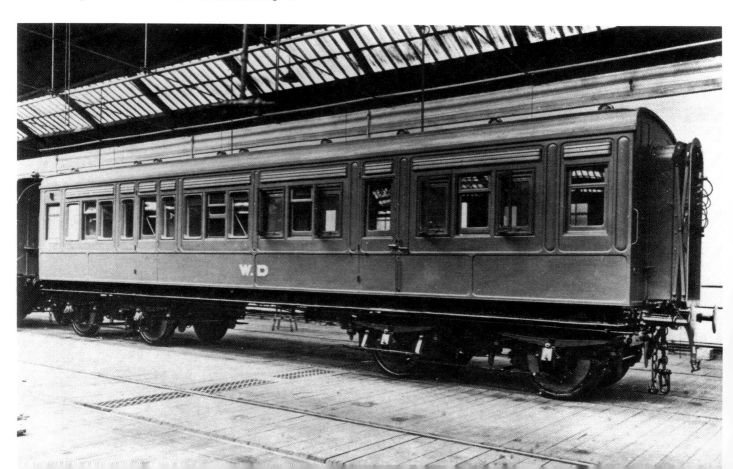

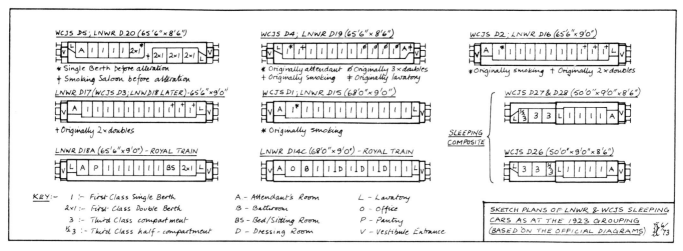

Figure 2 Sketch plans of sleeping cars. *(D. Jenkinson)*

with four seats. This feature was located in the centre of the vehicle and afforded opportunity to move the corridor across to the other side of the coach at the double berth end. The double compartments were arranged with a single bed on each side of a centre access area. Two were arranged with the berths across the coach but the compartment leading off the central area had its berths arranged longitudinally.

In addition to the sleeping compartments, these coaches had lavatories at both ends and an attendant's compartment next to the lavatory at the single berth end of the coach. The only significant difference between the LNWR and the WCJS version of this design was the slightly smaller attendant's compartment in the LNWR version.

Within the coaches, the fittings were elaborate in the extreme. Each berth was fitted with a horse-hair mattress on a spring base and courtesy shelves. In the double berths, the washbasins were placed between the beds and designed so that as the top was raised, waterproof curtains (to prevent splashing onto the beds) were raised on each side of the basin by means of studs working in brass quadrants. Two of the single berths had folding upper bunks for use at peak periods, thus anticipating by some years the modern type of twin berth compartment.

Compartment finishing varied. Framing was always in polished American walnut but the panels themselves were variously sycamore, bird's-eye maple, burr or Italian walnut set in ornamental inlaid frames with mouldings picked out

in gold. Bevel glass mirrors were also fitted. Windows had old gold figured tapestry blinds on sprung rollers, the same material being also used for the screening curtains provided in the double berths.

Upholstery was in crimson and brown saladin moquette with matching crimson silk laces. Floors were double thickness (and filled with hair felt for sound insulation) and were covered with linoleum and Wilton carpets. Ceilings were finished with flock paper to a floral pattern, picked out in cream and gold.

Outside the compartments, corridors were panelled in polished mahogany in a walnut framing above a dado of dark oak. The corridor ceiling was finished in polished sycamore panels while the central cross-vestibule, used as a smoking saloon, had a set of four revolving chairs and flap tables. Lighting was electric and all compartments had electrical communication with the attendant's compartment, there being a visible 'drop arm' signal outside each berth. By comparison with all this modernity, heating was by circulating hot water pipes connected to a coke-fed stove in the attendant's compartment.

The underframe adopted for these coaches was of composite timber and steel construction. The main side members and trussing were steel but the central longitudinal chassis members and headstocks were made from massive timber sections. Cross-bracing was a combination of timber struts and steel plates. The coaches ran on six wheel bogies of 11ft 6in wheelbase. *(Text continued on page 31)*

Plate 44 LNWR Sleeping Saloon No 129 (later 5129, 1st LMS 10371) to D20. The WCJS version of this type is given overleaf at *Fig. 3*, which also illustrates the opposite side of the cars.

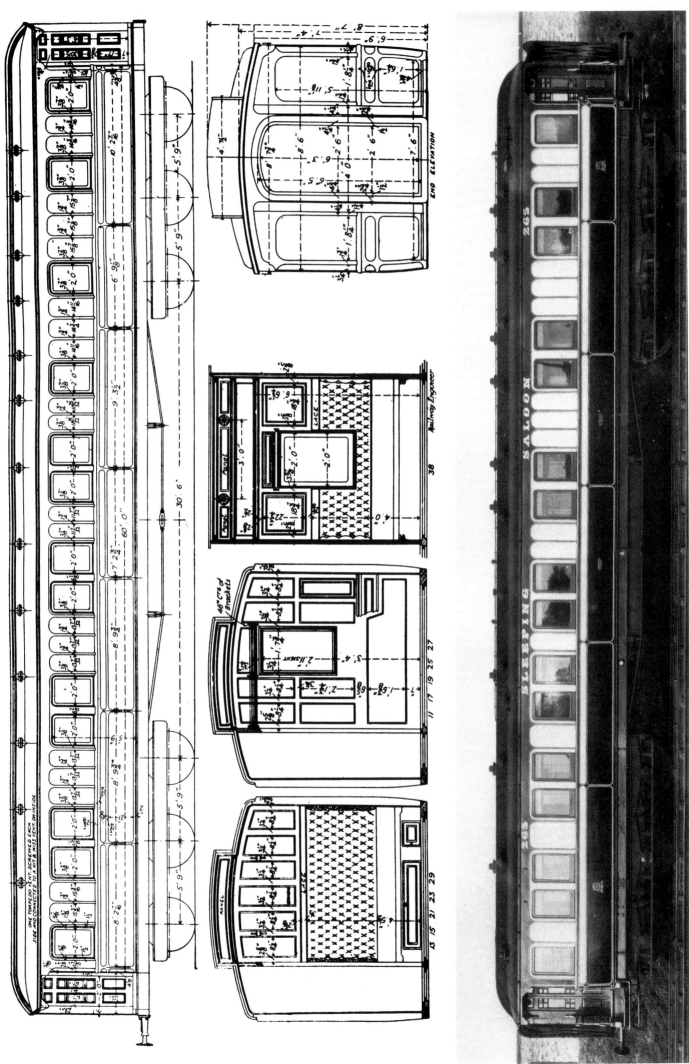

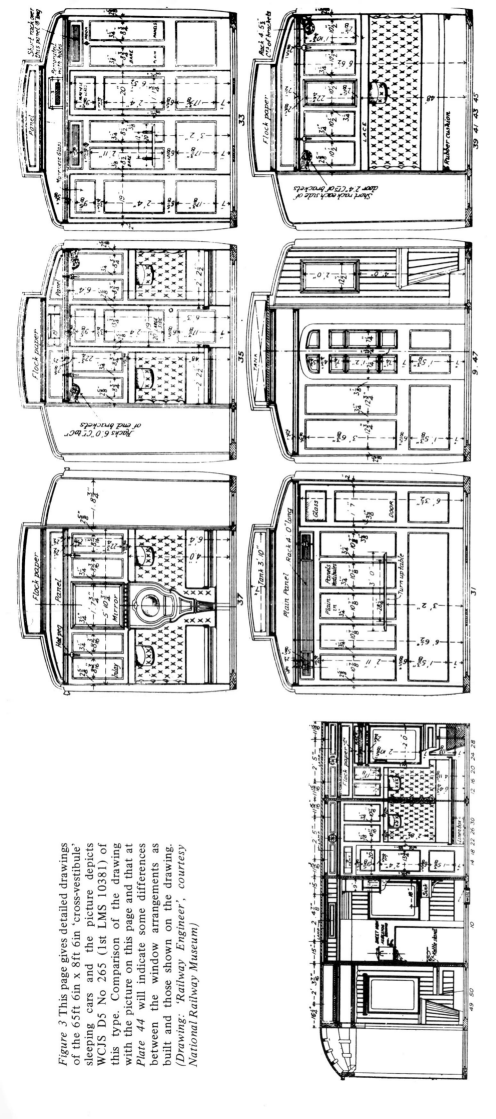
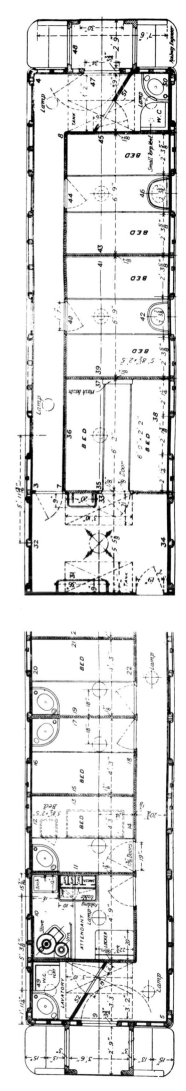

Figure 3 This page gives detailed drawings of the 65ft 6in x 8ft 6in 'cross-vestibule' sleeping cars and the picture depicts this type. Comparison of the drawing with the picture on this page and that at *Plate 44* will indicate some differences between the window arrangements as built and those shown on the drawing. *(Drawing: 'Railway Engineer', courtesy National Railway Museum)*

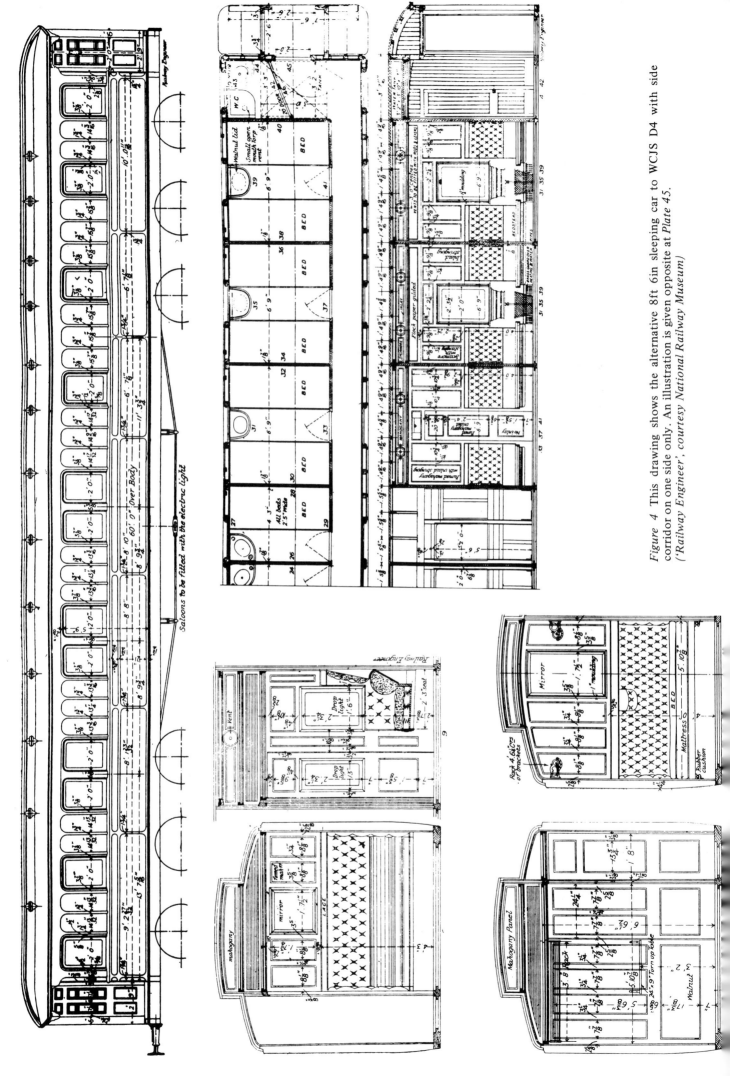

Figure 4 This drawing shows the alternative 8ft 6in sleeping car to WCJS D4 with side corridor on one side only. An illustration is given opposite at *Plate 45*. ('*Railway Engineer*', courtesy National Railway Museum)

30

Plate 45 LMS engineers' sleeping van No 297238. This coach started life as a WCJS sleeping saloon to WCJS D4 and this view clearly shows the elaboration at the vestibule entrances of the first generation of 65ft 6in twelve-wheelers.

(Author's collection)

At a later stage, a major modification was made to these cars. The single berth adjacent to the smoking area was converted to a longitudinally arranged double berth compartment. This took up floor space at the expense of the central vestibule which now degenerated into little more than a transverse passageway to enable the corridor to change sides. This modification cannot be dated with certainty but was probably just before the grouping at a time when most of the pre-1914 sleeping cars were re-furbished to bring them to the standards of the final elliptical roof designs built during the first world war.

These early sleeping cars had the very narrow type of entrance vestibule with the elaborate scrollwork handrails, first introduced on the 1893 dining cars (see page 13). The cars lasted until the early 1930s, being eventually replaced by the first of the Stanier pattern LMS 69ft coaches.

The second basic category of 8ft 6in clerestory sleeping car design appeared very soon after the pioneer cars had been introduced. These vehicles were to LNWR D19 and WCJS D4 and saw a change to a layout without the transverse central passageway. They were still 11 berth cars (five single, three double) but all the beds were now arranged in transverse fashion. As before, two lavatories, an attendant's compartment and a smoking saloon were also provided. The smoking saloon was now a genuine compartment and was located between the attendant and the sleeping berths. These cars were finished in exactly the same manner as the earlier cross-vestibule sleepers but there were far fewer of them.

When, like their predecessors, these later cars came to be modernised, an all single berth layout was adopted. The attendant's and smoking compartments were converted into single berths and, by shifting the inside partitions, four single berths were fitted into the area previously occupied by the three double berths. This in turn, involved altering the position of some of the outside windows, which was carried out so skilfully that photographs afford no evidence at all of these modifications. To accommodate the displaced attendant, the lavatory at the erstwhile double berth end of the car was converted into a service compartment. In this modified form, the cars continued to sleep 11 passengers and survived until 1933.

The diagram book evidence indicates that there was no difference between the LNWR and WCJS versions of these cars. However, judging from photographs, on at least one of them, almost certainly the LNWR example, the entrance vestibule was widened to the intermediate size and received the slightly less ornate handrails.

The years between 1902 and 1905 witnessed the most concentrated pre-group building of sleeping cars at Wolverton and all were of the later 9ft width. This extra six inches afforded a real improvement inside the coach by enabling a full length bed to be achieved more easily and yet still allow a reasonable side corridor to be provided. The 8ft 6in cars had been very restricted in this respect. A further improvement was yet another increase in the size of the entrance lobby. The end doors were still set back from the main body line but to nothing like the same extent as previously.

Five separate diagrams were involved (three LNWR and two WCJS) but the bulk of the cars were built either to LNWR D17 in 1903-4 or to WCJS D2 in 1904. One diagram was issued in 1902 (WCJS D3), which was the prototype vehicle for the whole series and two further diagrams are listed in the book for cars built in 1905 (LNWR D18 and D18A). This trio had a rather interesting history of which more in due course.

The prototype 9ft clerestory sleeping car to WCJS D3 (WCJS Car No 147) was, initially, a 10 berth car (six single and two double) and, other than the change in number of

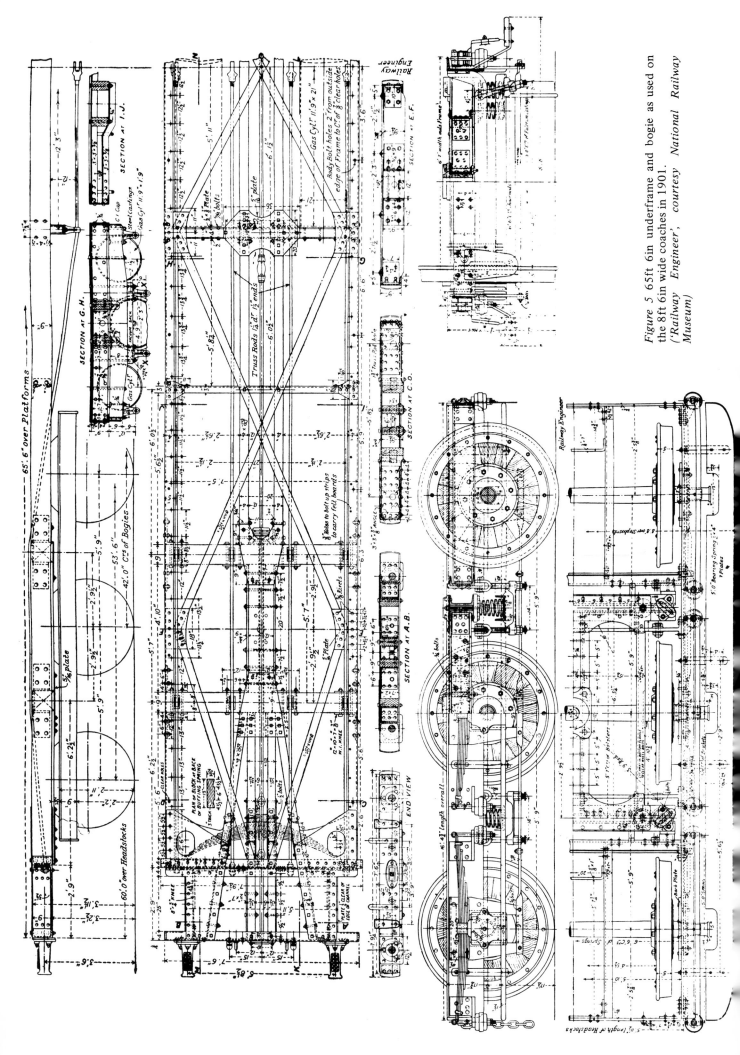

Figure 5 65ft 6in underframe and bogie as used on the 8ft 6in wide coaches in 1901. ('Railway Engineer', courtesy National Railway Museum)

berths, followed the layout set by the final batch of 8ft 6in cars before modification, having a separate smoking compartment, two lavatories and an attendant's compartment. When it too was modified to an 11 single berth style, the arrangement was very similar to the rebuilt 8ft 6in coaches except that the attendant was placed at the opposite end – see Fig. 2.

The main batch of 9ft clerestory sleeping cars was built from the outset with but one lavatory. The attendant was at the other end of the car and this single lavatory arrangement probably established the precedent for the subsequent modification of the earlier cars. The first of the main groups of coaches was to LNWR D17 (Figure 6). This was a 12 berth design (eight single and two double) with no separate smoking saloon. The matching WCJS D2, which was built in some quantity (15 cars), retained the traditional separate smoking compartment at the expense of the extra 12th berth in the otherwise all but identical LNWR version. When these two batches were modernised, the two double berths were converted to three singles and the WCJS version had its smoking compartment converted to a single berth. In both cases, apart from fractional differences in compartment size, the end product was substantially the same.

Turning now to the interiors of the 9ft clerestory sleeping cars, some slight changes were made compared with the 8ft 6in coaches. In general the effect was to lighten the decor compared with the more sombre wood finishes used in the earlier cars. Thus, the dado panels were now of white mahogany rather than dark oak and, in the compartments, both the top panels and ceilings were usually lincrusta finished in white enamel. Wood framing was usually mahogany in the compartments while in the corridors, top panels were oak with a white lincrusta ceiling above.

Although the double berths (before conversion to single) continued to be given washbasins of the traditional type, the single berths were given a new style of combination toilet cabinet set into the compartment wall opposite the bed. These were double sided fitments serving two adjacent compartments and, in consequence, appeared in the

(Text continues on page 37)

Plates 46-48 Three interior views of the elaborate decor of sleeping saloon No 151 (see next page). Although an LNWR vehicle, it is interesting to note that the sleeping compartment is furnished with WCJS blankets.

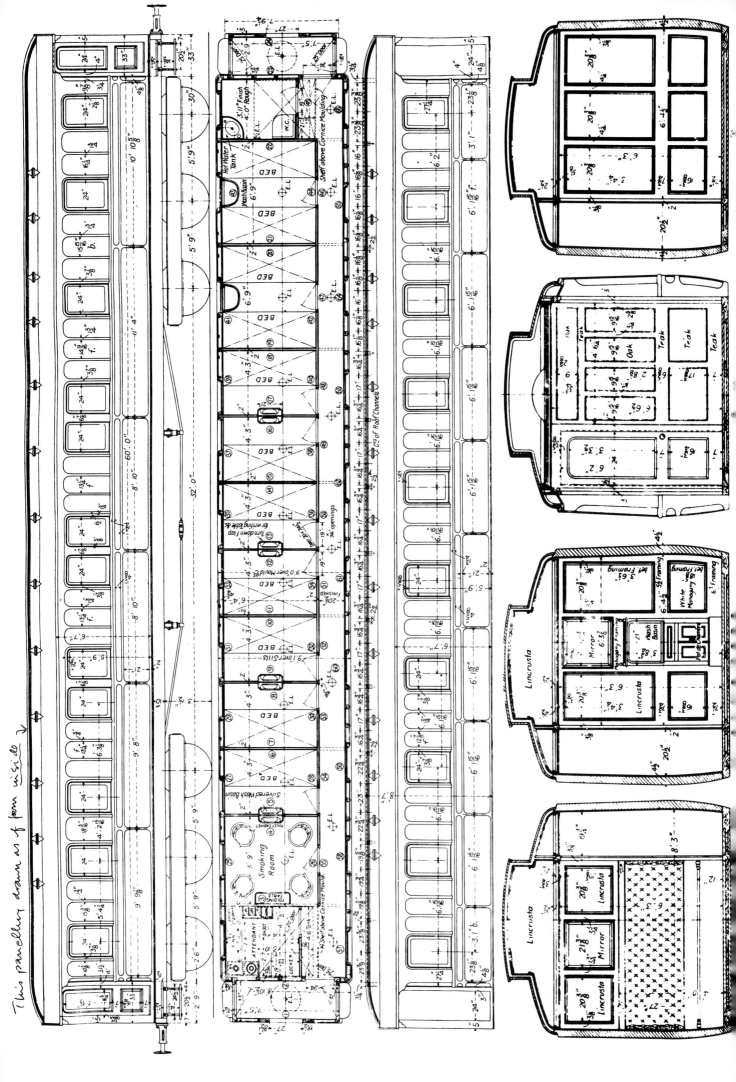

This panelling drawn as if seen inside

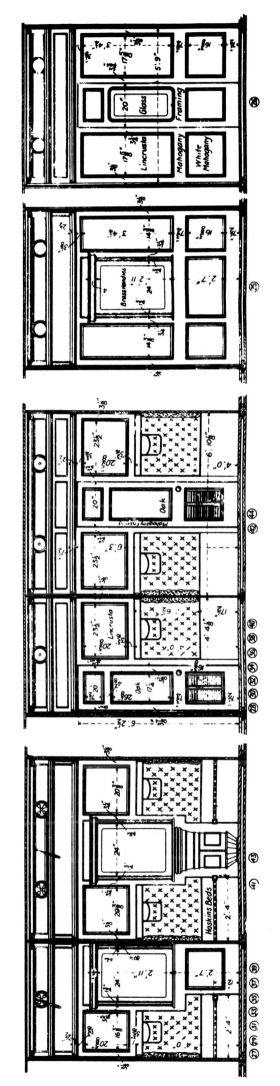

Figure 6 This page gives detailed drawings of the 9ft wide sleeping cars to WCJS D2 — see Appendix I. The photograph shows the LNWR D17 variant (built with an extra berth in place of the smoking saloon). Car No 151, later 5151 became LMS 10361, later 474 and was scrapped in 1936. (*Drawings: 'Railway Engineer', courtesy National Railway Museum*)

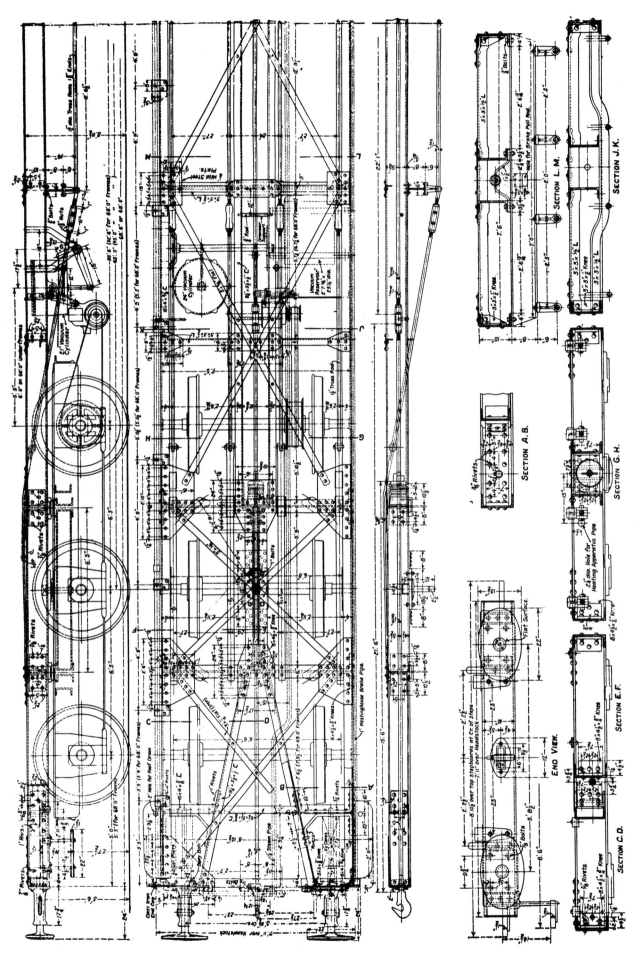

Figure 7 The later 12-wheel underframe arrangement for elliptical roof 65ft 6in and 68ft stock. *('Railway Engineer', courtesy National Railway Museum)*

smoking saloon as well. This materially simplified the subsequent conversion of this area into a genuine single berth. Prior to conversion, the smoking compartment, if present, was given four chairs and folding tables.

The service facilities were more elaborate too. Lavatories made extensive use of white, green and gold lined porcelain with heavily enamelled WC hoppers. The coaches were now heated by steam drawn from the locomotive of the train.

The final 9ft clerestories were three coaches to LNWR D18 in 1905. When built, these three reverted to the 10 berth, two lavatory layout of the pioneer WCJS D3 but they did not last long in this form. One of them was completely written off at Quintinshill, a second was converted to the 'standard' LNWR D17 pattern and, although its internal dimensions were slightly different, was inserted on that diagram; while the third car was completely refitted for the LNWR Royal Train becoming D18A in the process.

This car (LNWR 5114; LMS 10365, later 477) retained the partition layout of the D18 design but with some alterations in the use to which the various compartments were put. The two lavatories were retained, as was the attendant's compartment. The smoking saloon became a pantry and the two double berths were considerably altered. One became an enlarged single berth of bed-sitting room type while the second was used as a twin berth service compartment for the train staff. As a result of these modifications, the car retained only six genuine first class sleeping berths. It ran until 1968 in the Royal Train and was the last

Wolverton clerestory twelve-wheeler to be retained in capital stock. A second clerestory sleeping car was also selected for the Royal Train at a later date. This was a WCJS D2 car but in standard trim (WCJS 103; LMS 10342, later 461). It lasted until 1960.

With the exception of the two Royal Train cars, the 9ft clerestories were withdrawn from capital stock in the late 1930s, although several survived for many years as departmental dormitory coaches, migrating far and wide in the process. Some of them got as far as Lyme Regis on the Southern Region.

Final Developments

In 1907, the LNWR adopted the full elliptical roof and in the overnight travel sphere, this resulted in the final 65ft 6in sleeping car design to LNWR D16. There was no equivalent WCJS diagram. The six coaches concerned were elliptical roof versions of WCJS D2 with an identical layout both before and after modification and very similar finishing both inside and outside the cars. In fact, it is quite possible that they were ordered as clerestories. Apart from the roof, the only other major change was in the bogie design. On these ears, a new 12ft 6in bogie was fitted which was to be the final LNWR standard for twelve-wheel coaches. These elliptical roof sleeping cars seem rather to have eluded latter day photographers but one of them took on quite a lengthy new lease of life after withdrawal from capital stock by being converted into a mobile cinema coach.

Plates 49 & 50 Interior and exterior views of the only 65ft 6in elliptical roof sleeping car design to LNWR D16 (Car No 112, later 5112 – LMS 10337, later 481). The double berth arrangement was later modified to a single berth configuration – see main text.

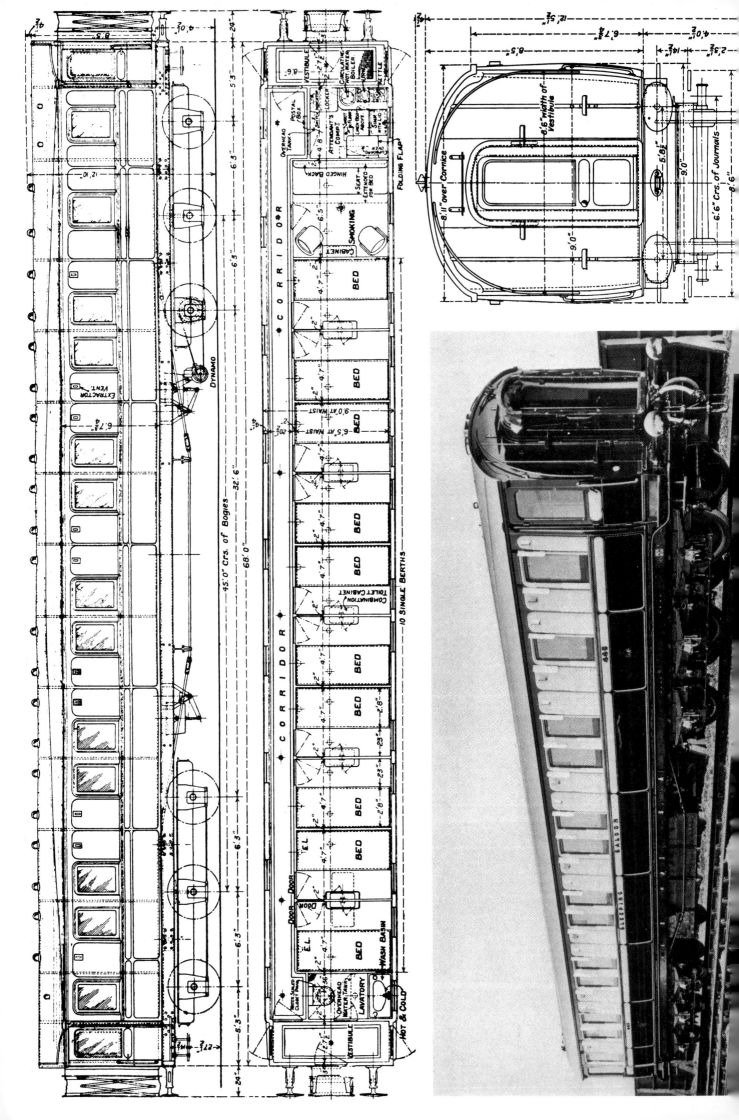

Plates 51 & 52 Two detail views of Royal Train sleeping car No. 495 (D14C), immediately prior to breaking up in October 1968. (D. Jenkinson)

The final LNWR/WCJS sleeping car design emerged in 1914. In most respects it was directly derived from D16 but there were a few significant innovations. The length became 68ft and this allowed a slight increase in compartment size and also set the standard length for new LMS construction after 1922. These new 68ft cars displayed the very wide entrance vestibules and the exterior panelling, although still of classic twelve-wheel style, did not exhibit quite as many separate panel sections between the windows as did the earlier cars.

With one exception (see below), all the 68ft LNWR/WCJS sleeping cars were identical although, as usual, two diagrams were issued (LNWR D15 and WCJS D1). The cars all had ten single berths from the outset although all adjacent pairs of berths had lockable inter-connecting doors to enable double berths to be arranged if need be. As usual, the coaches were given a separate smoking saloon which soon became appropriated as an additional sleeping berth. There was but one lavatory and this, with the attendant's compartment, occupied the extreme ends of the vehicle.

Once again, interior fittings exhibited some changes from the immediately preceding design. Dado panels now became Italian walnut with figured mahogany veneers in the upper panels, while the ceiling and all areas above the cornice level were now plain white.

Trimmings round the bed area were reduced to a minimum and all plain wood panels, together with all wall angles, were coved for ease of cleaning. All berths were now fitted with folding tables and the old familiar roller blinds and curtains gave way to rolling shutters which were better for

Figure 8 (opposite) The final LNWR/WCJS sleeping cars, the 68ft coaches to WCJS D1/LNWR D15. Note the 'full width' entrances. ('Railway Engineer', courtesy National Railway Museum)

excluding draughts. Mirrors and beds were all fitted with courtesy lights and carpets, of course, were still provided.

Upholstery continued to be in moquette of, if memory serves aright, a rather attractive green floral pattern much used on other first class stock of the period. The smoking compartment was similarly finished and even before conversion to a genuine sleeping berth, was so arranged that the seat could be drawn out to make an extra bed if needed.

The all single berth layout of these 68ft cars probably set the pattern for the modernisation of the older cars, already mentioned. By using the principle of lockable doors, the interior layout could be varied to suit the traffic needs. Fixed double berth compartments were much less flexible features in cases where the majority of travellers were journeying singly.

A refinement of D15 was the one car to D14C — again a Royal Train vehicle. It is not clear whether this car (LNWR 5132; LMS 10321, later 495) was originally built to D15 or whether it was designated for the Royal Train from new. Built as a replacement for the Quintinshill victim already mentioned and given the same running number, it seems to have gone to the Royal Train at a very early stage if it was not always thus employed.

Inside the car, the partition layout of D15 was maintained but the number of sleeping berths was relatively small. Of the original ten single berths, three were retained while six more were refitted as three suites of bed and dressing rooms. If necessary, beds could also be located in the dressing rooms. The tenth berth was converted to a bathroom. The smoking saloon provided in D15 as built was used as a service compartment in the Royal car but the location of attendant and lavatory was unchanged. This fine coach had the distinction of being the very last LNWR or WCJS twelve-wheeler in capital stock. It was withdrawn in 1968, only a few days after its clerestory running mate.

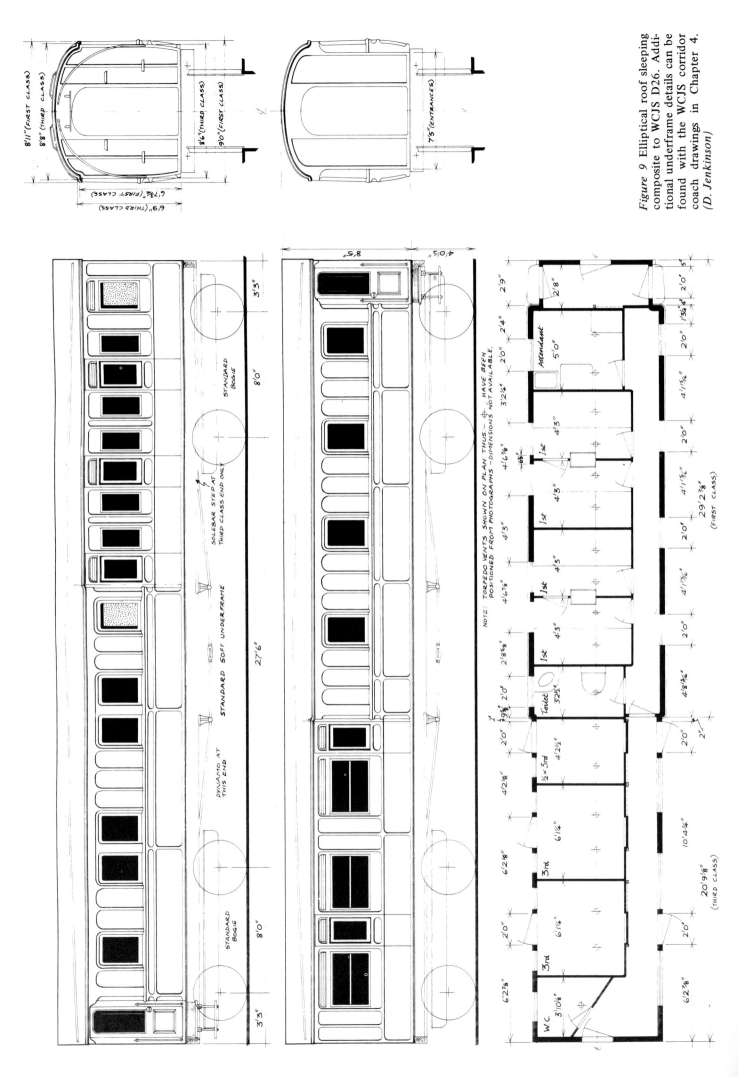

Figure 9 Elliptical roof sleeping composite to WCJS D26. Additional underframe details can be found with the WCJS corridor coach drawings in Chapter 4. (D. Jenkinson)

Plates 53 & 54 Photographs of the unorthodox composite sleeping coaches are rare and often of indifferent quality. Nevertheless, the unusual nature of the vehicles justifies the inclusion of these two pictures. *Plate 53 (above)* is a reproduction of an official LNWR postcard and shows the clerestory conversion to WCJS D28 while *Plate 54 (below)* shows the second elliptical roof variety to WCJS D26, the type drawn opposite.
(F. W. Shuttleworth's collection, R. J. Essery's collection)

It has been mentioned that until well after the grouping, only the first class passenger was provided with proper sleeping accommodation. However, there were several services on which the number of potential first class customers would not justify the use of a full twelve-wheel sleeping car. For these passengers, a so-called 'Sleeping Composite' was created at Wolverton — the coaches can hardly be said to have been designed for they were surely amongst the most peculiar passenger vehicles ever to run in Britain.

Basically, all had started life as 50ft arc roof WCJS corridor coaches of 1899-1902 vintage, the types involved being composites and brake composites — see pages 72-6. At a later stage, probably between about 1905 and 1908, some of them were converted into sleeping composites by removing the first class end of the body and replacing it with a sleeping section whose amenities exactly matched those of the current twelve-wheel sleeping cars. The third class end remained unaltered except for the fitting of a new roof to match the profile at the rebuilt end.

Since, at the time of conversion, the twelve wheel stock had reached the 9ft wide stage, these hybrid composites were built to match. One thus had a 9ft wide first class end somewhat uncomfortably married to the existing 8ft 6in third class end on the original 50ft chassis. Furthermore, halfway along the coach, the exterior panelling changed from the typical twelve-wheel style to the conventional Wolverton standard type. Moreover, in at least some cases, the first class sleeping portion was given a different running number from that of the vehicle itself. Plans of the coaches are included at *Fig. 2*.

Three diagrams were issued for these conversions, one with a clerestory roof and two with elliptical roofs. The clerestory version (WCJS D28) and the first of the elliptical roof coaches (WCJS D27) both started life as corridor brake composites to WCJS D41 and hence shared identical interior layouts after conversion. In fact, it seems reasonable to assume that the change from clerestory to elliptical style took place during the period when this batch of coaches

was undergoing conversion — hence the two diagrams.

The later elliptical roof conversions (WCJS D26) originated as corridor composites to WCJS D30. These coaches were opposite handed in relation to the brake composites involved in the first conversion. Hence, the sleeping composites created out of this batch presented almost a mirror image of the first series in terms of interior layout. This final design outlived the earlier two types and in the early 1930s, the LMS turned six of them into true composite sleeping cars by fitting the third class end with proper berths. This was done by removing all the third class seats and interior partitions and forming two larger compartments out of the original two plus coupé. Four third class sleeping berths were arranged longitudinally in each of these larger compartments. These four berth compartments, with upper and lower bunks, were of approximately similar standard to those provided in the LMS built third class sleeping cars proper but the ex-WCJS composites did not last very long, being withdrawn at the end of 1936.

The classic Wolverton sleeping cars had a long and honourable life, spanning more than half a century in revenue service. From them were directly derived the first LMS standard sleeping car designs which, in turn, contributed a large quota of features to the Stanier and BR standard sleeping cars. The survival of two genuine pre-group examples in the Royal Train for almost ten years after the general service vehicles had all gone to the scrap heap was ample testimony to their rugged construction and fine riding qualities. It can only be a cause for regret that no-one saw fit to rescue at least one of them for one of the several collections of preserved vehicles. To see these lovely coaches being crudely hacked to pieces and then burnt on their frames in late 1968 was a sight which the author would rather have been spared. Some consolation can be gained from the fact that the sleeping compartments in the Duke of Sutherland's private saloon (preserved in the national collection) are very similar to the standard Wolverton pattern at the turn of the century.

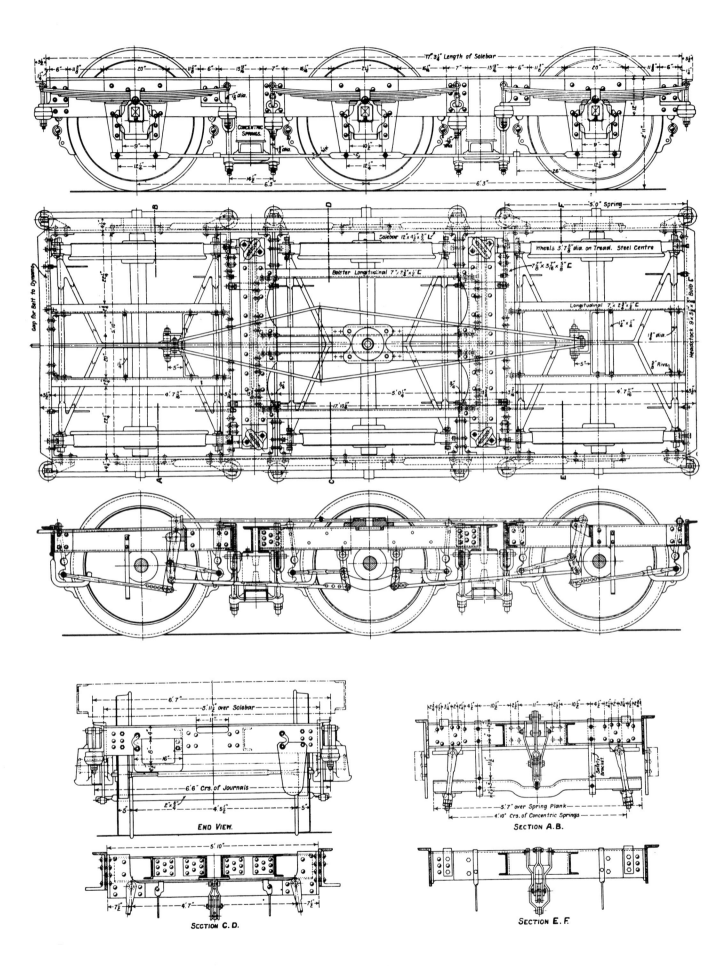

Figure 10 12ft 6in bogie as used on elliptical roof twelve wheel coaches.
('Railway Engineer', courtesy National Railway Museum)

Chapter 3 Dining Cars

Establishing the Style

West Coast dining cars were something of an institution. Acclaimed by many as the finest refreshment vehicles ever to run in this country, their characteristic lineaments were a feature of main line trains long after the contemporary general service coaches had been relegated to lesser use and replaced by the more modern outlines of the LMS standard coaches. Many indeed lasted long enough to see service with BR some forty years or more after first taking to the rails.

As with sleeping cars, dining cars first made their appearance from Wolverton before the start of the period with which this book is primarily concerned. It will, therefore, be helpful to take a brief backward look to see what had happened in the catering field before the first corridor trains made their appearance.

Dining car services were somewhat later arrivals on LNWR metals than sleeping facilities and this may have been because the contractual nature of many of the station refreshment rooms obliged certain trains to stop for meal breaks. Although the Great Northern Railway had pioneered dining cars in Britain in 1879 with a single Pullman car running between London and Leeds, it was not until some few years later that the first LNWR dining cars were put into service. These were 34ft six-wheel clerestory coaches and exhibited a somewhat modified version of the traditional Wolverton panelling and rather tall narrow windows *(Plate 56)*. They were the first LNWR general service coaches to be fitted with clerestories, known at the time as 'elevated roofs'. They ran as a pair with the kitchen vehicle seating eight passengers and the non-kitchen coach having fourteen seats. They went into service between London and Lancashire but, by all accounts, did not ride too well and were later, in spite of their short length, rebuilt with bogies. However, they did form the prototypes for some rather similar 42ft twin dining cars in 1892. These cars were almost contemporary with the pioneer twelve-wheel coaches and probably established some of their interior features. They were gas lit and their interior finishings matched those of the early twelve-wheel stock described below.

(Text continues on page 47)

Plate 55 Although but 34ft long, the pioneer LNWR diners lacked nothing in opulence and splendour as this 1890 interior view indicates — an exterior view is at *Plate 56*.

44

Plates 56-59 Pre-twelve-wheel dining cars. *Plate 56 (opposite — upper)* shows the twin 34ft diners 117 and 118 converted from the saloons shown at *Plate 4/5*. The exterior body is little altered but the coaches are now on bogies. *Plate 57 (opposite — lower)* shows a pair of the 42ft twin dining saloons for the Manchester-London service. The 45ft twelve wheel coaches for the Edinburgh portion of the pioneer WCJS corridor train were rather similar in aspect to these cars.

None of Wolverton's diners lacked ornamentation but if anything, the 42ft cars could arguably claim to have been the most elaborately decorated of all, as the two typical interiors on this page indicate. The somewhat over-stuffed Victorian pomposity of these cars cannot disguise the superb quality of craftsmanship displayed in the inlays, carving and other decoration.

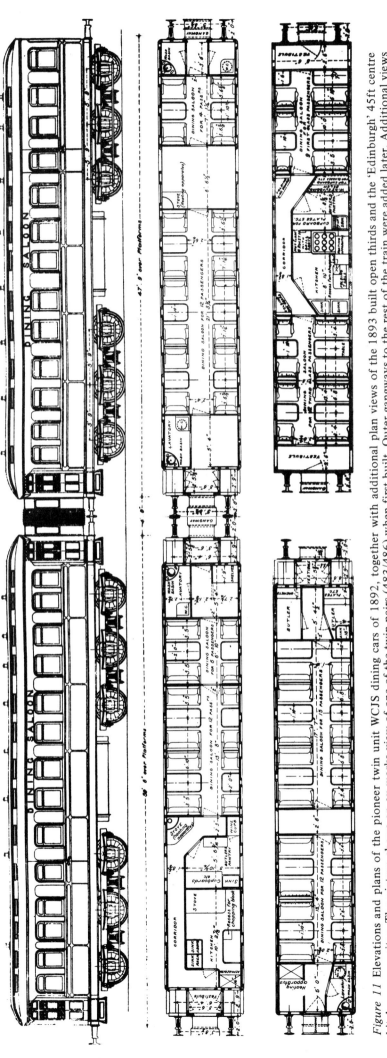

Figure 11 Elevations and plans of the pioneer twin unit WCJS dining cars of 1892, together with additional plan views of the 1893 built open thirds and the 'Edinburgh' 45ft centre kitchen composites. The picture shows an ex-works view of one of the twin pairs (483/486) when first built. Outer gangways to the rest of the train were added later. Additional views of car 483 are on pages 12/13. (*Drawing: 'Railway Engineer', courtesy National Railway Museum*)

The twelve-wheel dining car made its bow from Wolverton in 1892-3, shortly before the introduction of the first corridor trains on the West Coast route. As has already been stated, these early cars more or less established the basic exterior styling features of all subsequent LNWR and WCJS twelve-wheel designs. The subsequent evolutionary sequence from the 8ft 6in wide clerestory to the final 9ft wide elliptical style has also been described elsewhere so need not be repeated here. Suffice it to say that these changes in styling frequently, but not invariably, tended to appear on dining cars a year or two before being adopted for sleeping cars.

There was only one exception to the normal twelve-wheel exterior styling and it was to be found on one batch only of these early twelve-wheel diagrams. This was a truly transitional design between the older 42ft dining cars and what might be called the 'proper' Wolverton diners. The design was shown as LNWR D36 by the time the diagram book was prepared but the cars were, in fact, originally built for the WCJS. Three vehicles were constructed and were 45ft long. They had clerestories and their exterior styling largely combined that of the 34ft and 42ft dining cars, although the clerestory ends were now given a downward curve. Unlike later dining cars, these coaches had end entrances totally enclosed within the main body of the coach. They were composites and built for the Edinburgh section of the pioneer corridor train. Their plan view is shown with most of the later dining cars, at *Fig. 12* and the centre kitchen layout was to set the pattern for many subsequent composite dining cars from Wolverton, including all those built for the WCJS.

The remainder of the twelve-wheel dining cars built in 1892-3 were also in the WCJS book when first put into service. Three cars were built to each of three different designs namely kitchen-firsts, open firsts and open thirds. All three designs exhibited the new 'twelve-wheel' style of exterior panelling and introduced the characteristic entrance vestibules with all the associated wrought iron tracery.

The coaches themselves were of two basic types. The kitchen-firsts were 50ft 6in long with an outside entrance vestibule at both ends while the non-kitchen coaches were 47ft 9in long with an outside vestibule at one end only. As will be appreciated, all three types were, in effect, 45ft coaches with outside entrances added. It was, as will be recalled, the short-lived 45ft period of coach evolution when these pioneer dining cars were built.

Turning now to the coaches themselves, the kitchen-firsts of 1892, which later became LNWR D41, had an end kitchen layout and are shown on the works drawing as having 18 seats in three bays arranged with two seats on one side of the gangway and single seats on the other. This arrangement is confirmed in contemporary accounts of the cars but the same contemporary accounts also record that the cars were converted to a wholly single seat first class arrangement very soon after they were built so as to match the open firsts. It is, therefore, possible that they were actually designed as kitchen-thirds to run in pairs with the open firsts, being upgraded to first class when the open thirds emerged in 1893. At the opposite end to the kitchen was located a lavatory which was entered from a fairly capacious circulating area outside the entrance to the dining saloon.

The open firsts of 1892 (later LNWR D31A) seated 16 passengers, all in single seats. A four seat one bay saloon was located at the end opposite the main entrance to the car and was separated from a 12 seat, three bay saloon by a transverse vestibule with outside doors. Between the 12 seat saloon and the main entrance there were luggage racks and a lavatory. When transferred to LNWR D31A, the four seat saloon was stripped of its fittings, the outside doors to the transverse vestibule were sealed up and a small kitchen was built into the area so vacated. They thus became 12 seat kitchen-firsts and in this form went into ambulance use during the first world war. They never returned to book stock.

The open thirds appeared in 1893 and allowed the twin dining car sets to be enlarged to triple units. They were rather similar to the open firsts except that the lavatory was located beyond the smaller saloon at the non verandah end. Their introduction seems to have been the reason behind the upgrading of the aforementioned 50ft 6in cars. According to the diagram book, the saloons in two of the open thirds (later LNWR D42) seated 10 and 14 in two plus two and a half bays respectively while the third car (later LNWR D43) had 12 and 15 seats with the same bay arrangement. The coaches with reduced seating capacity are shown with single seats on both sides of the gangway adjacent to the vestibule partitions.

Contemporary accounts and pictures are at variance with the diagram book for these open thirds. The 'Railway Engineer', of 1893 records them as 18 seat coaches with single seats throughout and the picture at *Plate 63*, generally believed to be an interior view of one of them, would confirm this fact. However, a contemporary drawing, also in the 'Railway Engineer', shows a 27 seat arrangement. The most probable explanation seems to be that two of them started as 18 seat vehicles and one as a 27 seat coach. The latter may have been a spare unit. It seems probable that the 18 seaters were soon altered to two plus one seating, retaining the central gangway at the partitions and thus giving rise to the 24 seat variant.

Although the precise original seating arrangement of these coaches is a little uncertain, considerable information has survived concerning their internal finishing, which was based on that established in the 42ft twin saloons. It can only be described as opulent. In the first class sections, chairs and tables were of mahogany with ornamental panels and carved legs. Upholstery was in green figured moquette with green fringed velvet headcloths, while the roofs were covered in heavy gold ornamented flock paper with a floral design or with white on gold ground lincrusta. Floors were carpeted.

Third class upholstery was in patterned button down rep, the Edinburgh cars having brown on a dark blue ground and the Glasgow thirds being finished in red on a dark blue ground. In both cases, the buttons were bright red. Third class ceilings were pink on white ground lincrusta and floors were covered in linoleum.

Throughout the cars, extensive use was made of American walnut and polished mahogany mouldings and panels, with carved pilasters and inlaid marquetry work at the sides of door and window openings. Lighting in the cars was by gas, utilising ornamental brass pendant lacquered gaslamps with opal shades, suspended from the clerestory. Lavatories were panelled in polished sycamore and were fitted with silvered basins. Cooking was by gas and a self-contained gas-fired water apparatus provided the carriage heating.

The choice of a twelve-wheel chassis for these early WCJS dining cars may seem rather strange. However, according to contemporary accounts, six-wheel bogies were adopted solely because of the short length of point locking bars at that period.

These pioneer diners have been described in detail since one can detect in them the seeds of many features which were later to become widespread in the 65ft 6in dining cars. A study of the plans at *Fig. 12* will reveal that both end and centre kitchen layouts were employed from the outset and almost from the start, one saw the introduction of single seating for first class cars and two plus one in the thirds. Those few interior pictures which have survived indicate that the elaborate fittings which were so characteristic of Wolverton's dining cars were established in all essentials at a very early stage. The basic style changed but little over the next twenty or more years.

(Text continues on page 50)

Plates 60 & 61 The interiors on this page depict the No 1 and No 2 saloons of the 50ft 6in diner No 483 (*Fig. 11*). They clearly confirm the 2+1 seating arrangement when first built. Apart from the fringed seat headcloths, which were not repeated, these cars virtually established most of the decor ideas for the next decade or more.

Plate 62 (above) Interior view of 47ft 9in open first No 486 (*Fig. 11*). The decoration is all but identical to car 483 *(opposite)* but the seats are single on both sides of the gangway.

Plate 63 (below) This interior view of the 47ft 9in open thirds of 1893 shows, for the first time, the type of dining seat which became standard on all cars for the next ten years. Note the universal use of single seats in a *third* class coach. It seems that this feature may not have lasted long — see page 47.

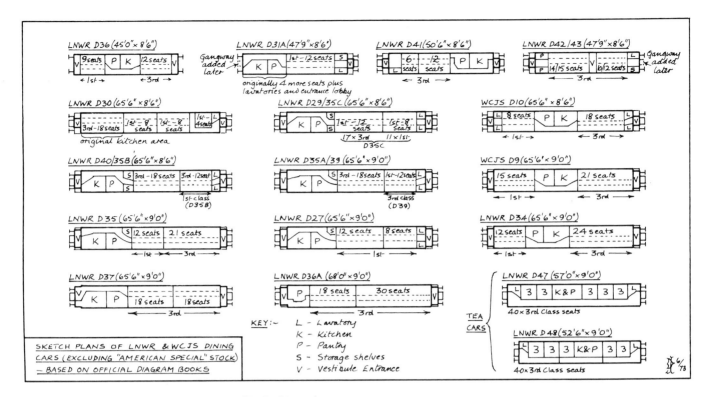

Figure 12 Sketch plans of dining cars. *(D. Jenkinson)*

When the WCJS was provided with its final quota of 65ft 6in dining cars in 1905, the 1893 coaches were divided between the LNWR and the Caledonian Railway. At least eight of the twelve seem to have reached the LNWR stock list and are recorded in the summary table of types at Appendix I. It is probable, though not confirmed, that the balance went to the CR. One of the Caledonian quota, probably a 50ft 6in kitchen version, underwent a whole series of successive rebuilds to fit it out as a departmental saloon and was in use in Scotland well into BR days as No. Sc 45018M. It even acquired a pair of Gresley bogies but, in its latter days, there was little, apart from some residual 'Wolverton' panelling, to enable the observer to appreciate its original nature. It is now privately preserved in this form, but in Caledonian livery, at Steam Town, Carnforth.

The 65ft 6in phase was ushered in only two or three years after the first twelve-wheel cars had started work. Again a batch of three cars was built but since only one was dual fitted, they cannot have been intended for Scottish workings. They were end kitchen first class cars with a total seating capacity for 20 passengers. Inside the vehicles there were two 8 seat saloons occupying the four bays adjacent to the kitchen. There was then a transverse vestibule from which access was gained to a further 4 seat saloon in the form of an orthodox compartment with side corridor alongside. This semi-private saloon was for ladies only or small private parties and was a popular feature in Pullman

cars of a later era; but it was not repeated in any other dining car designs from Wolverton. The interior of the coach was completed with a lavatory between the small saloon and the entrance lobby. Interior finishings did not differ significantly from the earlier cars.

All three of these coaches survived to the LMS and in 1927 had the kitchens removed to be replaced by a three bay third class saloon seating 18 passengers. They thus became 38 seat open composites but seem to have retained their original diagram number (D30). They saw little service in this form, being withdrawn in 1930.

These three dining cars mark the end of the development phase in dining car design at Wolverton. From this point onwards, cars tended to be built in larger batches and, until the rather specialised dining vehicles were built for the American Special stock in 1908, Wolverton concentrated exclusively on the combined kitchen and dining saloon and built no more non-kitchen vehicles. By direct contrast with the Midland Railway which, at about the same period, tended to favour a kitchen-first plus open third arrangement, the prevailing view on the LNWR seems to have been that a genuine kitchen-diner should be offered to every type of customer.

The adoption of this policy was to give rise to what was, perhaps, Wolverton's finest carriage building decade — a true golden age when elegance, style and, above all, craftsmanship were as important, if not more so, than mere functional convenience.

Plate 64 The pioneer 65ft 6in twelve-wheeler, first class diner 196, later 5196. It became LMS 10413 and was later converted to a 38 seat open composite (LNWR D30).

The Golden Age of Dining Cars

Mention a North Western dining car to students of railway history and the chances are that the minds of the majority will immediately turn to the image of a 65ft 6in twelve-wheel clerestory coach — and this is not really surprising. Between the end of 1896 and the middle of 1905, the famous clerestory diners were rolling out of Wolverton works at an average rate of almost ten per year. Never before had so much emphasis been placed on catering vehicles. Even the LMS in its peak dining car building phase (1930-7) only managed to build some thirty more cars for the whole of its system than had Wolverton alone more than thirty years previously for merely the West Coast part of it. When this activity is put alongside George Whale's restocking of the locomotive department, not to mention the tremendous steps being taken at Wolverton to improve the quality of the normal general service coaches, it will be appreciated that the LNWR did not so much enter the twentieth century as erupt into it!

During this period, 82 clerestory dining cars were built, masterpieces of craftsmanship and representing all that was best in late Victorian and early Edwardian travel. Of this grand total, no less than 50 were built during the years 1897-1901, a building rate approaching one per month. These were the 8ft 6in wide cars whereas the remaining 32 coaches which emerged between 1903 and 1905 were of the 9ft pattern.

Only two basic 8ft 6in designs were produced, one for the LNWR and the other for the WCJS. As far as can be deduced, the WCJS design was the first to appear. This was a centre kitchen composite design, fifteen of which were built in 1897 to WCJS D10. The interior layout was clearly inspired by the pioneer 45ft WCJS diners and consisted of a two bay, 8 seat first class saloon at one end and a three bay, 18 seat third class saloon at the other. The extreme corners of the car were occupied by lavatories and the coaches had the same narrow entrance vestibules as the 1893 and 1895 cars.

Almost coincident with the introduction of WCJS D10, the standard LNWR 8ft 6in diner made its appearance. This was an end kitchen five bay design clearly derived from the pioneer 65ft 6in cars of 1895 but without the little private saloon. Lavatories were located between the dining area and the entrance vestibule. The first of this type to appear were 20 seat kitchen-firsts to LNWR D29, and 25 cars were placed in service between 1897 and 1901. Although the diagram book indicates that they had narrow entrance vestibules, most pictures located by the author illustrate examples with intermediate width entrances. It is, therefore clear that only the early examples had the narrow entrances; how many has not been confirmed. Some sources record a WCJS example of this type of car but the final WCJS diagram book does not confirm this supposition. The explanation of this discrepancy is given by the account of LMS Car No. 76 (below).

Supplementing the first class cars were ten, externally identical second and third class cars to D40 which were built in 1901. These had the same interior layout as the first class coaches but with two/gangway/one seating. They thus accommodated 18 + 12 passengers. Although no first/third versions of these cars were built as such, at about the time of the grouping, seven of the first class coaches were rebuilt with two and one seating (except

(Text continues on page 57)

Plate 65 The fine lines of the first generation 65ft 6in cars are well exemplified by this picture of WCJS 561 to Diagram W10 when first built. A broadside view is given at *Plate 20.*

Plates 66-69 The interiors of Wolverton's twelve-wheel coaches were used as the inspiration for the design of menu cards wherein a certain amount of artistic licence was clearly allowed! On this page, the WCJS menu card is seen *(above)* while below is the interior of the real coach — the third class end of WCJS D10 *(Plate 65)*. Note the original gas lights, soon to be replaced by electric fittings.

Opposite is illustrated an LNWR menu card cover together with an interior view of first class diner 245, later 5245 of LNWR D29. This car became LMS 10407, later 71. Note the additional ventilation duct added below the clerestory on the right hand side lower roof. The reason for this modification is not known. The coach is electrically lit.

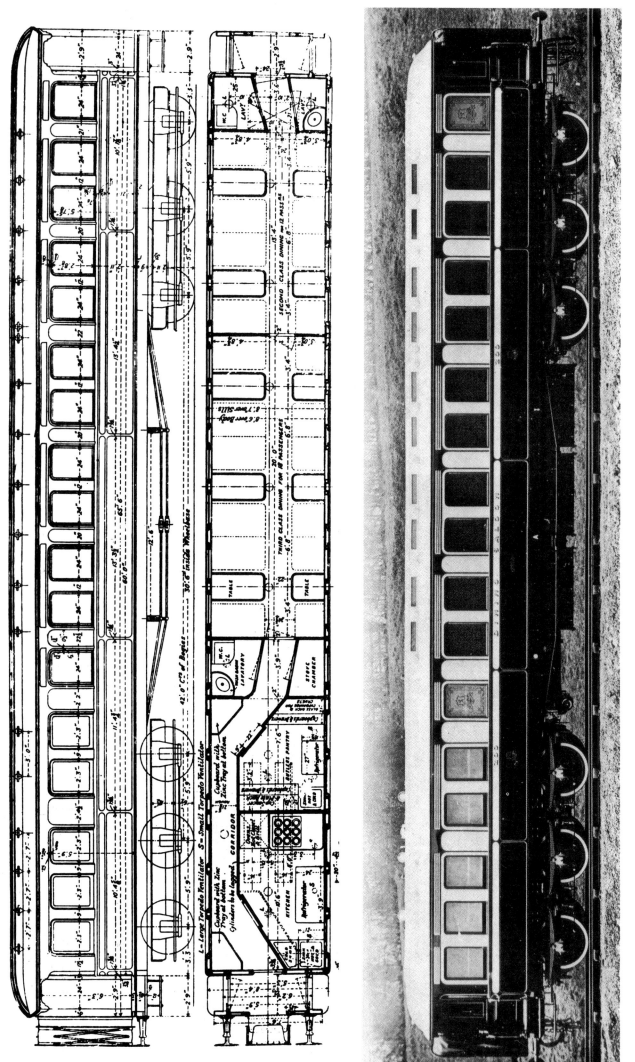

Figure 13 Standard 8ft 6in wide LNWR end kitchen composite dining car to D40. The drawing shows the arrangement of the intermediate width entrances and the photograph depicts the first class car 200 as first built for WCJS use. This coach is now preserved in the National Railway Museum and its more detailed history is given on page 57.
(Drawing: 'Railway Engineer', courtesy National Railway Museum)

Plates 70 & 71 (above) Interior views of two different saloons to LNWR D29. The view with the lighter ceiling shows No. 200 (opposite) as built. As preserved in the National Railway Museum, the car has been re-trimmed with later pattern LNWR upholstery and different light fittings. The left hand view shows an early example from D29, probably with narrow entrances. The electric light fittings are clearly derived if not converted from the earlier gas pattern — see, for example, Plates 60-3.

Plate 72 (below) Ex-LNWR Royal Train dining saloon No 76, seen in its final form in March 1956, shortly before withdrawal for preservation. It is coupled to Semi-Royal saloon to D1, No 807 (see Chapter 6). Note the replacement LMS pattern underframe on the dining saloon and the intermediate width vestibule entrances. This vehicle is now preserved at the National Railway Museum, York.

(F. W. Shuttleworth)

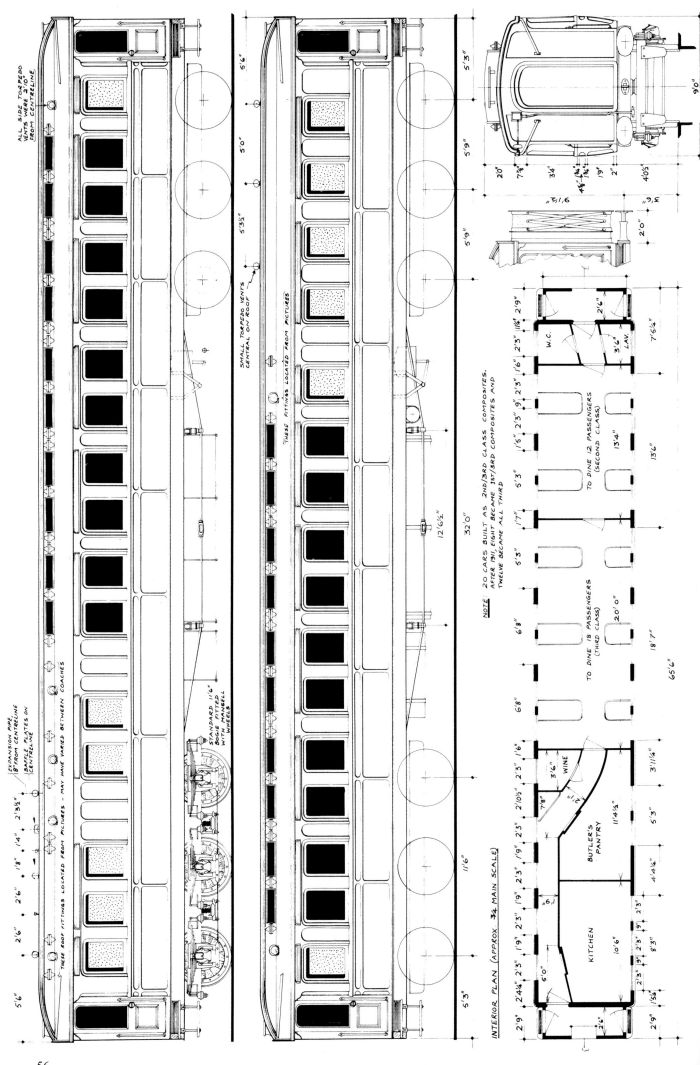

ALL SIDE TORPEDO VENTS WERE 2'0" FROM CENTRELINE

EXPANSION PIPE, 8" FROM CENTRELINE

BAFFLE PLATES ON CENTRELINE

THESE ROOF FITTINGS LOCATED FROM PICTURES - MAY HAVE VARIED BETWEEN COACHES

5'1" 2'6" 1'8" 14" 2'3½"

STANDARD 11'6" BOGIE FITTED WITH MANSELL WHEELS

SMALL TORPEDO VENTS CENTRAL ON ROOF

THESE FITTINGS LOCATED FROM PICTURES

5'6" 5'3"
5'0"
5'3½"
5'9"
5'9"
12'6½"
32'0"
11'6"
5'3"

9'0"
2'0" 7⅞" 34" 1'9" 2" 4'0½"
6'1½" 6'3"
2'0"

NOTE: 20 CARS BUILT AS 2ND/3RD CLASS COMPOSITES. AFTER 1911, EIGHT BECAME 1ST/3RD COMPOSITES AND TWELVE BECAME ALL THIRD

2'9" 1'6" 2'3" 11¼" 2'6" 2'9" 7'5¼"

W.C. 3'6" LAV.

1'5" 2'3" 9" 2'3" 1'6" 5'3"

TO DINE 12 PASSENGERS (SECOND CLASS)

134" 13'6"

1'7" 5'3"

6'8" 20'0" 18'7" 65'6"

TO DINE 18 PASSENGERS (THIRD CLASS)

6'8" 1'6" 2'3" 1'9" 2'3"

WINE 3'6" 1'0" 3'11¼"

BUTLER'S PANTRY 11'4¼"

7'8" 2'10½" 5'3" 4'4¼"

KITCHEN 10'6"

6'1" 2'3" 1'9" 9" 8'3"

2'9" 2'4¼" 2'3" 5'0" 2'3" 1'9" 1'5½"

2'6" 2'9"

INTERIOR PLAN (APPROX ¾ MAIN SCALE)

Figure 14 (left) Elevations and plan of the 65ft 6in x 9ft 0in clerestory composite dining car to LNWR D35A.
(D. Jenkinson)

Plate 73 (above) LNWR 9ft wide clerestory dining saloon No 290 (later 5290) was one of twenty handsome vehicles to D35A/D39 *(opposite)* and built in 1903-4. It became LMS 10455, later 269 and lasted until 1936.

adjacent to the interior partitions) and were reclassified as composites to D35C with 17 third class and 11 first class seats. In this role, they tended to be in great demand for weekend extra services. At about the same time as these seven cars were rebuilt and reclassified, six of the D40 composites were uprated to first/third. This does not seem to have involved much rebuilding and the cars retained their original seating capacity, now arranged as 18 third plus 12 first. This reclassification was allocated D35B. In 1929, these six cars had their lower step boards removed to enable them to work to Ramsgate under the restricted loading gauge of the Southern Railway.

The end kitchen 8ft 6in diners had a long and varied history. Undoubtedly the best known are the two vehicles which were allocated to the Royal Train (LMS 76 and 77) which, by great good fortune, have survived for posterity to see. LMS 76 is preserved in the Royal Train livery at the National Railway Museum and is a particularly celebrated coach. It was built in 1900, was allocated No. 200 in the WCJS series and appeared in the WCJS diagram book for a while. However, it was sent to the Paris Exhibition in the same year and eventually became LNWR No. 200 (later 5200) early in the reign of King George V. Very soon afterwards, the car had its smaller interior saloon modified by being given individual chairs and a table for use with the Royal Train. It is in this condition that it is preserved although it is now mounted on a replacement LMS pattern underframe with angle iron trussing and 12ft 6in wheelbase bogies. The LMS also made slight changes to the window ventilators. It is this car which, it is thought, has given rise to the belief that the WCJS made general use of end kitchen dining cars.

A much more genuine LNWR running condition is represented by the other preserved dining car (LMS 77). This coach retains its LNWR round bar and queenpost underframe together with the original bogies and interior fitments. It has a few minor changes to the exterior bodywork but basically portrays a very accurate picture of the style of car built at the turn of the century. At the time of writing (1977), it is housed at Quainton Road.

Reverting now to a consideration of general service coaches, it will be appreciated that before the conversion of many of the 8ft 6in cars to composite form, there was a considerable preponderance of first class dining accommodation within this group of vehicles and this had been the case since about 1901. At that time, in order to cope with the demands for refreshment services of the humbler traveller, the company experimented with odd 50ft side corridor coaches fitted out as second and third class dining composites. This involved placing tables in the compartments and marshalling the coach next to the dining car. How many coaches were thus treated is not known but the idea seems to have been only a stop-gap measure and in 1903-4, a batch of twenty new clerestory dining cars emerged from Wolverton to cater for the second and third class passenger. They were well worth waiting for *(Plate 73)*.

These cars (LNWR D35A) were built to the new 9ft wide style and were in essence directly derived from the 30 seat 8ft 6in cars to D40 (above). They seated 18 third class and 12 second class passengers and were very handsome looking coaches. When the second class was abolished on the LNWR, twelve of these cars were marked down to all third, becoming D39 and the other eight were re-classified as first/third composites, retaining their original diagram number. As far as is known, no major rebuilding was involved in these alterations of class. The eight composites were the first to be scrapped (1933-5) but the all thirds lingered on until 1938 during which year, the LMS converted the last three survivors into ARP lecture cars.

The final clerestory dining cars to emerge from Wolverton were, in some ways, the most famous of all these celebrated vehicles. They were composites and built in 1905 to WCJS D9. Twelve coaches were constructed and their external lines matched those of the final LNWR series; but their interior layout followed the classical WCJS centre kitchen pattern. The design was an almost exact repetition of the 8ft 6in WCJS D10 except that the four corner lavatories were omitted to make room for an extra half bay of seats at each end. Furthermore, the 9ft width enabled two and one seating to be provided at both ends of the car, thus

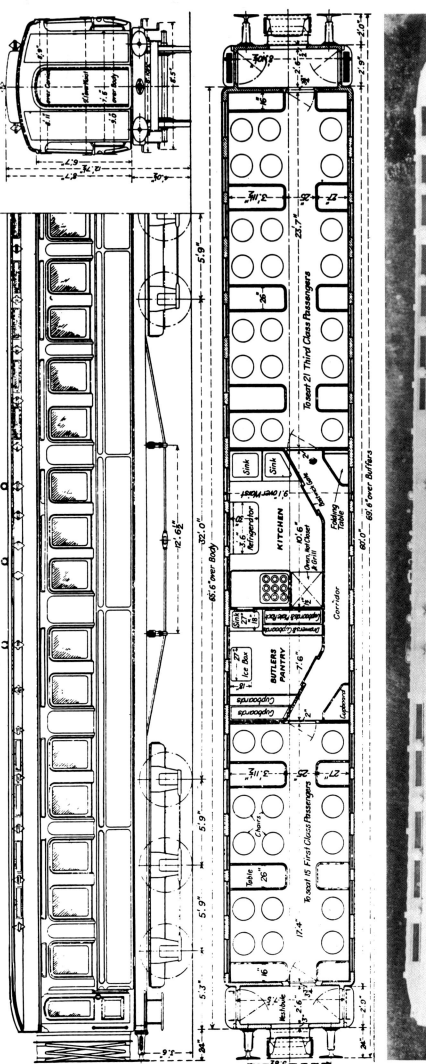

Figure 15 This page gives elevation and plan of the 9ft wide clerestory WCJS centre kitchen composites to Diagram W9. Note the general similarity to the earlier 8ft 6in coaches of Diagram W10 (*Plate 65*). The picture shows WCJS 531 ex-works in 1905 (LMS 10430, later 283). (*Drawing: 'Railway Engineer', courtesy National Railway Museum*)

Plate 74 First class saloon of WCJS 531 *(opposite)* showing the 'loose' seating adopted for these cars. This was the first real change in dining car interior design for over ten years.

boosting the seating capacity to 15 first plus 21 third. The building of these elegant coaches was responsible for the division of the pioneer 1893 diners between the LNWR and the Caledonian.

The interior finishing of these final clerestories saw the first significant departure from the styles established in the mid-1890s. They were designed with the object of increasing the dining accommodation and reducing the tare weight. It was not intended that passengers should use them for 'all the way' travel — hence the omission of lavatories.

The inevitable wood panelling was, of course, retained. The first class end had mahogany top panels in American walnut frames banded with dark walnut, green ebony and tulip wood. Tables were mahogany with red leather tops and dado panels were Italian walnut. In the third class end, the saloon was finished with oak top panels and mahogany mouldings in teak frames, dado panels being light oak vertical slats and the tables were teak with brown leather tops. Ceilings in both areas were flat white painted lincrusta with the floral design picked out in bright white enamel.

It was in the seating that the major change was visible. Seats were in the form of movable dining room chairs with arms, their materials matching those of the dining tables as appropriate. Some references state that at a later date, these armchairs were replaced by fixed seating of more conventional type but this has not been confirmed.

Ancillary fittings matched the contemporary sleeping cars. Although cooking continued to be by gas (as, indeed was generally the case with new dining cars right through the LMS period too), the coaches were electrically lit with both wall and centre lights and fitted with steam heating.

These final WCJS clerestory cars became very well known as a result of their presence in the celebrated 2 pm 'Corridor' from Euston to Edinburgh and Glasgow. At first they ran with the traditional arc roof stock but when, in 1908, Wolverton produced complete trains of twelve wheelers for this service, the clerestory diners became an integral part of the formation. Two diners were present in each set of eight coaches and further cars of the same type were also used on the 10 am Euston-Glasgow/Edinburgh trains. It was many years before they were replaced on these prestige trains and they did not become displaced from the mid day service until about 1930. After this date, the coaches were generally relegated to 'common' use for extra trains, especially at weekends. For this purpose, six of them were slightly modified to run the Ramsgate services in succession to the aforementioned 8ft 6in clerestory cars of LNWR D35B.

The WCJS 9ft cars were, by a long margin, the last Wolverton clerestory diners to run in general service and the last was not withdrawn until mid-1950. They were the last dining cars to be built for the WCJS.

Plate 75 Apart from the lighter woodwork and the lack of carpets below the tables, the third class end of WCJS 531 hardly differed from the first class saloon.

Plate 76 (above) LNWR D35 was almost an elliptical roof version of the clerestory design illustrated at *Plate 73*. The vehicle depicted here (LNWR 85, later 5085) became LMS 10450, later 288.

Plate 77 (left) Interior view of dining saloon No 85. Note the somewhat simpler decorative treatment compared with the clerestory interiors at *Plates 70/71*.

The Elliptical Roof Phase

Not surprisingly, the tremendous building of clerestory dining cars during the 1897-1905 period left the LNWR and WCJS in a very healthy position for catering vehicles. In consequence of this, together with a cessation of dining car services during the first world war, only twelve further combined kitchen and dining cars were built before the grouping. However, by contrast with the 82 clerestory vehicles to only two basic layouts, the elliptical diners involved four diagrams, all differing in layout. Furthermore, during the same period the LNWR also introduced three futher types of catering vehicle which broke away from the kitchen-diner concept. One cannot, therefore, avoid concluding that Wolverton felt itself able to experiment a little more than it could at the turn of the century.

Dealing first with the kitchen diners, the first to appear were four composites to LNWR D35 in 1907. These had a traditional end kitchen layout but, unlike all previous end kitchen designs, there were no lavatories provided. These were replaced by an extra half bay of third class seats

giving a capacity of 12 first class and 21 third class passengers.

This composite design was followed in 1908 by the most spacious dining car ever built at Wolverton before the grouping. It was to D27 and only one example was built. The car itself, a 20 seat kitchen-first, was built initially for the experimental Birmingham-London (Broad Street) businessman's service and in spite of its 9ft width, it reverted to the exclusively single seat style of the 8ft 6in clerestory cars. In view of the short lived nature of the service for which it was built and the unique and spacious interior layout, it is rather surprising that this non-standard car was not permanently re-allocated to the Royal Train as a substitute for one of the somewhat more cramped clerestory coaches. It did run from time to time in the Royal Train but always tended to remain something of an odd man out until withdrawn in 1941, at which time it was somewhat demoted by being turned into a salvage exhibition vehicle.

Plate 78 The palatial 'one-off' first class dining saloon to D27, No 302 (later 5302). It became LMS 10391, later 78.

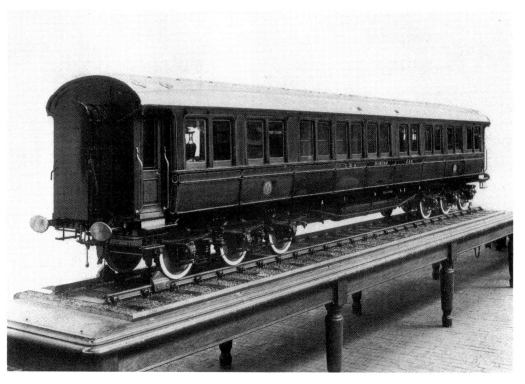

The third variety of elliptical roof kitchen-diner was to D34 in 1910. This was a batch of four centre kitchen composites, very similar to the final WCJS clerestory design but not fitted with dual standard braking. By comparison with the WCJS coaches from which they were clearly derived, these coaches had three fewer first class and three extra third class seats which gave a two bay plus four bay layout with 12 first and 24 third seats respectively. There were no lavatories. A superb model of one of these cars can be seen at the National Railway Museum and the vehicles themselves were very long lived. The final survivor was withdrawn in 1960 and was the last LNWR dining car to run in general service. It is not known for what services these cars were originally intended but the LMS and BR used them a great deal in Scotland. It is mildly surprising that these cars were not dual fitted and built to a WCJS diagram. Incorporated in the twelve wheel 2 pm sets, they would have exactly matched the side corridor vehicles.

Plate 79 (above) Quarter scale model of centre kitchen composite dining saloon to D34. This superb model is thought to have been built at Wolverton, contemporaneously with the real coaches (1910) and is seen here in LMS livery as displayed for many years at the old Euston station. As now displayed at the National Railway Museum, York, it is fully repainted in its original LNWR livery.

Plate 80 (below) Former LNWR composite dining car to D34 No Sc290M seen in Scotland in early BR days, hardly changed, save in livery, from its earliest days. It began life as LNWR 5087, 1st LMS 10417.

(F. W. Shuttleworth)

Plate 81 (above) The final LNWR kitchen/dining saloon design was to D37 in 1914. This design had six seating bays and almost full width vestibule entrances. Of the six examples originally envisaged, only three seem to have been built and the other three allocated numbers were given to the pantry thirds *(below)*. Saloon No 5026 became LMS 10477, later 295 and was scrapped in 1946.

Plate 82 (below) The only 68ft dining vehicles built by the LNWR were the pantry thirds to D36A in 1920. Saloon No 5035 (LMS 10474, later 199) was the last of the three to be built.

Plate 83 Interior view of 68ft pantry third to D36A *(Plate 82 – opposite)*. The fixed seats are to a new design and the whole interior is markedly less cluttered than that of the original clerestory cars, though still obviously from the same family line.

The last of the LNWR kitchen dining cars emerged in 1914 to D37. Three coaches were built of six bay, end kitchen design seating 36, nominally third class passengers. In fact, they ran for most of their life as composites seating 18 firsts and 18 thirds with the third class seats adjacent to the kitchen. The six bay layout was a new departure for an end kitchen design and was only achieved at the expense of toilet space. These dining cars were fitted with the very wide entrance vestibules also used on the 68ft sleeping cars of similar vintage. The diagram book suggests that six of these D37 cars might, originally, have been envisaged. However, the three extra running numbers allocated to D37 were, in the event, given to the 68ft pantry thirds to D36A (below).

All the kitchen-diners built during the elliptical roof period reverted to the traditional fixed style of seating.

During the elliptical roof period, the LNWR also experimented with other methods of providing catering accommodation. The most noteworthy innovation was the provision of three sets of dining coaches in 1908 to run in the American Special trains. Each set was in the form of an open first/kitchen only car/open composite triplet. The kitchen cars were 50ft vehicles on four wheel bogies but styled to match the twelve wheel dining saloons which latter followed normal practice. The coaches are described in more detail in Chapter 6, along with the rest of these set trains, but it is worth mentioning here that their seating

style was very similar to that used on the final WCJS clerestory cars and employed loose armchairs rather than fixed traditional seats.

The last open dining cars built in the traditional manner, were three 68ft pantry thirds to D36A in 1920. They appear to have been built in place of three further examples of D37 (above). Their interior layout is given at *Fig. 12* and they are illustrated on this page. The traditional end vestibule was present as usual but, rather surprisingly in view of their late date of building and the 68ft length, the vestibules reverted to the pre-1914 width of the older cars rather than the new style of D37. It is for this reason that they are thought unlikely to have been rebuilds of D37; furthermore, it seems unlikely that the LNWR would rebuild a dining car to an increased length! One possible reason for the reversion to the older type of entrances is that they may have been intended to provide extra dining accommodation on the American boat trains and were built to match that style of coach. Although the LMS did use them on the Liverpool service in the 1920s, paired with a kitchen-first, their first recorded workings in 1920 were on the Euston-Wolverhampton trains. They had traditional fixed seats. These coaches were the only LNWR 68ft dining cars and although they did not have kitchens, the LMS numbered them in the dining car series and not with the open third class group of coaches.

The third catering innovation during the final pre-group phase was the development of the corridor third class tea car. The exact date of introduction of this type of vehicle cannot be determined but two styles of coach were involved. The purpose behind these cars was to provide a corridor service of light refreshments — in effect, the precursors of the modern miniature buffet cars.

The first vehicles (to LNWR D47) were eight 57ft coaches of orthodox 1906-7 cove roof style. It is not clear whether they were built as tea cars from new or were later conversions from existing stock. Essentially, the coach was an orthodox seven compartment corridor third with two compartments removed to make way for the kitchen and pantry. Above this area was a small raised roof section, rather like a miniature clerestory, to assist in ventilation.

The second tea car design to D48 was similar in concept. Built in 1915, these later coaches had full elliptical roofs and no clerestory and are thought to have been built new as tea cars. They were the last LNWR catering vehicles to be built with cooking facilities.

Plate 84 57ft cove roof corridor third class tea car to D47, No 442. Note the short clerestory above the pantry. The later numbering of this car is not known.

Plate 85 (below) 52ft 6in corridor third class tea car to LNWR D48, seen running as LMS 4656 (later LMS 184). It had started life as LNWR No 230.

Chapter 4   General Service Corridor Stock

The side corridor coach is the only major type of vehicle whose pre-group growth and development is wholly encompassed within the main period covered by this book. In consequence, it is the only style of vehicle where the diagram book evidence is, for all practical purposes, complete. The quantities built are summarised at *Table 1*.

The corridor coach probably exhibited more visible changes in style than any other single category of vehicle to emerge from Wolverton during 1893 to 1923. In a sense, therefore, one can use the corridor vehicle as the barometer of change at Wolverton during this period. As explained in Chapter 1, the design of general service stock passed through three basic phases, most easily identified by the roof style adopted. From the point of view of corridor stock, these changes in roof style also coincided, as often as not, with other and perhaps more significant changes within the vehicle. It seems logical therefore, to base the study of these coaches on this basic threefold division.

Arc Roof Stock: 1893-1903
Although the first corridor coaches were built at Wolverton in 1893, the use of side corridors on the LNWR proper did not become very widespread until the turn of the century. In fact, apart from an odd batch of third class coaches, the first corridor vehicles built purely for the LNWR did not even enter service until 1898-9. Thus, the first phase of corridor development at Wolverton is essentially the story of the West Coast Joint Stock.

The first corridor vehicles to emerge were built to the then standard 42ft length in 1893. All except one design were for the WCJS and were 8ft 6in wide over the body, brakes being 9ft 2in over the projecting lookouts. All things considered, these were quite lavish dimensions for the time and the 8ft 6in width remained virtually standard for WCJS

vehicles until the widespread introduction of 9ft wide coaches in the early 1900s. The odd men out were the corridor thirds to LNWR D269. These were 42ft long by 8ft wide and may well have been the very first corridor coaches to be built at Wolverton. They were probably ex-7 compartment non-corridors and on rebuilding, six compartments and one lavatory were provided. To make room for the centre gangway adjacent to the end compartment, the latter was of slightly peculiar shape, having room for only four passengers instead of the usual six (see plans of types at *Fig. 16*). It is not known how many were built, but three are shown in the diagram book and this may have been the sum total. Only one of them reached the LMS — see Appendix I. Some brakes were also converted (see page 7).

On most British railways there were six basic varieties of side corridor coach namely first class, third class and composite, in each case either with or without a guard's and brake compartment. As far as the LNWR was concerned, however, the second class passenger had also to be catered for — at least until 1911; but since all the second class compartments had been downgraded to third class by the time the diagram book was prepared, it is simpler to refer to two classes only in this narrative. The provision of second class accommodation will, however, be mentioned where relevant. Second class accommodation was not provided in WCJS corridor coaches.

Five of the possible six varieties of coach were represented in the WCJS 42ft list, the omitted type being the brake first. This may have been a significant omission because the brake first was never a popular LNWR type, even in later days when corridor coaches were much more common. It is interesting to note that more recent BR practice tends to favour the brake first for inter-city workings. However, the lack of brake firsts was amply compensated by the presence of no fewer than four brake third designs together

---

TABLE 1 SUMMARY OF LNWR/WCJS GENERAL SERVICE CORRIDOR COACHES

The figure shown under each category is the number of such vehicles listed in the diagram books. In most cases, this is the same as the number built, but there may be odd discrepancies.

	ARC ROOF			COVE ROOF		STANDARD ELLIPTICAL			TOPLIGHT ELLIPTICAL			Totals
	42'	45'	50'	50'	57'	50'	52' 6"	57'	50'	52' 6"	57'	
First	—	—	9	—	9	—	—	6	—	4	2	30
Brake First	—	—	9	—	4	—	—	—	—	—	—	13
Composite	—	27	175	—	9	—	16	32	—	51	111	421
Brake Composite	3	10	84	10	60	—	—	38	—	—	56	261
Third	27	19	269	—	30	68	—	183	91	103	83	873
Brake Third	12	—	118	2	30	—	—	125	—	4	148	439
Totals	42	56	664	12	142	68	16	384	91	162	400	2037

Footnote: Coaches re-classified (usually downgraded) before the diagram books were issued are listed in this table in their re-graded form. For further details, see Appendix I.

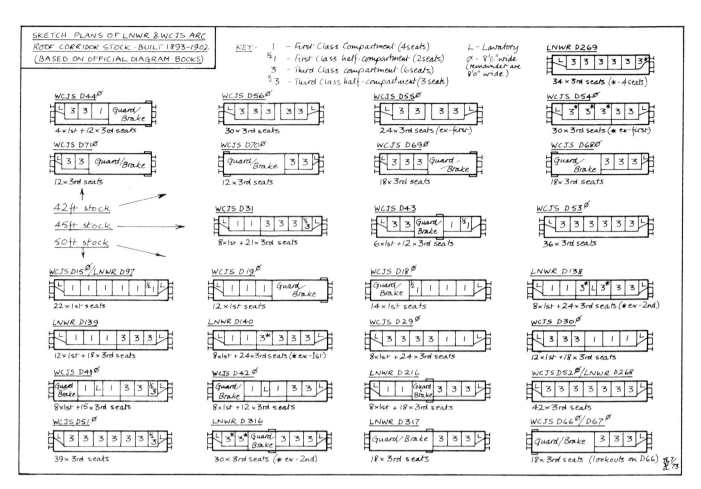

Figure 16 Sketch plans of arc roof corridor stock. (D. Jenkinson)

Plate 86 A specially posed picture of a train of WCJS 42ft corridor stock, together with a trio of the pioneer clerestory dining saloons. The locomotive is the famous Webb compound No 1304 *Jeanie Deans*.

with one brake composite diagram. The plans are given at *Fig. 16* from which it can be seen that both two and three compartment third brakes were built in both left and right handed versions (WCJS Diagrams 68-71). Only twelve coaches were involved all told. The matter of 'handed' brakes was also rather a prophetic move, rather akin to the omission of the brake first as a type. Throughout the whole of the corridor era on the LNWR, frequent attempts were made to maintain the corridor down one side only of the train in the more important services. This idea worked quite well where definite sets of coaches were provided but, as can be imagined, the ramifications of coach rostering amongst the common user vehicles rendered the scheme somewhat over-optimistic.

The fifth of the brake ended 42ft designs was a three compartment composite to WCJS D44. Three only were built and they were the only 42ft corridor coaches to retain first class accommodation for the whole of their working life.

The non-brake coaches in the 42ft series were all running as thirds by the time the final diagram book was issued and are listed as WCJS Diagrams 54-6. Originally, they were firsts, thirds and composites. All three types were very similar in aspect having end toilets and standardised compartments and seating. Because of the standardised compartment sizes, the first and thirds were each provided with a centrally located transverse vestibule. There was, of course, no space for such a vestibule in the composites which were also the most numerous of the three types. The transverse vestibules in the firsts and thirds were used for luggage storage since they had no outside doors.

The interior amenities provided in these 42ft coaches tended to set the style for the whole of the arc roof period and beyond. Third class compartments seated six and first class compartments had four seats. American walnut mouldings were favoured in both classes with sycamore panelling in the firsts and pine in the thirds. Both classes of compartment had white lincrusta ceilings and most metal fittings, including corridor handrails were brass.

Upholstery material is less certain. First class compartments were doubtless finished in the favoured moquette while one source quotes the thirds as being finished with upholstery in bright emerald green which it describes as 'a somewhat staring colour'. An interesting inclusion in the coaches was the provision of sprung flap seats in the corridors — presumably for use at busy periods. Lighting was initially by compressed oil gas although many (probably all) were later converted to electric light.

Published sources are at variances as to how the first corridor train was marshalled but the accompanying picture at *Plate 86*, almost certainly posed specially, at least gives a very good impression of the appearance of these 42ft coaches, along with the pioneer dining cars. It is clearly not the 'Corridor' itself since there is no sign of the Edinburgh dining car. Similar coaches which can be identified by type are also given in the picture caption to *Plate 16*.

A short time after the 42ft coaches were built, Wolverton had a mild flirtation with 45ft vehicles. Some published accounts seem to impart a greater degree of significance to these 45ft carriages than their numerical strength would indicate. It was, of course, the basic length for the early twelve wheel dining cars (disregarding the outside entrances) and was quite popular for saloons, but as far as side corridor stock is concerned, the length was not very common. Only three designs were introduced — again all to WCJS diagrams. One was a corridor third, one was a composite and the third design was a brake composite.

Little needs be said about the six compartment thirds. They were very similar to the 42ft coaches and had a long life in general service, the last survivor being withdrawn in 1942. The other two varieties were rather more interesting.

They appear to have been introduced in 1898, which is surprising, since by then the first of the 50ft coaches had been built. Moreover, some of the 45ft coaches were to the LNWR 8ft width rather than the WCJS standard of 8ft 6in.

The composites to WCJS D31 were orthodox vehicles with two first and three and a half third class compartments but the brake composites (WCJS D43) were rather different from the earlier 42ft coaches. They had two third plus one and a half first class compartments but the brake compartment was in the centre separating the two classes of accommodation. This centre brake arrangement was not uncommon on non-corridor stock but this was the first time it had appeared in corridor vehicles. It later became widespread on corridor stock built for LNWR use but was never repeated for the WCJS.

The side corridor coach only became an important feature on the purely LNWR routes at the turn of the century with the considerable building of 50ft stock. Large numbers of these coaches were placed in service between 1897 and 1903 for both LNWR and WCJS use. There were, however, fundamental differences between the coaches built for the LNWR and those constructed for the WCJS. It is therefore simpler to consider the two lines of development separately, starting with the LNWR series.

The LNWR coaches were all 50ft x 8ft and, in the case of brake coaches, 9ft over the projecting lookouts. Many, but not all, were dual fitted. As with the earlier WCJS 42ft coaches, five of the six possible types were produced, the exception once again, being a brake first. Except for corridor composites, of which there were two variants, only one basic design for each generic type was produced.

The full first to D97 was a five and a half compartment coach seating ?? passengers, all in corner seats. Six only were produced, vacuum fitted only and fitted with lavatories at each end.

By contrast with the small number of full firsts, corridor composites were very numerous, totalling 118 coaches. The commonest design was D138 which had 80 representatives, all built during 1898-9. These started as tri-composites with two compartments for each of the three classes and an additional lavatory in the centre of the coach. Within the compartments, finishing materials were, it is thought, very similar in both seconds and thirds — for example, armrests were not provided. Second class seats were, however, a little softer and probably upholstered in rather superior material to those in the third class areas. On the abolition of second class in 1911, the coaches were reclassified as first/third with four third class compartments.

The second composite design to D139 was again a six compartment vehicle, this time three first plus three third and no centre lavatory. At a later stage, some 22 were altered to D140. This merely involved altering one of the first class compartments to third class by changing the seats and the position of the connecting door between the two ends of the coach.

The brake composite design to D216 was another numerous type and perpetuated the centre brake arrangement first seen in the 45ft WCJS coaches but with considerably greater seating capacity. Sixty of them were built between 1900 and 1901.

The LNWR 50ft arc roof corridor third had the distinction of being the most numerous single type of side corridor coach ever to be built at Wolverton during the pregroup period. Between 1898 and 1903, 240 were built, some dual fitted and it was this type of coach which was occasionally used as a dining composite — see page 57. Early examples of the design had horizontally divided lavatory windows and on these particular coaches, the corridor side had droplights between every long window rather than in the outside doors only as in the later coaches (see *Figure 17* on page 68).

(Text continues on page 72)

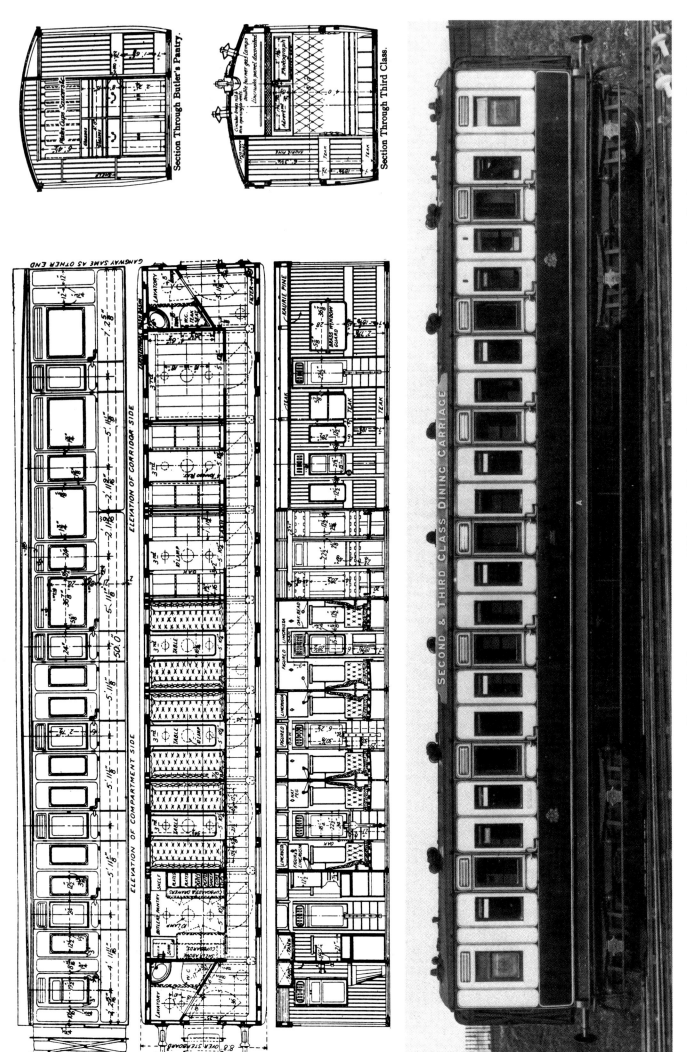

Figure 17 Standard 50ft arc roof corridor third to D268 modified for use as a second/third class dining carriage. Note the alternating large and small windows on the corridor side and the horizontally divided lavatory windows, typical features of early examples to this diagram — see also *Plate 17*. The coach illustrated, LNWR 2269, became LMS 4943, later 2331.

NOTES

1. UNDERFRAME DETAIL IS FOR ELECTRIC LIGHT. FOR GASLIT CONDITION OMIT BATTERY BOXES AND DYNAMO AND REPLACE WITH TWO GAS CYLINDERS 9'6"×1'6"(DIAM) SET 4'0" BETWEEN CENTRES IN POSITION SHOWN BY DOTTED LINES.

2. END ELEVATION OMITS HANDRAILS &. FOR THESE SEE DRG J.W.G.

3. INTERIOR PLANS ARE HALF MAN SCALE. ROOF VENTS AND GASLAMPS ARE NOTED. GAS LAMPS BEING RINGED THUS :- ⊕

4. DIMENSIONS QUOTED FOR COMPARTMENTS ARE LENGTH BETWEEN PARTITIONS.

5. UNDERFRAME/BOGIE DETAIL ALSO APPLIES TO W.C.J.S. 50'×8'6" CORRIDOR STOCK (SEE PAGES 73-75).

6. ON FULL BRAKE, GUARDS DOORS AND LOOK-OUTS WERE DIRECTLY OPPOSITE EACH OTHER AND NOT DIAGONALLY OPPOSITE.

NOTE: TORPEDO VENTS ON FULL BRAKE ROOF LOCATED EITHER SIDE OF ROOF HATCHES & 2'0" FROM CENTRELINE.

8'6" END ELEVATION
(FULL VAN ONLY)

6'9"

8'6" (SOLEBAR STEPS)
8'9" (BOGIE STEPS)
9'2" (OVER LOOKOUTS)

7'10"

4'0"

COMPOSITE
FIRSTS: 7'1¼"
THIRDS: 5'10½"
TOILETS: 4'0½" AND 3'2"

BRAKE COMPO.
FIRSTS: 7'1¼"
THIRDS: 5'10½"
GUARD: 9'1½"
TOILETS: 4'0½"

THIRD
THIRDS: 5'10¼"
TOILETS: 3'11¾"

← THIS SECTION ORIGINALLY 2ND CLASS

W.C. | 1st | 3rd | 3rd | 3rd | W.C.
8'0"

W.C. | 1st | GUARD/BRAKE | 3rd | 3rd | W.C.
8'0"

W.C. | 3rd | 3rd | 3rd | 3rd | W.C.
8'0"

50'0"

CORRIDOR THIRD (WOLVERTON DRAWING 3298)

← CORRIDOR SIDE

CORRIDOR THIRD WAS EXACTLY SYMMETRICAL ABOUT THE CENTRELINE, THEREFORE ONLY HALF ELEVATIONS ARE SHOWN ON THIS DRAWING.

6'2⅝" | 2'0" | 5'11½" | 4'11½" | 8'10½" | 7'10½" | 2'6" | 6'2⅝"

COMPARTMENT SIDE →

CORRIDOR FULL BRAKE (THIS DESIGN WAS 8'6" WIDE OVER BODY PANELS)

G.L. :- GAS LAMP (10") CENTRELINES

INWARD OPENING DOOR (BOTH SIDES) WITH HANDLE ALWAYS ON SIDE FURTHEST FROM LOOKOUT

GAS CYLINDER (SEE NOTES)

BATTERY BOX ON BOTH SIDES

VACUUM CYLINDER FAR SIDE 2'1" FROM LONGITUDINAL

BODY SUPPORT BRACKETS FOR 8'6" WIDE STOCK

REPEAT BOGIE

BOGIE STEPS FITTED ONLY WHEN BOGIE LOCATED UNDER GUARDS DOOR

REPEAT VAC CYLINDER THIS SIDE

3'3" | 9'6¼" | 2'6" | 7'11½" | 2'6¾" | 2'6" | 7'11½" | 2'6" | 9'6¼" | 3'3"
2'0" | 8'0" | 27'6" | 8'0"

3'6"

Figure 18 (above). This drawing shows the alternative version of LNWR D268 plus the 8ft 6in wide arc roof full brake to D378 and W79. The drawing also gives plans for the further LNWR arc roof stock, elevations of which can be found on page 70. *(D. Jenkinson)*

69

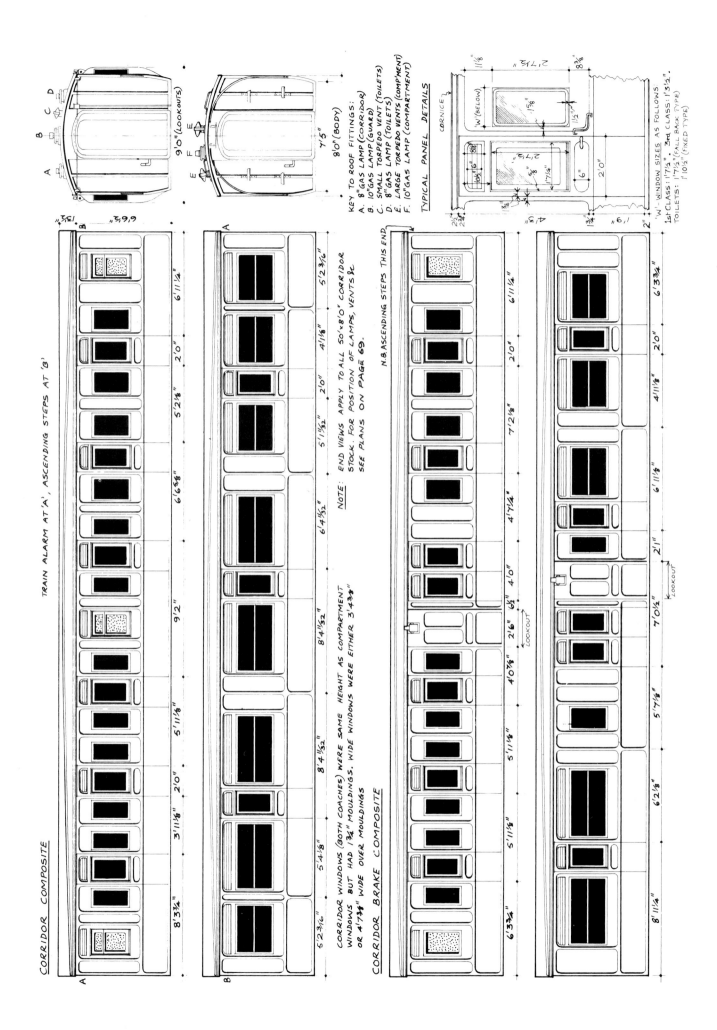

CORRIDOR COMPOSITE

TRAIN ALARM AT 'A', ASCENDING STEPS AT 'B'

CORRIDOR BRAKE COMPOSITE

N.B. ASCENDING STEPS THIS END

KEY TO ROOF FITTINGS:

A. 8" GAS LAMP (CORRIDOR)
B. 10" GAS LAMP (GUARD)
C. SMALL TORPEDO VENT (TOILETS)
D. 8" GAS LAMP (TOILETS)
E. LARGE TORPEDO VENTS (COMP'MENT)
F. 10" GAS LAMP (COMPARTMENT)

TYPICAL PANEL DETAILS

'W' WINDOW SIZES AS FOLLOWS:
1st CLASS: 1'7½". 3rd CLASS: 1'3½".
TOILETS: 1'7½"(FALL BACK TYPE)
1'10½"(FIXED TYPE)

NOTE: END VIEWS APPLY TO ALL 50'x8'0" CORRIDOR STOCK. FOR POSITION OF LAMPS, VENTS &c SEE PLANS ON PAGE 69.

CORRIDOR WINDOWS (BOTH COACHES) WERE SAME HEIGHT AS COMPARTMENT WINDOWS BUT HAD 1¾" MOULDINGS. WIDE WINDOWS WERE EITHER 3'4⅜" OR 4'7⅛" WIDE OVER MOULDINGS

Figure 19 On this page are shown further examples of LNWR 50ft arc roof corridor stock. Opposite are elevations of the composite and brake composite to Diagrams D138 and D216 respectively, together with end elevations and an enlarged view of typical LNWR panelling. On this page (top) is a four coach train of 50ft coaches consisting of a 2nd/3rd class (later all third class) centre brake coach leading (LNWR D316), followed by two composites of the type drawn opposite and a 50ft brake to D378. The other picture (left) shows a typical corridor side elevation of a converted tri-composite to D138, now in engineer stock as LMS 46031 and without gangway connections. *(Drawing: D. Jenkinson)*

Plate 87 Although shown in LMS livery and after conversion to a caravan coach, this picture of No 46000 gives a very clear impression of the standard LNWR arc roof corridor third to D268. It was probably one of the later batches built and shows the alternative form of a lavatory window — compare with *Fig. 17*.

Like their matching full thirds, the 50ft arc roof third brakes were also the most numerous LNWR side corridor examples of the type. They were five compartment, centre brake coaches, originally built as second and third class composites and 100 were put into service to D316 from 1898 onwards. At a later stage, 36 of them were altered to D317 by the removal of the two original second class compartments and their lavatory, thus converting the coaches to an end brake arrangement. The lookouts, however, remained centrally placed.

Most of the LNWR arc roof corridor stock was gaslit when new, but at a later date many were converted to electric lighting. The process was not a speedy one and many gaslit examples passed to the LMS. It cannot be stated with certainty whether all coaches were converted to electric lighting before scrapping.

From the relatively simple pattern of the LNWR arc roof corridor stock, it is now necessary to turn to the rather more complex situation which existed in the WCJS variants. In this case, all six generic types of corridor coach were provided and in all but one instance there were two designs involved for each type. In part, this may have been because the 50ft length was introduced on the WCJS before being adopted for LNWR stock as well and this may have caused some of the early WCJS designs to be somewhat experimental.

With but a few exceptions, the WCJS coaches differed from the LNWR series in four main respects. Firstly, they were generally 8ft 6in wide rather than 8ft; secondly, third class compartments were usually rather more generous in leg room; thirdly, most of the brake coaches were built without projecting lookouts and finally, the centre brake layout was not adopted. All the coaches were, of course, dual fitted and, like the LNWR designs, many of the earlier examples were gaslit.

The few brake ended coaches which did have projecting lookouts were introduced in 1897, along with the rest of the pioneer 50ft coaches. In all, 15 vehicles were built in this year to a total of no less than four diagrams (first; first brake; third; third brake). Six full thirds were built and three each of the other types. They were built as five coach sets to run with some of the newly introduced 65ft 6in dining cars (WCJS D10 — see page 51) on the 11.30 am train from Euston. The building of multiples of three was a

common LNWR/WCJS practice and was followed in similar fashion by the LMS on several occasions. It was based on the idea of two sets in service and one set spare. It is interesting to recall that the last noteworthy instance of building spare sets was the case of the BR 'Blue Pullman' diesel trains. In our more cost-conscious present era, the building of a spare set is sometimes embarrassing.

Turning now to the WCJS 50ft coaches in more detail, the full first for the above sets, to WCJS D15, was an 8ft 6in precursor of the already mentioned LNWR D97 with precisely identical facilities and carrying capacity. It was introduced some two years before the LNWR design and its contemporary brake first to WCJS D19 was a three compartment design with projecting lookouts. A later and slightly more numerous brake first was to WCJS D18 which appeared in 1902. This coach had an extra half compartment and no raised lookouts. The six which were built ran for more than 40 years as first class coaches and the last survivor was withdrawn in 1943, long after the rest of the arc roof full firsts and, indeed, some later stock, had either been withdrawn or downgraded. By all accounts, their riding was superb.

Although no corridor composites were built for the 1897 sets, the type itself was a very common WCJS corridor design of which almost sixty were built to two diagrams between 1902 and 1903. The two varieties were substantially similar. WCJS D30 was the more numerous and had a three first/three third layout seating 30 passengers while WCJS D29 had a two first/four third arrangement seating 32. It was, of course, some of the coaches from D30 which were involved in the sleeping composite conversion recorded on page 41.

Like the full composites, the two brake composites had much in common. The earlier of the two was WCJS D41 which managed to pack four and a half compartments, two lavatories and a guard's compartment into the 50ft length. These coaches were built as a batch on their own in 1899, midway between the 1897 sets and the rest of the WCJS 50ft corridors. They are described in the diagram in their original state as 'sleeping composite brake', the sleeping accommodation being provided by means of pull-out seats in the first class compartments to provide a bed for night use. Of the twenty or so which were built, nine were later converted to the 'half and half' sleeping composites of

(Text continues on page 76)

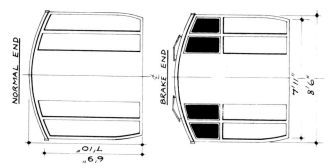

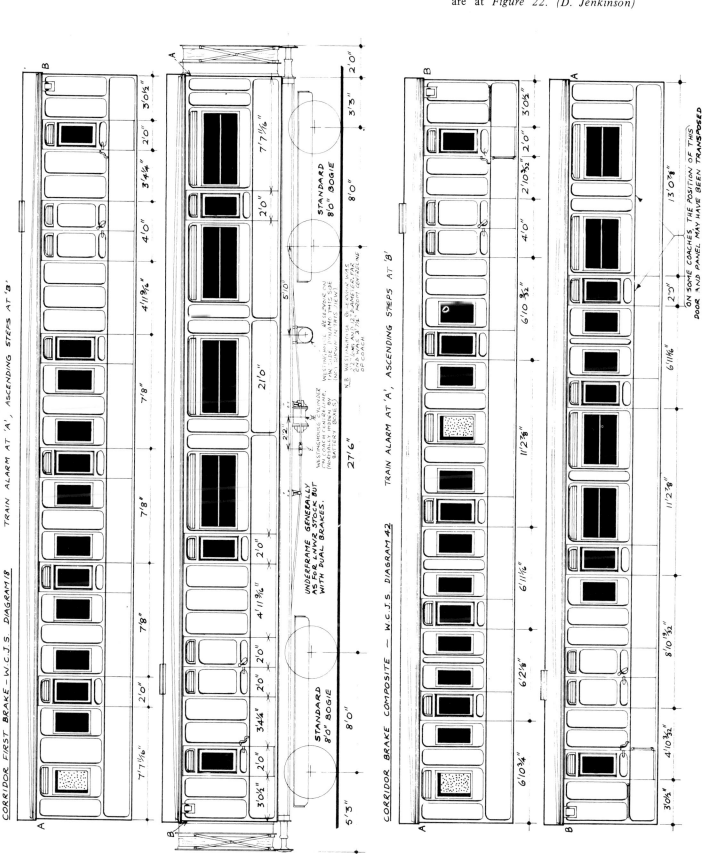

Figure 20 This page gives two varieties of WCJS 50ft stock. End details and panel dimensions were generally similar to those given at Figure 19. The additional underframe detail for WCJS working is shown, other details being as given at Figure 18. All these coaches were electrically lit from new and plans are at *Figure 22. (D. Jenkinson)*

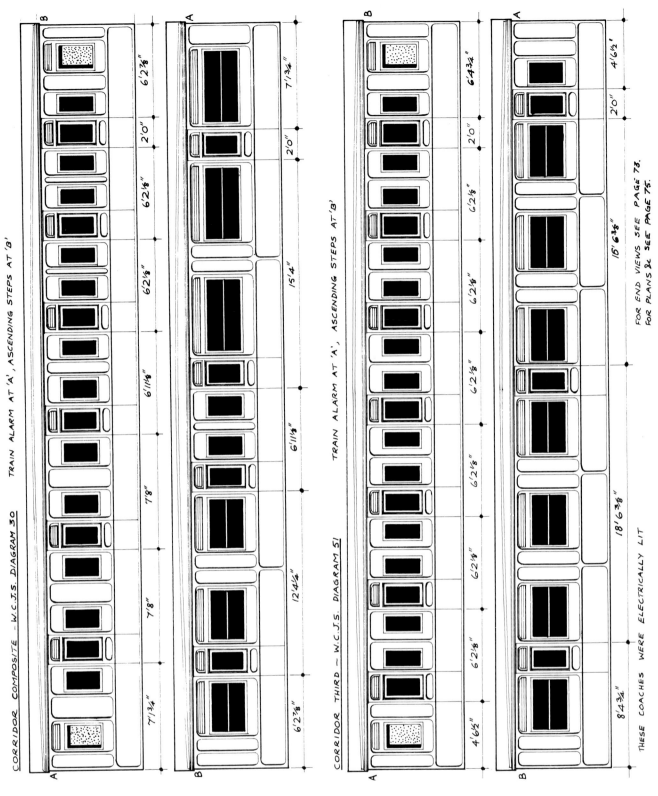

CORRIDOR COMPOSITE – W.C.J.S. DIAGRAM 30

TRAIN ALARM AT 'A', ASCENDING STEPS AT 'B'

CORRIDOR THIRD – W.C.J.S. DIAGRAM 51

TRAIN ALARM AT 'A', ASCENDING STEPS AT 'B'

FOR END VIEWS SEE PAGE 73.
FOR PLANS & SEE PAGE 75.

THESE COACHES WERE ELECTRICALLY LIT

Figure 21 The full composite and full third of the WCJS 50ft arc roof corridor series are shown on this drawing while the picture *(left)* shows a brake composite (LMS 6983) to WCJS Diagram 42 running in later years as part of an extra train set. The coach began life as WCJS 140, 1st LMS 9724. *(Drawing: D. Jenkinson, Photograph: Author's collection)*

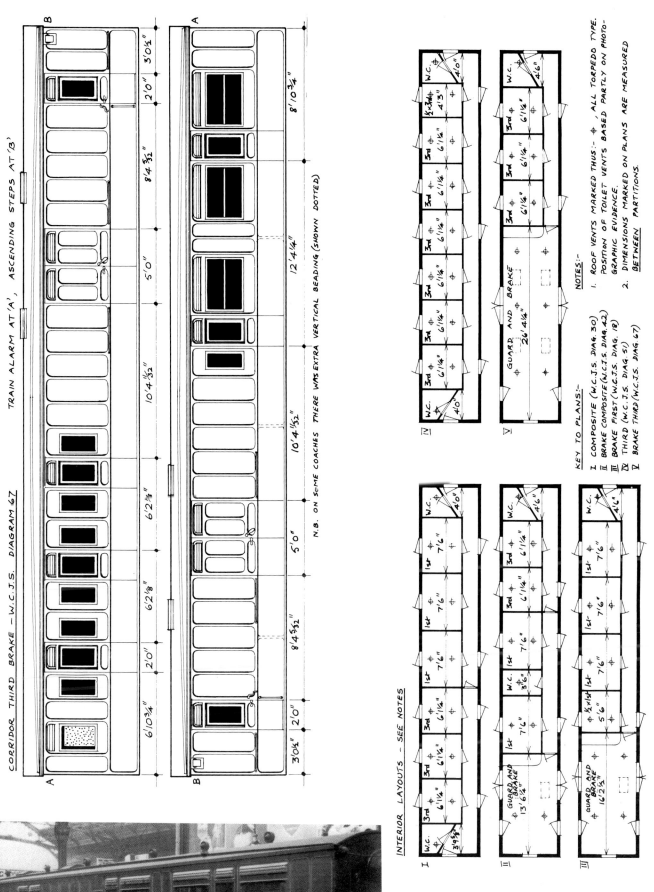

CORRIDOR THIRD BRAKE — W.C.J.S. DIAGRAM 67

TRAIN ALARM AT 'A', ASCENDING STEPS AT 'B'

N.B. ON SOME COACHES THERE WAS EXTRA VERTICAL BEADING (SHOWN DOTTED)

INTERIOR LAYOUTS — SEE NOTES

KEY TO PLANS:-

I COMPOSITE (W.C.J.S. DIAG. 30)
II BRAKE COMPOSITE (W.C.J.S. DIAG. 42)
III BRAKE FIRST (W.C.J.S. DIAG. 18)
IV THIRD (W.C.J.S. DIAG. 51)
V BRAKE THIRD (W.C.J.S. DIAG. 67)

NOTES:-

1. ROOF VENTS MARKED THUS:- ⊕ , ALL TORPEDO TYPE. POSITION OF TOILET VENTS BASED PARTLY ON PHOTO-GRAPHIC EVIDENCE.
2. DIMENSIONS MARKED ON PLANS ARE MEASURED BETWEEN PARTITIONS.

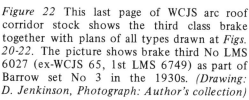

Figure 22 This last page of WCJS arc roof corridor stock shows the third class brake together with plans of all types drawn at *Figs. 20-22.* The picture shows brake third No LMS 6027 (ex-WCJS 65, 1st LMS 6749) as part of Barrow set No 3 in the 1930s. *(Drawing: D. Jenkinson, Photograph: Author's collection)*

WCJS D27 and D28. The unconverted coaches had a longer life than the sleeping conversion and survived until 1944. The second brake composite design to WCJS D42 was built along with the main batches of WCJS 50ft corridors in 1902 and differed from the earlier version solely in the omission of the third class coupé compartment. These coaches were very long-lived and only became extinct in 1952.

The first of the two 50ft corridor third designs was the above mentioned batch of six vehicles built in 1897 for the 11.30 am sets. These were to WCJS D52 and, except for their extra width, they set the pattern for the standard seven compartment LNWR corridor third already considered. In 1902-3, these six coaches were supplemented by what might best be described as the WCJS 'standard' corridor third to WCJS D51. This design was built in some quantity and had half a compartment less than the previous version which enabled slightly more leg room to be provided. They were electrically lit from new.

Like the full thirds, the brake thirds followed a similar line of development. There was the usual trio of 1897 coaches with projecting lookouts (WCJS D66), which was followed in 1902-3 by the much larger batch of coaches without lookouts and with slightly larger compartments to WCJS D67. The building of these and all the other final batches of WCJS 50ft corridors was to bring the construction of arc roof corridor stock to a close.

Cove Roof Stock: 1903-7

It is not altogether surprising that after the considerable building of gangwayed stock during the arc roof period, there should have been a slight pause in activity before the construction of corridor coaches was resumed in any quantity. As a result, the cove roof period made only a small contribution in numerical terms to the grand total of LNWR corridor coaches. However, the period is more significant than its numerical total would imply because the coaches built during this phase established most of the more modern ideas in passenger travel which were to achieve full fruition when the company adopted a high elliptical roof.

Cove roof corridor coaches were built solely for the LNWR but their basic features formed an essential part of the ancestry of both LNWR and WCJS elliptical roof vehicles. The most significant change in style was the increase in overall dimensions, particularly in terms of body width and compartment legroom. With but two minor exceptions — see page 83 — the body width went up to 9ft and, in many cases, third class compartments were increased in size to 6ft 6in between partitions. The first class compartments were exceptionally roomy being 7ft 6in between partitions and some six feet from the corridor to the compartment outside door — yet they still seated only four passengers. Windows became a little wider on both compartment and corridor side of the coaches and the projecting guard's lookouts were abandoned. The final change from the arc roof era, except for the very first batch of all, was the universal adoption of a new standard 57ft length for the vehicles. Early 57ft examples continued to use the 8ft wheelbase bogie of the 50ft stock but by the close of the period, a new 9ft bogie had been introduced which became the standard for the vast bulk of all LNWR and WCJS 57ft vehicles. Since the 57ft coach on a 9ft bogie only became obsolete in the 1950s when the final LMS design coaches were put into service, the cove roof stock can truly be said to have had far reaching consequences.

The first examples of the new style appeared in 1903 and were very neat brake composites to D214, some, at least, being used for the Central Wales services — see *Plate 88*. They were to a 50ft design but whether this was a legacy of the arc roof period or deliberately adopted for loading gauge reasons is not known. The centre brake compartment and the disposition of the passenger seating areas exactly followed the layout of the arc roof design to D216. At a later stage, one of the cove roof brakes had one first class compartment altered into a typist's office and was reclassified as D215.

The remaining cove roof corridor coaches were all 57ft designs and all six generic classes of coach were represented. The brake ended vehicles exhibited some variety but the non-brake coaches were relatively straightforward.

The full first to D95 was a palatial vehicle. With seats for only 24 passengers and taring 32 tons, it is as well that by the time of its introduction, the Webb compounds had

Plate 88 50ft tri-composite corridor brake No 900 to LNWR D214, the pioneer cove roof corridor type. It later became LNWR 5885, LMS 9733 and 7057. Drawings of this type are given opposite.

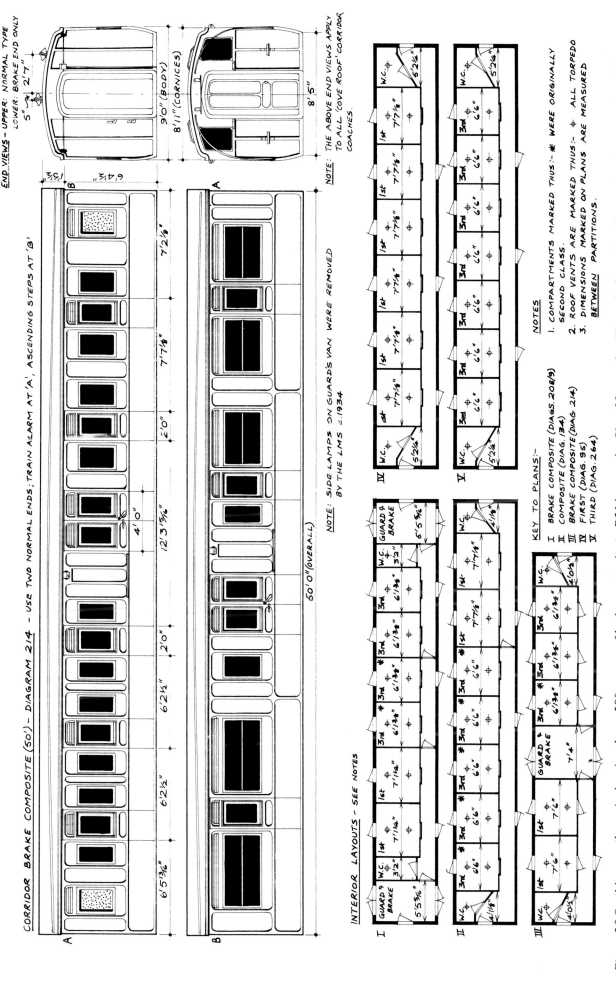

END VIEWS – UPPER: NORMAL TYPE
LOWER: BRAKE END ONLY

5'2⅛"

9'0"(BODY)
8'11"(CORNICES)

8'5"

NOTE: THE ABOVE END VIEWS APPLY
TO ALL 'COVE ROOF' CORRIDOR
COACHES.

CORRIDOR BRAKE COMPOSITE (50') – DIAGRAM 214 – USE TWO NORMAL ENDS; TRAIN ALARM AT 'A', ASCENDING STEPS AT 'B'

1'3½"
6'4½"

7'2½" 7'7⅝" 2'0" 12'3⅝" 4'0" 2'0" 6'2½" 6'2½"

50'0"(OVERALL)

NOTE: SIDE LAMPS ON GUARD'S VAN WERE REMOVED
BY THE LMS c.1934

INTERIOR LAYOUTS – SEE NOTES

I GUARD & BRAKE 3'2" W.C. 1st 7'1¼" 3rd 6'1¼" *3rd 6'1¾" 3rd 6'6" 3rd 6'6" 1st 7'1¼" W.C. 5'5⅝" 4'1¼" 5'5⅝"

II W.C. 3rd 6'6" 3rd 6'6" 3rd 6'6" *3rd 6'1¾" *1st 7'7⅝" 1st 7'7⅞" W.C. GUARD & BRAKE 3'2" 4'1⅛" 5'5⅝"

III W.C. 1st 7'6" 1st 7'6" 3rd 6'1¾" *3rd 6'1¾" 3rd 6'1¾" W.C. GUARD & BRAKE 7'4" 4'0¼"

NOTES

1. COMPARTMENTS MARKED THUS:- ✳ WERE ORIGINALLY
   SECOND CLASS.
2. ROOF VENTS ARE MARKED THUS:- ✛ ALL TORPEDO
3. DIMENSIONS MARKED ON PLANS ARE MEASURED
   BETWEEN PARTITIONS.

KEY TO PLANS:-

I   BRAKE COMPOSITE (DIAGS. 208/9)
II   COMPOSITE (DIAG. 134)
III BRAKE COMPOSITE (DIAG. 214)
IV   FIRST (DIAG. 9s)
V   THIRD (DIAG. 264)

IV W.C. 1st 7'7⅝" 1st 7'7⅝" 1st 7'7⅝" 1st 7'7⅝" 1st 7'7⅝" W.C. 5'2¼" 5'2¼"

V W.C. 3rd 6'6" 3rd 6'6" 3rd 6'6" 3rd 6'6" 3rd 6'6" 3rd 6'6" W.C. 5'2¼" 5'2¼"

Figure 23 On this page, the main drawing shows 50ft cove roof brake composite to D214 — see also *Plate 98* opposite. The underframe detail was as for the arc roof stock already given. The other drawings give interior plans of this coach and end elevations for all cove roof corridor stock, together with plans of four types of 57ft cove roof corridors, other details of which are at *Fig. 24* (overleaf) and *Fig. 25* (page 80). *(D. Jenkinson)*

77

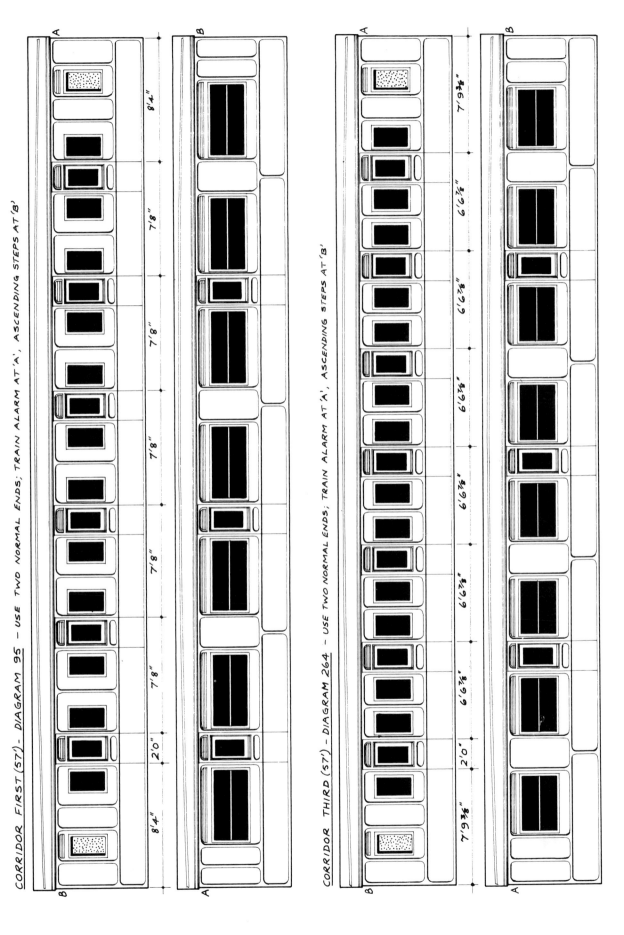

Figure 24 Side elevation drawings of the 57ft cove roof firsts and thirds. Plans and end views are at *Fig. 23*, underframe at *Fig. 25*. *(D. Jenkinson)*

CORRIDOR FIRST (57') – DIAGRAM 95 – USE TWO NORMAL ENDS; TRAIN ALARM AT 'A', ASCENDING STEPS AT 'B'

CORRIDOR THIRD (57') – DIAGRAM 264 – USE TWO NORMAL ENDS; TRAIN ALARM AT 'A', ASCENDING STEPS AT 'B'

Plate 89 (above) BR camping coach No M020453M in April 1952. This coach was originally a seven compartment cove roof corridor third to D264 and was one of the earlier examples fitted with 8ft wheelbase bogies.

Plate 90 (right) 57ft cove roof corridor first to D95 shown running as LMS 2244, downgraded to third class.

(R. J. Essery's collection)

been largely displaced by more potent motive power. In 1936, the LMS adopted the somewhat unusual course of marking these coaches down to third class. They were, of course, some thirty years old and marking down as such was not uncommon; but bearing in mind that some of the far less roomy arc roof corridor coaches retained first class seats into the 1940s and even the 1950s, one cannot but regard the downgrading of D95 as a little odd. It is not known whether they were fitted with new third class type seats at the time of marking down.

The full third to D264 had the same seven compartment layout as its arc roof predecessor and the extra length was mostly given to the passenger in the shape of compartments 6ft 6in between partitions. The increase in width enabled four per side seating to be offered at peak periods without undue discomfort. This seating standard was to remain normal in 9ft wide corridor stock until well into the LMS period when Stanier introduced third class armrests for new construction. Three of the cove roof thirds were motor fitted before grouping to Diagram M75 — see Chapter 7 — and there was, of course, the tea car version of the design — see page 64.

The final non-brake cove roof corridor design was the composite to D134 which started life offering two first plus five second class compartments. The seconds later became thirds without change in seating capacity — see *Fig. 26*.

Only three corridor brake first designs were ever built for the LNWR proper and the cove roof period had the distinction of introducing two of them. Most of the coaches were to D126, a four compartment end brake design seating 16 passengers. They did not last long in this form and well before grouping had been altered to brake composites (D210A) by fitting third class seats into the two compart-

(Text continues on page 83)

Plate 91 Third class compartment interior of brake composite No 900 — see also *Plate 88*.

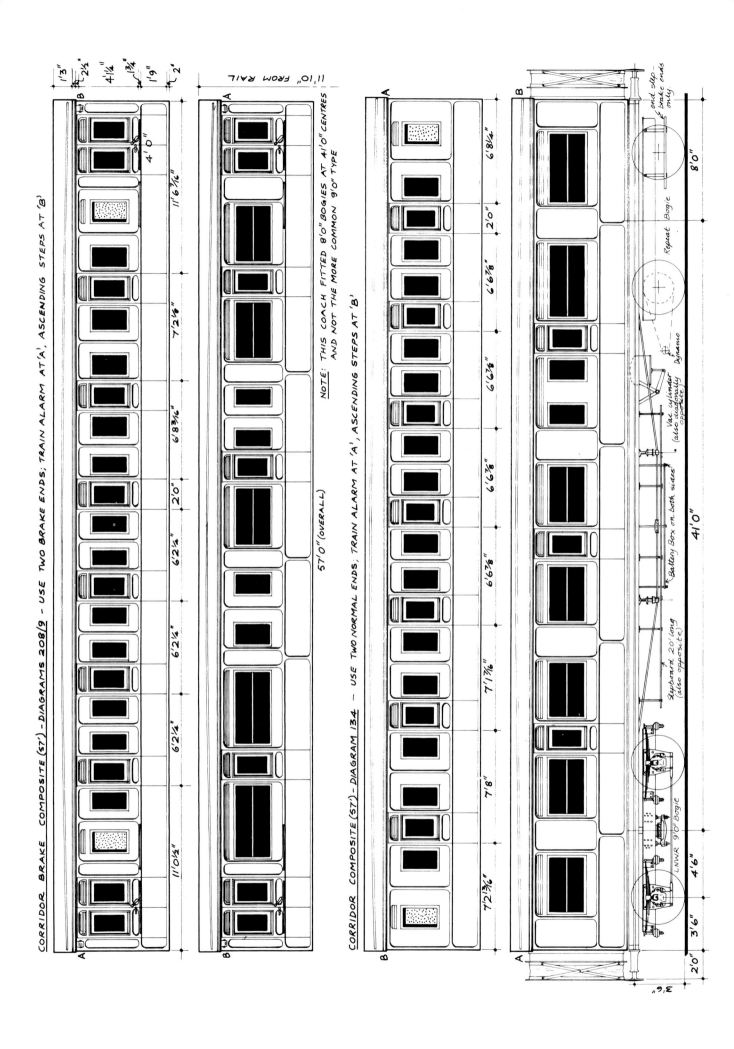

CORRIDOR BRAKE COMPOSITE (57') - DIAGRAMS 208/9 - USE TWO BRAKE ENDS; TRAIN ALARM AT 'A', ASCENDING STEPS AT 'B'

NOTE: THIS COACH FITTED 8'0" BOGIES AT 41'0" CENTRES AND NOT THE MORE COMMON 9'0" TYPE

CORRIDOR COMPOSITE (57') - DIAGRAM 134 — USE TWO NORMAL ENDS; TRAIN ALARM AT 'A', ASCENDING STEPS AT 'B'

Plate 92 Double ended tri-composite brake No 1833 to LNWR D208. The subsequent LNWR and LMS numbers of this vehicle are not known. Interior views of the compartments are given at *Plates 28-31*.

Plate 93 First and second class cove roof corridor composite No 1815 to D134, built in 1907. Its second LNWR number has not been identified, or its LMS numbers.

Plate 94 End view of a cove roof corridor brake coach — vehicle not identified, but probably a brake first to D127 as originally built.

Figure 25 (opposite) These final 57ft cove roof drawings depict the composite and brake composite designs further illustrated on this page. They also give underframe and bogie detail applicable to most 57ft cove roof corridor coaches. *(D. Jenkinson)*

Plates 95 & 96 Royal Train corridor brake first Nos 5155 *(above)* and 5154 *(below)* seen at Town Green and Wolverton in 1955 and 1958. These vehicles, to D127A, were converted from the standard brake first design seen at *Plate 27*. Note the clerestories, lack of gangway at the brake ends and the replacement LMS pattern underframes. These coaches, having been replaced in 1977 by new vehicles are now preserved in their original colours by the National Railway Museum.

ments nearest to the van portion into which was also fitted a second lavatory. It is in this form that they are shown on the sketch plans at *Fig. 26*. The other brake first design was to D127 — a somewhat extravagant two compartment brake of which only four examples were built. One of them can be seen as the leading coach of the train illustrated at *Plate 27*. One cannot really see much purpose in the introduction of such a wasteful vehicle in terms of passenger space and this may have been the reason why two of them were subsequently altered to D127A and D127B for use in the Royal Train.

This modification took the form of converting the two compartments into staff sleeping areas and fitting the large brake compartments with a variety of additional equipment for use in the more exalted role to which they were now put. Additional lavatories were also added. The coaches had the gangways removed at the brake ends and were fitted with dual brakes and provided with clerestories to match the rest of the train. The date of conversion is not known — it is shown as an LMS insertion in the diagram book — but a picture exists showing them in the Royal Train as early as 1923-4 so the alterations were probably carried out by the LNWR. In 1937, the LMS fitted them with new angle trussed LMS standard underframes and bogies. Economical as ever, the company saved the old LNWR chassis and during the second world war mounted new Stanier pattern full brake bodies on them. The Royal Train brakes were, by quite a long margin, the last of the pre-group coaches to run regularly in the train but at the time of writing (1977), they have just been replaced.

Like the brake firsts, two brake third designs were produced in the cove roof style. One was a three compartment coach (D310) and the other a four compartment vehicle (D313), but no reason can be offered why two types were built. In this respect it is worth mentioning

that the LNWR never really settled upon a consistent layout for corridor brake thirds and the multiplicity of types continued through until the grouping. It was probably related to the amount of luggage space required on individual services.

Perhaps the most significant cove roof corridor coaches were the brake composites to D208 shown at *Plate 92*. Not only were they the most numerous of the cove roof designs but they introduced a 'double ended' layout which remained standardised for virtually all further LNWR coaches of the type until the grouping. The double ended layout was not adopted for the WCJS. The D208 coaches started life as tri-composites with two compartments each for the three classes of passenger. As in the case of the 50ft brake composites, one of these 57ft coaches was later given a typist's office, becoming D209 in the process. As will be explained in the next section of this chapter, some of the elliptical roof double ended brake composites were built for slip coach working and given raised lookouts on the carriage roof. The diagram book gives no evidence that any of the cove roof coaches were thus employed but the possibility cannot be excluded.

Two final cove roof corridor coaches remained to be considered. These were, in fact, rather peculiar rebuilds of World War I ambulance coaches and they re-entered service as corridor third brakes in 1919, one coach each to D318 and D319. They were dual fitted 50ft x 8ft 6in vehicles and the only difference between them was that they were opposite handed. As ambulances, they had been used as 'cot coaches' in Naval Ambulance Train No. 6 but the diagram book does not give any earlier information than this. They may have started life as 50ft full brakes but on conversion to passenger carrying they were given toplight style features including full waist panelling.

Plate 97 (left) The curious 'one-off' corridor third brake to D319, seen running as LMS 6058. It was built in 1919 from a 'cot coach' from World War I Naval Ambulance Train No 6 as LNWR 6696 and became LMS No 6869 in 1923. *(Author's collection)*

Plates 98 & 99 (below) Two interior views of cove roof composite No 116 (later numbering not known). This vehicle is almost certainly another example from D208 — *Fig. 25.*

Plate 100 A typical mixture of cove and elliptical roof corridors, together with the inevitable dining saloons, is seen in this view of a northbound express near Bletchley behind a Claughton Class 4-6-0. Unusually, there are no arc roof coaches in the formation.

Figure 26 Sketch plans of cove and elliptical roof corridor stock. (D. Jenkinson)

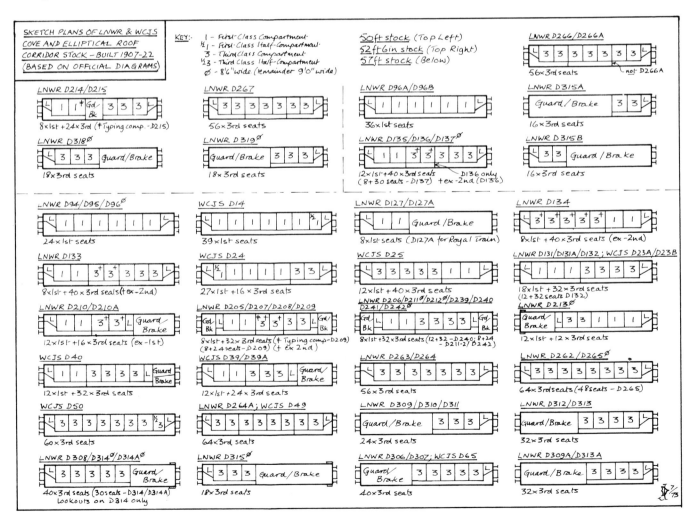

Elliptical Roof Stock: 1907-23

Unlike the two preceding periods of corridor coach development, the elliptical roof phase does not lend itself to straightforward analysis. The number of coaches built was considerable and many more diagrams were issued than for the earlier coaches. Moreover, there was no consistency in either dimensions or external styling. All types are fully listed in the summary at Appendix I but in this chapter, attention will be concentrated on the more general comments which can be made in explanation of the nature of the variations, if not the reasons for all of them.

Elliptical roof stock first appeared in 1907 and generally followed the pattern established by the cove roof coaches. There is, in fact, clear evidence that some of the first elliptical roof designs were conceived as cove roof vehicles. From an early stage, however, there was re-introduced an 8ft 6in body width for some of the elliptical designs. This superficially retrograde step was probably taken to enable corridor coaches of more modern type to be provided for routes with limited clearances. Some of these 8ft 6in coaches also reverted to having projecting lookouts for the guard.

Almost coincident with the abolition of second class travel on the LNWR (1911), there was the noticeable change in body styling which has been considered in Chapter 1. In most cases, the introduction of this new top-light styling involved the issue of new carriage diagrams but this policy was not always adopted. Further complicating the stylistic character of LNWR coaches at this time was the fact that early toplight carriages had square corners at the lower edge of the panelling whereas later examples had rounded corners throughout. The date of this change is not certain but seems to have been around 1912-13. *Plates 106* and *107* illustrate the two styles.

Not only were there stylistic variations to consider during this phase, but there was also the re-introduction of 50ft coaches for some types and the introduction of yet another length of vehicle, this time 52ft 6in. Furthermore, just as was the case during the arc roof period, it was usual for WCJS coaches to be slightly different in layout from their LNWR contemporaries. Rarely was the same design of vehicle built for both LNWR and WCJS use, even though the coaches were emerging from the works at much the same time. The final complicating factor was the first world war. Many coaches were appropriated for ambulance use at this time and although some were subsequently re-instated for passenger use, quite a number of them were converted to full brake form — see page 99.

During the elliptical roof phase, interior amenities continued to improve but not in quite so spectacular a fashion as had happened with dining and sleeping vehicles.

By the time of World War I, a typical first class compartment would be finished in polished walnut with flush panels of Italian walnut and would have the usual mirrors and pictures above the seats. Carpets, hat pegs and ashtrays were provided, together with brackets to permit the insertion of a portable table if required. Upholstery continued to be in the favoured moquette, a green pattern of Blenheim moquette being very popular. In general, first class compartments were upholstered with loose cushions on top of spring base seats. Another rather useful feature by now was the provision of courtesy lights over passenger headrests to supplement the ceiling lighting.

At the same time, the characteristic third class compartment would be finished in polished teak with mirrors, picture frames and, like the firsts, provision for the insertion of portable tables. Seats were frequently upholstered in crimson velvet and were in some coaches, pivoted at the back and made to turn up so as to facilitate cleaning. Floors were covered in linoleum and the only lights were at ceiling level. It was to be left to the LMS to provide armrests and courtesy lights for the third class passenger.

Outside the compartments, continued and liberal use was made of a variety of wood finishes viz: polished fumed oak, walnut, mahogany and teak. Lavatories were frequently equipped with earthenware basins, in succession to the earlier polished metal type, and were usually well supplied with hot and cold water and liquid soap containers.

In total, however, it is not possible to make very many valid generalisations which would apply to the whole range of elliptical roof coaches and the best way to consider the subject is by individual types.

First Class Coaches

The by now traditional reluctance to build corridor first brakes was well exemplified in the elliptical roof period. Only two were built (D125) and these were elliptical roof versions of the cove roof D126 — above. They were built in 1908 and, like their predecessors, were later converted to brake composite form and reclassified as D210.

Corridor firsts were almost as thin on the ground as brake firsts. Only a dozen were built to no less than five separate diagrams, one for the WCJS. The four LNWR diagrams were all six-compartment designs, clearly inspired by the cove roof D95. Six coaches were 57ft long and four were 52ft 6in. The 57ft coaches were built to D94 and D96 and were identical save for the body width, D96 being 8ft 6in wide. Both diagrams were marked down to all third in 1937. The shorter coaches were toplight vehicles built in 1917 to D96A and D96B. These two designs seated six per

Plate 101 Elliptical roof corridor composite to D133 No LMS 4627 (ex-LNWR 3930, 1st LMS 8116). This design, drawings of which are on the next page, was the first elliptical roof corridor type to appear and was originally a tri-composite.
(J. P. Richards)

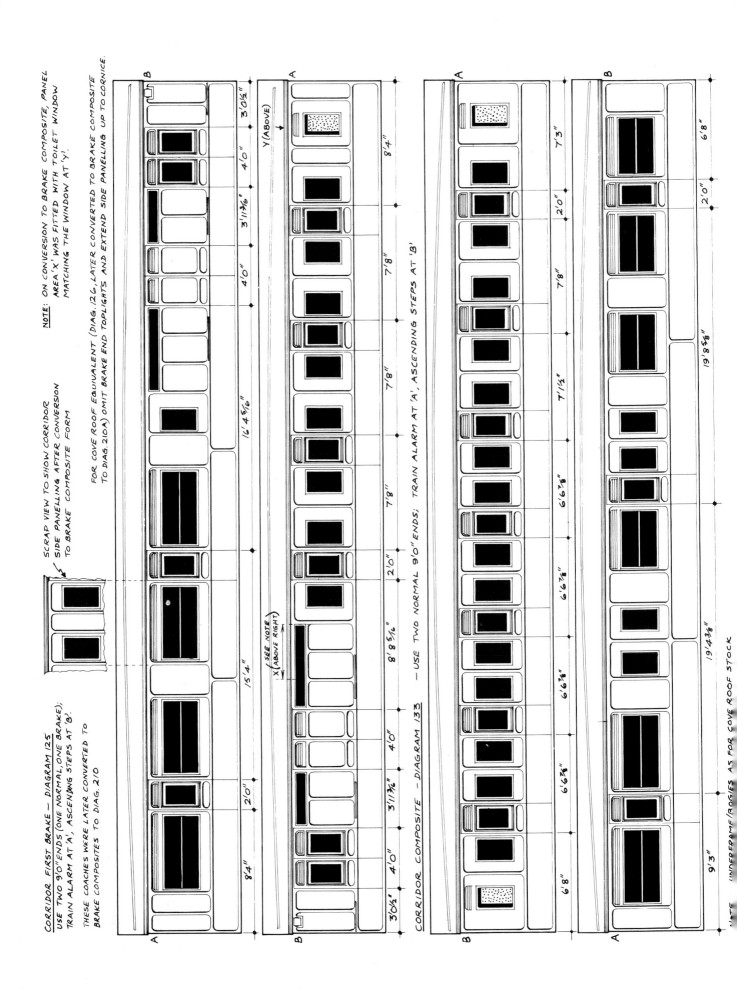

Figure 27 Standard elliptical roof 57ft corridor first brake and composite coaches. Underframes were as for cove roof stock (see *Fig. 25*) while plans and end views are at *Fig. 29* (page 90) and *Fig. 30* (page 92) respectively. *(D. Jenkinson)*

86

Plate 102 One of the recessed door Liverpool-Newcastle sets of 52ft 6in corridor coaches. *(J. P. Richards)*

compartment and the only significant difference was the recessed doors fitted to D96A. This rather unusual pair of coaches were built as part of two recessed door six coach sets for the Liverpool-Newcastle service *(Plate 102)* but the idea was not repeated for any other coaches which had to work on lines with limited clearances. At a later state in their history, the coaches were marshalled in one of the Maryport and Carlisle 'narrow' sets of coaches.

The fifth corridor first design was to WCJS D14. These coaches were built in 1913 as part of two completely new sets of toplight coaches for Anglo-Scottish workings at this time. The train thus re-equipped was the 10 am from Euston, later to become the 'Royal Scot' in LMS days. The coaches themselves had an extra half compartment compared with the LNWR designs — a curious reversal of the normal WCJS procedure — and the compartments were, in consequence, a little smaller than on the 57ft LNWR designs. Like the 52ft 6in LNWR coaches, the WCJS firsts seated six per compartment. It is interesting to note that the LMS adopted a six and a half compartment layout in its own pioneer corridor firsts.

Composite Coaches

With one exception, again a WCJS diagram, elliptical roof corridor composites followed one of two basic layouts.

Until 1913, a five third plus two first class compartment layout was the norm and after this date, a three first plus four third class arrangement was adopted. The one exception was also built in 1913. It should also be mentioned that some early examples of the two plus five pattern originally took the rails as tri-composites with two firsts, two seconds and three third class compartments.

The first elliptical composites were to D133 and built in 1907 *(Plate 101)*. The works drawing of these coaches shows a cove roof and it is likely that this particular group of coaches was, in fact, the first series to receive the full elliptical roof. They were a tri-composite version of the cove roof D134 — above — but built opposite handed. Seating capacity was as for the cove roof version. This design was followed in 1911 by a 52ft 6in equivalent (D136), again a tri-composite, in which the compartment sizes were reduced and the first class seating increased to six per compartment. Somewhat unusually, these coaches were gaslit when new. These vehicles had a toplight equivalent in D135, built during 1913-14. There was no significant change in the vehicles except that they were electrically lit and were not, of course, tri-composite at this date *(Plate 104)*.

Between the building of these two batches of 52ft 6in composites there was also introduced an 8ft 6in wide

Plate 103 This posed view of 4-6-0 No 2222 *Sir Gilbert Claughton* was taken to illustrate the train of new 'Top-light' style coaches built for the 10.00 a.m. Euston-Glasgow train in 1913. The coach immediately behind the van is a full first to WCJS D14. Needless to say, in spite of the newness of the train, the luggage van and dining car are of older design and stylistically different!

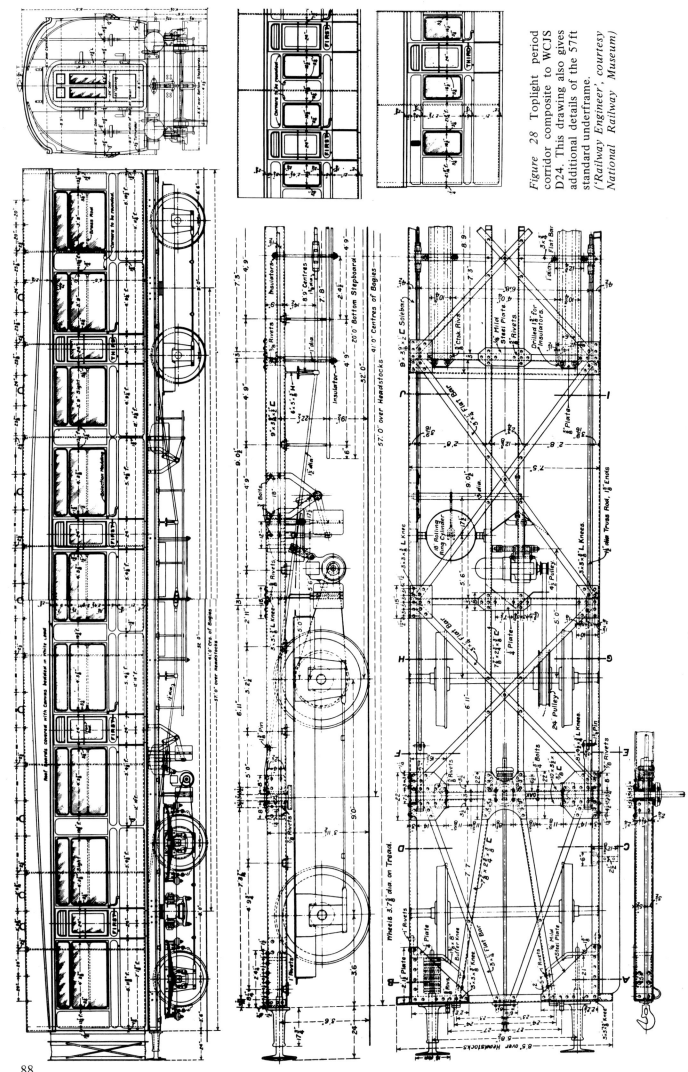

Figure 28 Toplight period corridor composite to WCJS D24. This drawing also gives additional details of the 57ft standard underframe. (*'Railway Engineer', courtesy National Railway Museum*)

88

Plate 104 'Toplight' corridor composite of 52ft 6in length to D135 No 2555 (LMS 8156, later 4577). Note the square lower corners of the panels above the waist.

version to D137. These were some of the earliest toplight coaches to be built and, being narrower, seated four passengers in the first class and six in the third class compartments. As with D135, they just post-dated the abolition of second class.

The matching WCJS corridor composites to the above LNWR types were also built in 1913. WCJS D24 had the non-standard layout (4½F + 2T), while WCJS D25 had the traditional five plus two pattern with the two first class compartments handed in the same fashion as the 57ft cove roof coaches. Both WCJS designs were 57ft toplights and only two of each type were built. As with the full firsts to WCJS D14 – above – the composites were built specifically for the new set trains of 1913.

Although the five third plus two first class arrangement was quite common, the nearest approach the LNWR came to a 'standard' corridor composite was the group of vehicles built during the 1914-20 period to D131 and D132. These were 57ft coaches of 9ft body width with four third and three first class compartments. The only difference between the diagrams was the two per side seating in the first class compartments of D132. Identical coaches to D131 were built to WCJS order and allocated WCJS D23A. There is evidence that some of the coaches in the D131/D132 series were built opposite handed to the plan as drawn at *Fig. 26*, but it has not been possible to establish how many or which coaches were concerned, nor can a reason for the variations be advanced.

The final corridor composites to emerge before 1923 (LNWR D131A and WCJS D23B) were built in 1922 and only differed from their predecessors in having slightly larger first class compartments at the expense of somewhat smaller lavatories. They retained the four third plus three first class layout which eventually became adopted, after a few experimental alternatives, as the LMS standard arrangement. Hundreds of examples were built between 1923 and 1950 to LMS designs – the direct descendants of the old LNWR coaches.

Unlike corridor composites, which were built in sizeable quantities, elliptical roof brake composites were built in quite small batches as can be seen from the summary at Appendix I. With but one exception, all the LNWR diagrams were double brake ended whereas all the WCJS diagrams were single brake ended. All the double ended coaches had the two first plus four third class compartment layout first introduced on the cove roof D208. As with the full composites, many of these vehicles started life as tri-composites and some of them were built to run as slip coaches. For this purpose, they were given raised 'birdcage' lookouts over each end and were, of course, allocated separate diagrams in this form.

There were, essentially, three series of elliptical roof double ended brake composites, all being 57ft long. The earliest coaches were to D205 and D207, built between 1908 and 1910 with traditional panelling. Both were tri-composites and the only difference was the fractionally

Plate 105 The 'standard' 57ft corridor composite of the 'Toplight' period to D131, taken from the compartment side. The coach is No 2532 (LMS 8006, later 4671) and a close-up view of a similar vehicle can be seen at *Plate 41*.

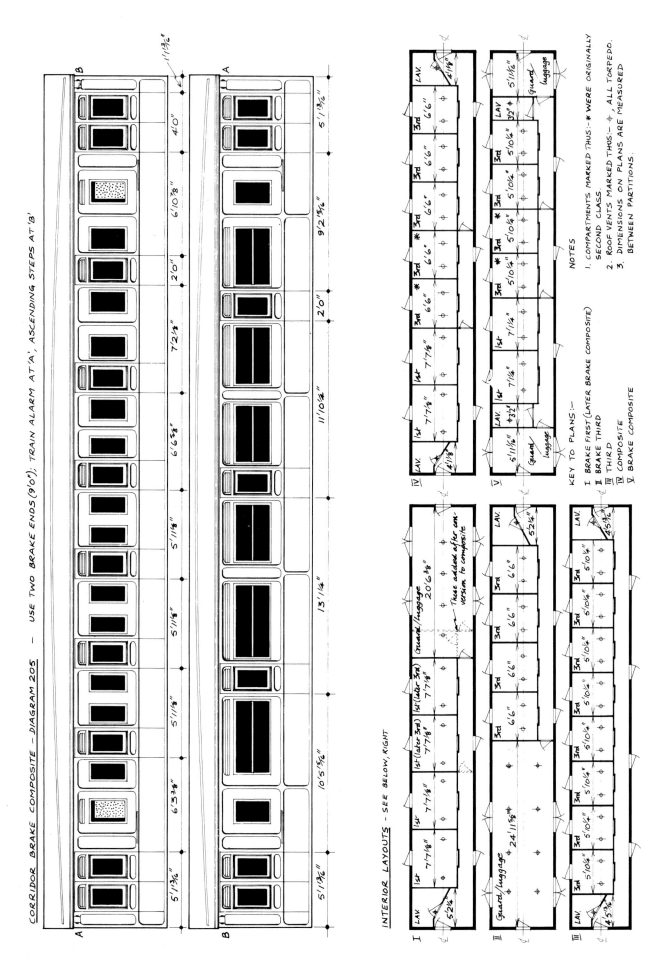

Figure 29 This drawing shows the standard elliptical roof 'Double-Ended' brake composite together with plans of additional types illustrated in more detail at *Fig. 27* and *Fig. 30*. Underframe detail is identical to that at *Fig. 25* and end views are at *Fig. 30. (D. Jenkinson)*

Plate 106 Toplight period double ended brake composite No 6048 to D240. Note the square corners at the lower edge of the upper panels. The vehicle became LMS 9626, later 7170, withdrawn in 1955.

smaller third class compartments of D205. All versions seated two per side in the first class compartments. The slip version in this series was D241, built in 1910 as part of the same order as D205. It does not, however, appear to have been a tri-composite.

The second and third series of double ended brakes were toplight coaches built during 1913-17. One series was 9ft wide and the other series 8ft 6in wide. None, of course, were built as tri-composites. The first of the toplight double enders were 9ft wide slip coaches to D240. Apart from the outside panelling, they were all but identical to the traditionally panelled D241 but the first class compartments seated six rather than four. The conventional coaches of the 9ft toplight series were to D206 and reverted to four seat first class compartments and these had a matching slip version to D239, also with four seat firsts. From the numbers built, it seems safe to assume that D206 and D239 were part of the same order.

The 8ft 6in wide double ended coaches were built to D211 and D212, D211 having slightly larger third class compartments. The slip version of this variant was to D242 which was ordered and built alongside D212 in 1913. These narrow vehicles included some examples with the earlier square cornered lower panel edges – possibly all the coaches built to D212 and D242.

A rather odd feature common to all the double ended brake composites was the apparent indecision regarding compartment sizes. Almost every diagram differed from its predecessor in this respect, but the changed dimensions were so small, generally less than 3in. that it is difficult to understand the purpose behind them. Its main contribution seems to have been to confuse the diagram book. Considering there were only two basic types of coach, nine separate diagrams seem a little excessive!

The single ended brake composites were far fewer in number. The first on the scene were the coaches to LNWR D213 in 1909. These were 57ft first and second class coaches of 8ft 6in body width and were given projecting lookouts for the guard. Apart from the downgraded brake firsts already considered, these vehicles were the only single ended brake composites built purely for LNWR use. They are illustrated at *Plates 109-10*. The building of narrower than standard corridor stock was quite common on the LNWR during the period when these coaches were introduced. It permitted through running to lines with limited clearances at a time when the LNWR was making considerable efforts to stimulate such travel. It cannot be stated, with certainty, just where all these coaches worked, but one well known service on which they were used was the 'Sunny South' special.

The two WCJS corridor brake composite designs were both introduced in 1913 along with the other new coaches for the Scottish services. The more numerous type was WCJS D40 and was much in demand for individual through coach working from provincial centres to Scotland. The only significant difference between this design and WCJS D39, was the one less third class compartment in the latter coaches. One of the D39 examples is illustrated at *Plate 107*.

(Text continues on page 95)

Plate 107 'Toplight' brake composite No 207 to WCJS D39 (LMS 9683, later 7081). Note that all the panelling is round cornered on this vehicle.

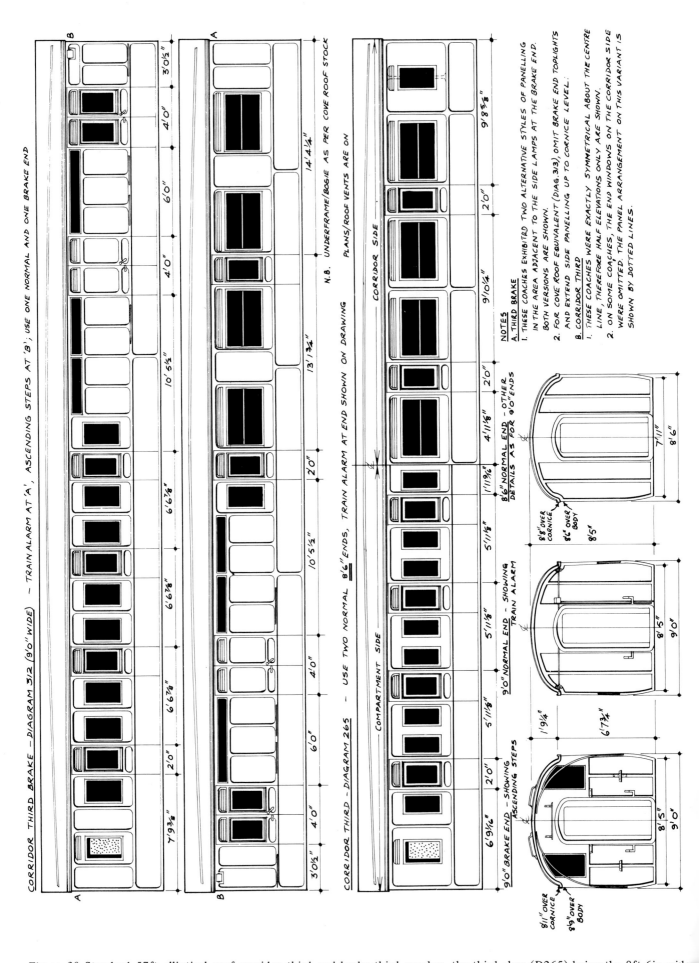

Figure 30 Standard 57ft elliptical roof corridor third and brake third coaches, the third class (D265) being the 8ft 6in wide version. Plans are at *Fig. 29* and underframe detail at *Fig. 25*. (D. Jenkinson)

Plate 108 57ft standard elliptical roof corridor third to D265 *(opposite)*. The coach became LMS 4549, later 2958 and was scrapped in 1951.

Plate 110 The opposite side view of another example to D213 — M7211M (ex-LNWR 5899, 1st LMS 9660), taken in 1956. *(F. W. Shuttleworth)*

Plate 109 8ft 6in wide end brake composite to D213, No M7209M (ex-LNWR 5791, 1st LMS 9658), seen in plain BR red livery just prior to scrapping in 1956. *(F. W. Shuttleworth)*

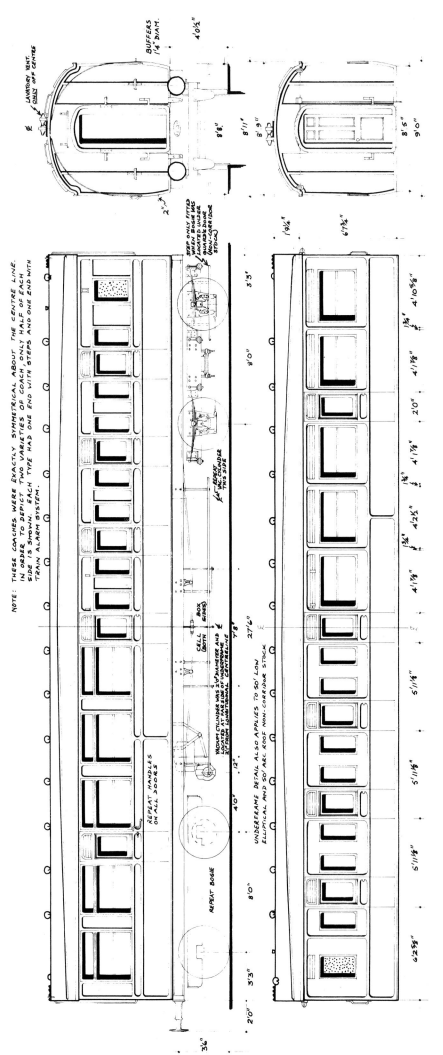

NOTE: THESE COACHES WERE EXACTLY SYMMETRICAL ABOUT THE CENTRE LINE. IN ORDER TO DEPICT TWO VARIETIES OF COACH, ONLY HALF OF EACH SIDE IS SHOWN. EACH TYPE HAD ONE END WITH STEPS AND ONE END WITH TRAIN ALARM SYSTEM.

BUFFERS 1¼" DIAM.

LAVATORY VENT. ONLY OFF CENTRE

REPEAT HANDLES ON ALL DOORS

REPEAT BOGIE

UNDERFRAME DETAIL ALSO APPLIES TO 50' LONG ELLIPTICAL AND 50' ARC ROOF NON-CORRIDOR STOCK

VACUUM CYLINDER WAS 2'0"DIAMETER AND LOCATED AT FARSIDE OF UNDERFRAME 2' FROM LONGITUDINAL CENTRELINE

CELL (BOTH BOX SIDES)

REPEAT VAC CYLINDER THIS SIDE

STEP ONLY FITTED WHEN BOGIE WAS LOCATED UNDER GUARDS DOOR (NON-CORRIDOR STOCK)

Figure 31 50ft corridor third to D267 on which both types of panel treatment were to be found. The drawing gives half elevations of each type and the picture shows a toplight example No 36 (LMS 4826, later 2640). Note that although built later than the traditional versions, the toplight examples were gas lit. (D. Jenkinson)

Plate 111 Traditional LNWR panelling on 50ft corridor third to D267 No M2620M (LNWR 1590, 1st LMS 4796).

(R. J. Essery's collection)

Third Class Coaches

It is commonly assumed and, indeed, has been frequently suggested in print, that the LNWR standard gangwayed coach from the early 1900s onwards was a 57ft x 9ft vehicle. Perusal of the corridor third class designs during the elliptical roof phase quickly gives the lie to such a simplification. It is true that 57ft was the most commonly adopted dimension for corridor stock in general but it was by no means the most usual dimension for the humble corridor third.

The first elliptical roof coaches of the type were, indeed, 57ft coaches of 9ft width, built to D262 in 1908. The latter had the same palatial seven compartment layout as the preceding cove roof D264, but only seven were built; they may even have been an uncompleted portion of the original cove roof order. At this juncture, it seems likely that the official view of these large third class compartments was moderated somewhat and the design of D262 introduced an eight compartment layout of otherwise identical style. The idea seems to have been mildly experimental and only two examples were built.

The first 'standard' LNWR elliptical roof corridor third was to D265, also introduced in 1908 and was basically an eight compartment 8ft 6in wide equivalent of the above mentioned D262. It eventually became the most numerous of all the elliptical roof corridor thirds but why such heavy emphasis was placed on 8ft 6in wide coaches when, relatively speaking, this width was not particularly common on other elliptical roof stock, is not known. Neither were they particularly cost-effective in terms of weight per passenger. They tared only two tons less than the 9ft wide D262 but carried only three quarters of the passenger load. Several of these coaches were motor fitted by the LMS.

The numerous D265 coaches were, of course, 57ft vehicles but the next design to appear exhibited a reversion to the classic 50ft, seven compartment style which was so popular in the arc roof period. This resulted in the introduction of D267 and in this case, by contrast with all other corridor designs, both the traditionally panelled and the toplight examples were included on the same diagram. Oddly enough, the toplight version was gaslit at first. The coaches were built between 1910 and 1913 and if the second LMS numbering is any guide, it would seem that some of the toplight coaches may have emerged before the last of the traditional vehicles. The toplight coaches to this diagram had the square panelling at the lower corners.

The next corridor thirds to appear were to WCJS D50 in 1913 and were associated with the already mentioned set trains of that year. The layout adopted followed the traditional WCJS practice of providing half a compartment less than in the corresponding LNWR coaches in order to give more leg room.

Following on these few 57ft WCJS coaches, Wolverton went back to shorter vehicles for LNWR use and produced the 52ft 6in coaches to D266. These were toplight carriages, identical in layout to the aforementioned 50ft elliptical thirds, but with slightly enlarged compartments. Some of these coaches were converted to ambulances during the first world war and most of these never came back. However, five of them finally returned after the grouping and were 'rebuilt' back to their original form. Somewhat surprisingly, they were not reinstated on the original LNWR diagram but were officially recorded as 'new' coaches to LMS D1710. Probably for this reason they were not numbered with the LNWR coaches either but were to be found in the LMS standard series. Six substantially identical 52ft 6in thirds were built with recessed doors for the Liverpool-Newcastle sets and allocated D266A.

It was not until 1917 that Wolverton began to build 57ft corridor third class coaches of the full 9ft width in any quantity solely for LNWR use. The coaches concerned were to D264A and were eight compartment vehicles seating 64 passengers. Although built in some quantity, nothing like as many were constructed as was the case with the 8ft 6in wide D265 or the two shorter than normal designs. Three of the 64 seat thirds were built for the WCJS and allocated D49 in the WCJS book — the only instance of the same design of corridor third being built for both LNWR and WCJS use. Judging by the WCJS numbers allocated to this trio, they seem to have been post-war replacements for premature withdrawals from WCJS D50 and D51.

With these eight compartment coaches, Wolverton had produced a design which, like its contemporary corridor composite, was to be adopted almost unchanged by the LMS in its early years. Although the LMS body panelling followed Midland Railway practice, the MR itself had not built very many 57ft coaches before the grouping so one can, perhaps, give Wolverton a major share of the credit for the LMS designs.

It has already been remarked that corridor third class brakes were probably the least consistent vehicles built at Wolverton both in the matter of 'handing' and in terms of the number of compartments provided. During the elliptical roof period, this matter was further complicated by matters of body length and width, not to mention the question of exterior styling. The only simple generalisation possible is that none of the elliptical roof third brakes were built with a central van portion.

Plate 112 Corridor brake third No 6742 to LNWR D306 (LMS 6483, later 6384) typifies the final LNWR standard 57ft corridor stock.

Dealing first with the traditionally panelled versions built during the 1907-10 period, no fewer than six diagrams were issued, two of them for 8ft 6in designs. The first type to appear was D308 in 1907. This was a five compartment derivative of the preceding cove roof styles and shared the same large compartment size with its predecessors. It was, however, opposite handed. This was followed by D312 and D309 which were the elliptical roof equivalents of the two cove roof designs and handed in the same way. The fourth 9ft wide diagram to D311 had an identical layout to the three compartment D309 but with much smaller compartments. Like its matching corridor third to D262, it seems to have been mildly experimental and only two were built.

The two 8ft 6in wide brakes to D314 and D315 were both, like their matching brake composites, built with projecting lookouts. They had five and three compartments respectively, handed in the same way as the five compartment D308. Five of the D314 brakes were later altered to D314A by removing the lookouts, thus giving them even greater route availability.

The most consistent brake third design was the first toplight example (LNWR D307). It had two derivatives, WCJS D65 and LNWR D306 *(Plates 39, 112)* and all three were five compartment coaches, the main difference being in compartment size (5ft 10¼in; 6ft 1³⁄₈in and 6ft 2½in respectively). There were also slight differences in the panelling, D307 having the squared-off bottom corners.

Two 52ft 6in designs were the next to appear – in 1917, to D315A and D315B. These were two compartment recessed door coaches built for the aforementioned Liverpool-Newcastle sets. Two diagrams were issued to cover the opposite handed nature of the coaches. Two of each type were built and they were the only non-57ft, elliptical roof, corridor third brakes.

The final pre-group corridor third brakes were four compartment coaches to D309A built during 1919 and 1920. They were very similar to the five compartment versions and, as before, different diagrams were issued to cover the fractional changes in compartment size. Only two coaches were built to D309A and these were ex-ambulance train vehicles.

As will be seen, the most common single style of corridor brake third during the elliptical roof period was a five compartment design. Once again, this seems to have established a pattern for the first LMS standard vehicles in terms of compartment numbers. The LMS brakes were handed in the Midland way rather than the LNWR fashion, but the Midland had tended to favour a three compartment layout so it does not seem too fanciful to postulate some Wolverton influence on interior layouts as in the case of the firsts, thirds and composites.

Passenger Full Brakes

With but a few exceptions, the passenger full brakes listed in the LNWR and WCJS diagram books were gangwayed types and designed to run in express trains, so it seems logical to deal with them here. In general, full brakes tended to follow the same lines of evolution as the

Plate 113 45ft full brake to WCJS D80 No 315 (LMS 2411, later 32338). This vehicle, an identical design to LNWR D381, had an interesting history. In 1937, it was transferred to the M & GN section of the LNER, becoming LNER No 84000.

Plate 114 (above) 50ft cove roof full brake No 743 (later 8743) was built with sliding doors and designated 'for milk traffic'. It was built to D380 and became LMS 2378, later 32528.

Plate 115 (above) Interior view of 50ft cove roof brake to D376. This coach was No 12, later 8012 and became LMS 2239, later 32576.

Plate 116 (below) This picture shows the neat design of cove roof brake built to the normal 9ft body width (D373). It is LNWR No 741, later 8741 and became LMS 2062, later 32525.

Plates 117 & 118 (left) Two common elliptical roof full brake designs. The version with projecting lookouts is an unidentified example of the 50ft D375, while M32223M (ex-LNWR number not known) is a later built example to D382, a 42ft design. Note the continued use of traditional panelling on this design.

(R. J. Essery's collection; J. E. Cull)

Plate 119 Another view of a 42ft full brake to D382, fitted for WD use in World War I with additional windows.

Plate 120 57ft full brake No 8981 (LMS 2034, later 32751) was a conversion from a ward car used in one of the World War I ambulance trains. This variant was to D370E.

passenger carrying coaches and most of the detailed information has been tabulated and is incorporated in the summary table at Appendix I.

Collectively, full brakes formed a numerous group of coaches and their development was steady if not spectacular. During the arc roof period, three types predominated. Most numerous were the hundreds of six wheelers to D385, a simple non-gangwayed design, probably very cheap to construct and highly standardised in its fittings. Apart from the two four wheel vehicles to D387 — see Appendix I — these six wheel coaches were the only non-gangwayed full brakes to be listed in the diagram books at the time of compilation.

The other two common designs during the arc roof period, both built in quite substantial quantities, were 45ft and 50ft bogie brakes. All told, rather more 45ft examples were put into service than 50ft coaches and it is rather surprising that this should be by far the largest instance in LNWR/WCJS carriage history of the multiplication of a 45ft design *(Plate 113)*. They were built for both LNWR and WCJS use as, indeed, were the substantially similar 50ft brakes which were 8ft 6in wide (both LNWR *and* WCJS) as opposed to the 8ft width of the 45ft coaches. Why 8ft 6in was adopted for full brakes in the LNWR diagram book is not known. Normally at this time, LNWR coaches were narrower than their WCJS equivalents. Both the 45ft and the 50ft designs seem to have stemmed from the much less numerous 42ft brakes to WCJS D81.

The cove roof period saw but a few full brakes added to the lists but, as so often was the case in this period of carriage building, the resultant vehicles were of particularly well balanced appearance (e.g. *Plate 116*). The most numerous of the cove roof brakes was a six wheel design to D384 and was intended for milk traffic.

Large scale building of full brakes resumed during the elliptical roof period and two designs were particularly numerous, both to LNWR diagrams (D375/D382 — *Plates 117, 118*). In fact, after the arc roof period, most full brakes were built to LNWR diagrams and very few additions were made to the WCJS lists.

An interesting feature of the elliptical roof vans was the use of shorter lengths and widths than was by now normal for gangwayed stock. The only 57ft brakes appeared right at the end of the story (LNWR Diagrams 370-370E) and these were the conversions to full brake form of the previous passenger carrying coaches which had seen service during World War I as ambulance coaches. As can be seen from the summary table, they were not very numerous.

Perusal of the summary table will reveal that as well as the large batches of what might be termed 'standard' full brakes, several diagrams were issued for much smaller numbers of coaches. Noteworthy amongst these were a number of 45ft clerestory brakes with sliding doors to D381A/D381B. These were also ex-ambulances which had, before the war, been used as parcels and cycle vans. A neat design of brake resulted from the conversion.

Another neat clerestory design was represented by the two 50ft brake vans to D374. These coaches were given clerestories to match the Royal Train coaches with which they ran and were clearly derived, if not rebuilt from the standard 50ft arc roof brakes.

The final group of full brakes worthy of comment are the very few full width elliptical roof brakes (other than the above mentioned ambulance conversions). Six of these were built with 'twelve wheel' style panelling for the American Special trains — see page 135 — while the bulk of the remainder (WCJS D77/D78) were classed as postal brakes and had typical offset gangways. Why they were not included in the TPO diagrams is not known, but the LMS finally resolved matters by giving them TPO series running numbers. The only truly 'standard' 9ft wide elliptical brakes built as such were two coaches to D372. These were high roofed derivatives of the standard cove roof 50ft brake — *Plate 116* — and may have been part of the same order.

LNWR Corridor Train Working (see also Appendix IV)

Although special sets of coaches were built for certain trains (e.g. WCJS 42ft stock, 1893; 50ft stock, 1897; 12 wheel stock, 1908; Toplight stock, 1913), most express trains on the system were formed of standard stock as required and to little set pattern. In fact, apart from the above mentioned WCJS trains, the only other set formations worthy of note were, of course, the luxurious American Special trains of 1908. Thus it was that, for the most part, LNWR trains tended to develop over the years their characteristic uneven appearance as the number of styles and lengths of carriages multiplied. Even so, there were some quasi-standardised practices.

Many services made basic use of branded sets of coaches, for example the Euston and Wolverhampton services which frequently saw a typical four coach formation (BTK, CK, CK, BTK) with a dining or tea car inserted in the middle. Strengthening coaches would be added at the end if required. This basic four coach formation of two third brakes and two composites was widely used on the LNWR and was known as an 'Inter Corridor Set'. The vehicles could be of almost any type and were not constant in the sets — the brakes being particulary liable to be of older design than the composites which were often of toplight type.

Another common formation was a two coach pairing (brake third plus composite), many times branded as a set and used for through coach working attached to trains bound for other places where a single brake composite was insufficient.

Finally, it should be mentioned that on some occasions, a mixture of corridor and lavatory stock was used (e.g. the Crewe and Llandudno sets) which utilised corridor brake thirds with lavatory non-corridor composites — a somewhat unusual combination.

Chapter 5   General Service Non-Corridor Stock

Preamble

When considering the non-corridor stock built for the LNWR, it is important to realise that this particular category of coaching stock had its origins well before the date adopted as the basic starting point for the detailed surveys in this book. In fact, the development of non-corridor stock was a fairly continuous process throughout the history of Wolverton so it is necessary to go back a little in time in order to put matters into perspective. At the same time, the choice of 1893 is not entirely arbitrary in relation to non-corridor stock. A study of the diagram book reveals some significant changes in emphasis in non-corridor coaches during the 1890s which were entirely attributable to the introduction of corridor vehicles on the more important trains. It is therefore not entirely irrelevant to continue to use the early 1890s as a basic reference point.

Essentially, the effect of the introduction of corridor coaches can best be appreciated by considering the figures given at *Table 2* wherein the coaches listed in the diagram book are summarised. From this table it can readily be seen that the introduction of corridor coaches had two effects. Firstly, the total production of non-corridor coaches slowed down quite appreciably, coincident with the build up of corridor types and secondly, of the non-corridor stock which was built, an increasingly high proportion of the vehicles were non-lavatory types. This is not too surprising, bearing in mind that in pre-corridor days, the need for lavatory accommodation was much greater on those long distance trains now being given over to corridor

coaches than it was on the more suburban type workings. It is not therefore surprising to find that about three quarters of the lavatory coaches listed in the diagram book are arc roof types and of these, the vast majority were built before 1893. Yet in spite of the fact that corridor coaches rendered much of the lavatory stock obsolescent, if not obsolete, it is astonishing how resilient some of these old coaches proved to be. A working life in the order of fifty years was not uncommon.

As far as non-lavatory coaches were concerned the total numbers built declined over the years but the seating capacity probably changed little as a result of the replacement of four and six wheel coaches by modern bogie stock. The capacity of a 57ft elliptical roof non-corridor third at 108 seats was over twice that of a 30ft six wheel coach with but 50 seats.

The total number of diagrams issued for non-corridor coaches exceeded 150, of which something over one third represented lavatory equipped vehicles. It will thus be clear that it is impossible to discuss every single type of vehicle put into service. Fortunately, however, many diagrams were for small batches only, sometimes as little as one vehicle being involved and a perusal of the summary information at Appendix I reveals that the bulk of the coaches were confined to considerably fewer types than the 150 above mentioned. It is not, therefore, too difficult to discover the main trends of development.

TABLE 2 SUMMARY OF LNWR GENERAL SERVICE NON-CORRIDOR STOCK

The figures shown under each category represent the number of such vehicles listed in the diagram books. In many cases this is the same as the number built but there are discrepancies in the case of older vehicles where some designs saw withdrawal commence before the preparation of the diagram book. Overall, therefore, the figures in this table are probably on the low side.

	ARC ROOF								COVE ROOF			STANDARD ELLIPTICAL			'TOPLIGHT' ELLIPTICAL				Totals
	28'	30'	32'	42'	45'	50'	56'	60'	50'	54'	57'	50'	54'	57'	30'	50'	54'	57'	
Lavatory Stock																			
First		8		15	15				10	1		1							27
Composite		8	64	206	87				4	10			1	10			7	85	480
Brake Composite			20	49	27	9					5							3	113
Third		42			55				24			1					7		129
Brake Third				3	7				10	20				20			8		68
Suburban Stock																			
First	23				4	93			26						3	7	4	4	164
Composite	37	170	82	3		64	11		38			41						176	622
Brake Composite		19		10	4														33
Third	104	500	3	54	4	139	11	5	76			26			6			93	1021
Brake Third	58	304	2	84	4	163	22		128			81			2		6	207	1061
Totals	222	1043	171	479	137	468	44	5	376	31	5	150	1	30	11	7	32	568	3720

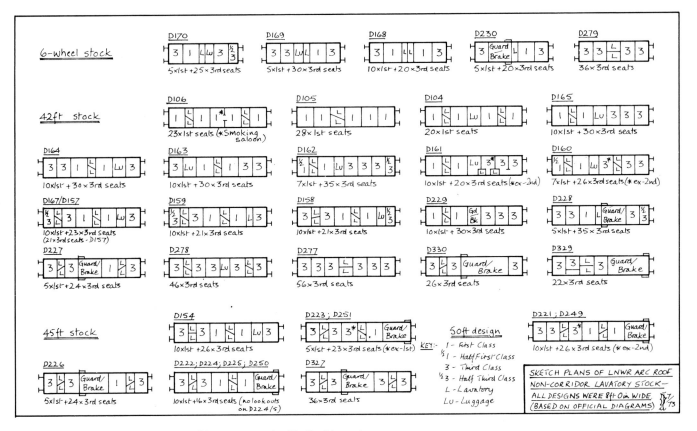

Figure 32 Sketch plans of arc roof lavatory stock. *(D. Jenkinson)*

Lavatory Stock

The typical LNWR lavatory non-corridor coach was a composite vehicle and these accounted for 593 out of the 817 coaches traceable in the diagram book. Thirds accounted for the bulk of the remainder and, as with side corridor stock, the full first was something of a rarity. Most lavatory coaches were built during the arc roof period, many dating from the 1880s and early 1890s, and the 42ft length was dominant but not exclusive. Many of the 42ft vehicles had evolved from earlier 32ft designs and were radial or ex-radial coaches. Some of them, undoubtedly, had their origins in the WCJS lists although all are shown as LNWR in the final diagram book.

The cove roof period saw little recognisable pattern emerge, beyond a slight preponderance of 50ft vehicles and a general tendency to build a higher proportion of third class coaches. However, during the elliptical roof phase the composite re-asserted its ascendancy and a marked preference was shown for the 57ft length.

Turning now to the designs in more detail, at *Fig. 32* are given sketch plans of all the arc roof lavatory coaches listed in the diagram book and the dominance of the 42ft length is apparent. However, the many permutations of layout within its length are, to say the least, confusing. As far as first class coaches were concerned, the only substantial and long lived batch were the five compartment vehicles built in 1893 to D105. These lasted until 1935 but, unusually for LNWR coaches of the period, lavatory access was limited to but two compartments. In fact, one of the noteworthy features of Wolverton built lavatory stock was the incredible ingenuity adopted by the designers to enable as many passengers as possible to gain access to the lavatories.

A particularly interesting example was the radial 42ft composite to D161. This design was, as far as can be deduced, the first occasion on which second and third class passengers were given lavatory access and was clearly derived from D165 wherein only the first class traveller

Plate 121 First class lavatory coach No 294 to LNWR D105. Its later numbering details are not known.

Plate 122 42ft radial chassis tri-composite 469 of LNWR D165. This coach only provided lavatory access for first class passengers but was the precursor of D161 which gave lavatory access to all. Its later numbers are not known.

Plate 123 This typical LNWR coach of the pre-corridor period was photographed c. 1923-4, still with a radial chassis. It is a 42ft luggage composite No 3248, later LMS 8761, to D164. Some examples of this type were eventually fitted with bogies but it is not known whether 3248 was thus equipped.

(F. W. Shuttleworth's collection)

Plate 124 This 42ft radial chassis WCJS tri-composite dates from the later 1880s when Anglo-Scottish trains still carried three classes of passenger. When the WCJS became wholly corridor, this design became LNWR D162. Note the half compartments with small end windows opposite the outward facing seats.

could attend to his bodily needs. The design of D161 may have been a rebuild in view of the curious box-like arrangement of the lavatories, incorporated as a sort of afterthought at the second and third class end. Amazingly, one of them survived until 1937!

However, it was to be a few more years after the building of D161 before a more satisfactory solution was found. A noteworthy attempt was made with D160, an early bogie coach which, built in some quantity, gave lavatory access to all but one compartment. This design was highly thought of in its day and one example was sent to the Chicago exhibition of 1893 — see also *Figure 33*.

One of the difficulties at this time was the frequent necessity to accommodate three classes of passenger within one vehicle and this led to numerous designs incorporating half compartments in order to cope with the problem. At this range of time, it is not always possible to spot the former tri-composites in the diagram book, but it seems fairly certain that many coaches which are shown with half compartments were originally tri-composites.

In the middle 1890s, two other composite designs (42ft and 45ft) were built in some quantity. The 42ft coaches to Diagrams 157, 159, and 167 were, in essence, identical and in the D159 version, incorporated no fewer than five lavatories. These coaches, together with the 45ft derivatives to D154, whose extra length permitted the elimination of the half compartment, formed the bulk of the long distance vehicles at this time.

Brake composites were numerically far fewer than non-brakes, but some particularly neat solutions were evolved with both centre and end brake arrangements adopted. With part of the coach length taken up by the guard's compartment, there was rarely space for more than four passenger compartments — which made it relatively easy to give lavatory access to all. Typical and fairly numerous examples of this period were the 42ft centre brake coaches to D227 (and its 45ft equivalent to D226) and the substantially similar end brake designs to D222 and D223, both 45ft coaches.

Many of these brake composites were originally built for slip coach working and were given raised 'birdcages' on the roof. This development culminated in the one and only 50ft arc roof lavatory design to D221. This was an ingeniously contrived five compartment tri-composite slip brake, later converted for normal working, and was virtually a complete train within one coach. Even so, the presence of the fifth compartment made it impossible to provide lavatories for all passengers.

Third class lavatory coaches were relatively few and far between during the arc roof period. Most of the designs which were built failed to give lavatory access to all compartments and the only types to be built in any numbers were the 42ft radial and the 30ft six wheel coaches to D277 and D279 respectively. In each of these designs, a pair of lavatories replaced the centre compartment of an otherwise perfectly orthodox suburban type coach and allowed lavatory access from the immediately adjacent compartments only.

(Text continues on page 106)

Plate 125 First class luxury in an arc roof lavatory coach of the late Victorian period. The lavatory door can be seen reflected in the mirror.

103

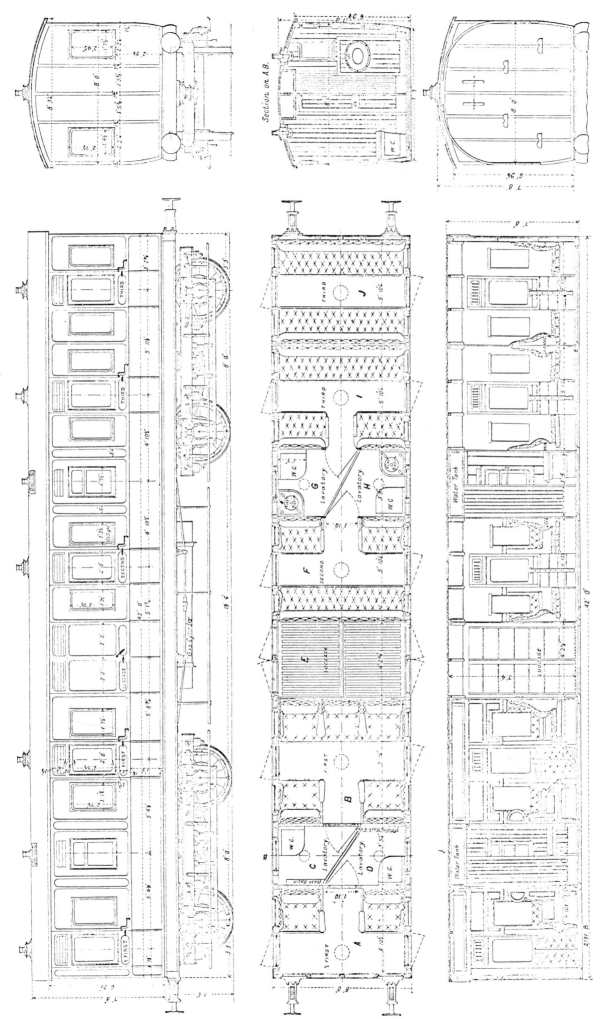

Plate 126 (opposite) A marvellous array of LNWR non-corridor coaches is shown in this evocative picture of Birmingham New Street in 1905. Perhaps the most interesting vehicle is the 42ft lavatory composite to D160 in the centre of the picture. Other readily identifiable types are the six-wheelers, the 50ft arc roof suburban coaches and the roofs of some cove roof coaches in the right foreground.

Figure 33 (above) 42ft bogie lavatory tri-composite (LNWR D160) as exhibited at Chicago in 1893. Underframe drawings applicable to this vehicle are given at *Fig. 1*, page 25. ('*Railway Engineering*', *courtesy National Railway Museum*)

The introduction of corridor stock brought lavatory coach construction almost to a stop in the late 1890s and it was not until 1905 that the first cove roof examples were built. However, with these coaches, a determined effort does seem to have been made to provide lavatory access on a rather more lavish scale — possibly influenced by the improved amenities now being offered in corridor coaches. Coupled with the rather more generous proportions of the cove roof period, this resulted, as with the corridor equivalents, in some spacious and attractive vehicles. Sketch plans of all types are given at *Fig. 34*.

The full first to D102 — *Plate 128* — was a particularly roomy coach. It was a 50ft design with no fewer than five lavatories and provided 35 comfortable seats. The class survived in first class use until after the second world war except for one downgraded example.

Unlike the previous period, composite lavatory coaches were not particularly emphasised during the cove roof phase but the few which did emerge were again, for the most part, spacious designs. The most numerous were the 54ft coaches to D149 and D150, identical save for first class seating capacity. The increase to 54ft, yet another new length, allowed provision for six compartments and six lavatories and, once again, the coaches ran for well over forty years before scrapping.

The only brake composite of this period was rather unusual (D248). It reverted to the previous 8ft width and was originally designed for slip coach working with raised roof lookouts. Presumably the reduction in width was to permit more widespread use on the system. Within the coach, the six compartments were served by only four lavatories but interior connecting doors allowed all passengers to gain access. This provision of interior doors was somewhat unusual for the LNWR. The coaches were originally tri-composites and were converted for normal use at a later stage by the removal of the roof lookouts.

The highest proportion of cove roof lavatory coaches were for third class use alone and repeated the design features found in the first class and composite vehicles. The 50ft full third to D276 had six compartments and six lavatories and the most numerous brake third (D324) was a 54ft coach with four compartments and four lavatories. There is no doubt that the provision of lavatories was by now becoming somewhat extravagant and it is rather surprising that the company did not more often adopt the idea of internal connecting doors. The seating space lost by fitting these features would have been more than regained by the reduction possible in the number of toilet areas.

From the numbers and types built, it is clear that the cove roof period saw the first deliberate building on a

Figure 34 Sketch plans of cove and elliptical roof lavatory stock. *(D. Jenkinson)*

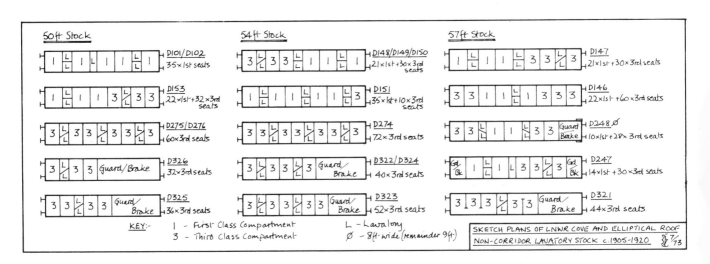

Plate 128 (above) The spacious cove roof lavatory first to D102, No 208, later 4636 (LMS 10091, later 18178). It lasted until 1951, having run as a first class vehicle for 45 years.

Plate 129 (below) A six coach set of 50ft cove roof lavatory non-corridors marshalled from the far end exactly as described in the last paragraph on this page. Drawings of three of the varieties represented are at *Fig. 35*.

reasonable scale of that familiar LNWR institution, the 'Inter-District Lavatory Set'. These were mostly short sets of coaches (usually three or four vehicles) for use on inter-mediate distance workings. Doubtless, the introduction of corridor coaches on the mainline trains had stimulated a demand for better facilities on cross-country workings. Many of the superseded arc roof lavatory coaches were, of course, utilised for these services and were often semi-permanently assembled into what might best be described as 'ad hoc' sets of coaches; but they had not been built for this purpose whereas the cove roof coaches often were. One suspects that demand was probably outstripping supply — hence the need for new coaches. In later years,

particularly after the grouping, this resulted in older corridor coaches being used on cross-country services; but until well into the 1920s, there were few surplus corridors available so it doubtless seemed sensible to build new lavatory stock for inter-district use.

The 54ft cove roof coaches were certainly thus designed, two brake thirds and a composite forming a standard set. It is less easy to detect set formations which account for all the 50ft coaches but a noted authority states that some of them were used to make up rather longer than usual six coach sets marshalled as follows: third brake/third/third/first/composite/third brake.

Plate 130 This coach almost makes a mockery of any attempt to form valid generalisations. It is a 54ft roof lavatory brake third No 127 to D324 but embodying exterior panelling only associated with the toplight period! It is not a rebuild since it carries a pre-1910 series number. According to one source, one set of coaches to this style may have been built for the Windermere services (other types not known) but it must have been experimental since all other known examples on D324 had conventional panelling. Later numbering details of 127 are not known.

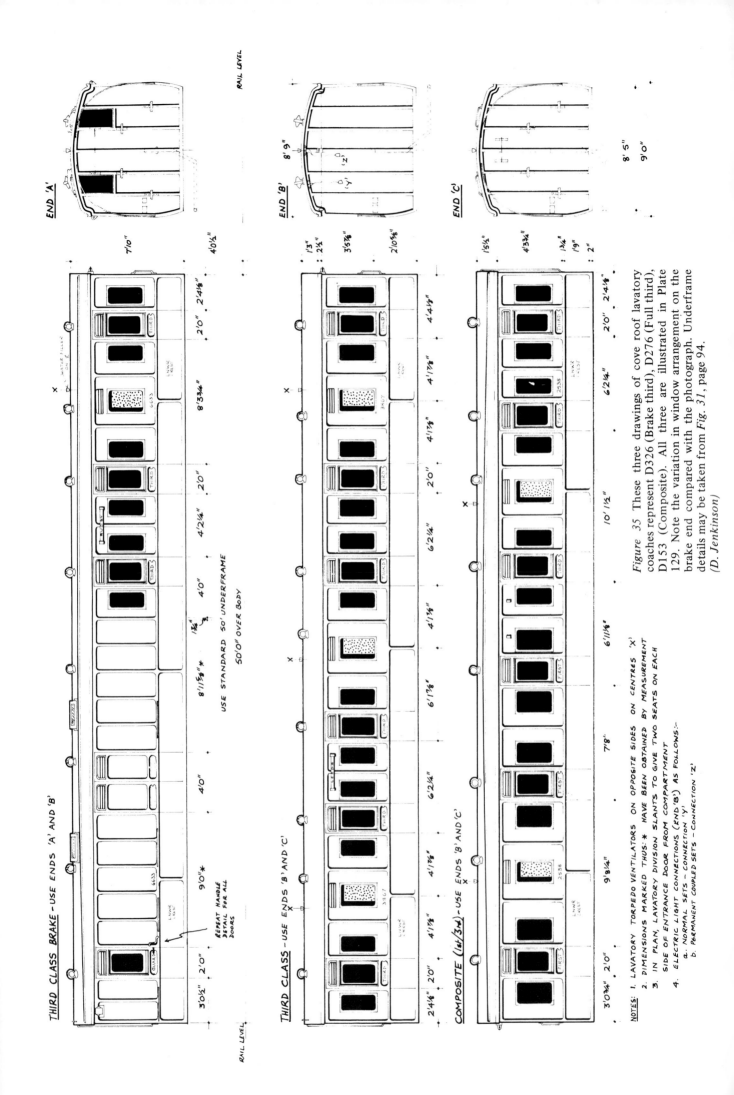

Figure 35 These three drawings of cove roof lavatory coaches represent D326 (Brake third), D276 (Full third), D153 (Composite). All three are illustrated in Plate 129. Note the variation in window arrangement on the brake end compared with the photograph. Underframe details may be taken from *Fig. 31*, page 94.
(D. Jenkinson)

Plate 131 'Toplight' period lavatory brake composite to D247 No 6078 (LMS 9812, later 25834). Note the raised 'birdcage' lookouts for slip working. More details of this design are given in the main text and an enlarged view of the brake end is at *Plate 40*, page 21.

During the elliptical roof phase, the construction of lavatory stock slowed down even more. The fact that, eventually, more elliptical roof stock was built than cove roof is merely because the style was in vogue for a much longer period. With few exceptions, the coaches which emerged during this phase were built in quite small batches and three quite separate stages can be discerned. During the early period, a batch of 30 coaches was built, 20 to D321 (third brake) and ten to D147 (composite). These were 57ft coaches and almost certainly intended as three coach sets. In the composites, six lavatories served six compartments, but in the brake ends, the five compartments had to make do with but two lavatories, access to which was gained by internal doors within the coach. There were also a few 'one-off' 50ft ellipticals which were probably ordered as cove roof coaches and certainly identical in facilities with their cove roof predecessors.

The next elliptical roof lavatory coaches reverted to 54ft length and emerged in small batches at the start of the top-light period. These were D151, D274, D322 and D323 and it is tempting to try and arrange them into sets, especially in the case of D151, a six compartment composite with but one third class compartment — which suggest some special services with a higher than normal percentage of first class.

The main batch of elliptical roof lavatory coaches were the 57ft composites to D146 of which 85 entered service during and after the first world war. Only two first class compartments had lavatory access and it is hard to understand why such a coach was built in such quantity. There were no matching brakes and if any were put into sets it must either have been with brake coaches of earlier vintage or with contemporary brakes without lavatories.

Finally, mention should be made of the lavatory brake composites to D247. These were the final non-corridor slip brakes to be built by the LNWR and had a double brake ended layout in common with their contemporary corridor coaches — see page 91. The fact that only three were built suggests some particular service, but no other information has been discovered. They displayed virtually the whole range of stylistic features representative of this period of non-corridor stock and were built at a surprisingly late date for *non-corridor* slip coaches (1913).

It can thus be seen that the evolution of non-corridor lavatory coaches on the LNWR system reflected very closely the changing fashions of the travelling public. In the early days they formed the main line trains, where a lavatory feature was both desirable and essential. Construction tailed off when this area of operation was given over to corridor stock, until the increasing demand for better facilities on the lesser services caused a slight revival of interest in the type.

By the start of the post-grouping era, however, even the need for new inter-district stock was diminishing as older corridor coaches became available and it is significant that the LMS itself built very few non-corridor lavatory coaches and the majority of these appeared before 1930. By this time, corridor coaches were plentiful and history, in a sense, repeated itself as these vehicles, like the original express lavatory coaches, were themselves relegated to lesser use when newer carriages took over the main line trains. It is hard to generalise about the final phase of non-corridor inter-district working. Many coaches survived well into BR days but scrapping was continuous throughout the 1930s and 1940s. The increasing use of multiple unit diesels, plus the closure of many lines, suggests that in general, the 1950s represent the terminal phase of a once familiar type of vehicles.

Suburban Stock

(*Note:* The word 'suburban', when applied to coaching stock is something of a misnomer, since many such coaches worked in rural areas; but it has been traditionally used for many years to describe high capacity, non-corridor, non-lavatory vehicles. The term will, therefore, be used in this survey of LNWR coaches in preference to the more cumbersome, if more correct phrase.)

Of the passenger carrying vehicles of LNWR and WCJS origin handed over to the LMS at the grouping, slightly more than half were of suburban type, in spite of the great developments and advances in the more glamorous field of corridor stock already considered. It will, therefore, be readily appreciated that for the ordinary man in the street, his most probable contact with LNWR passenger carrying facilities would be the humble suburban coach.

Almost 3000 vehicles were involved and nearly two thirds of them were of arc roof design. However, unlike the case of lavatory coaches, it should not be supposed that the considerably fewer cove and elliptical roof coaches represented any marked change in operating policy. When considering suburban coaches, the key factor is seating capacity and it must be borne in mind that of the arc roof coaches, well over 1000 were six wheelers and less than 500 were 50ft bogie coaches. Moreover, they were only 8ft wide whereas the bulk of the later coaches were 9ft wide. A perusal of the seating capacities of the various suburban coaches given as part of the information at *Table 3* clearly indicates the considerable increase in seating capacity per vehicle after the turn of the century.

Suburban coaches were most usually built against a requirement for a certain number of seats. Of course, the larger coaches were heavier, 28 tons for a 57ft x 9ft third compared with 24 tons for its 50ft predecessor and 13 tons for the 30ft six wheelers. But if these weights are compared with seating capacity (108, 80 and 40 respectively) the weight per passenger seat can be seen to be reducing with each increase in coach size, not to mention the reduction in maintenance costs as a result of fewer coaches being needed.

TABLE 3 SUMMARY AND SEATING CAPACITY OF LNWR SUBURBAN STOCK LISTED IN FINAL DIAGRAM BOOK

Key to coach types: A – Arc Roof; C – Cove Roof; E – Elliptical Roof; T – Elliptical Roof (Toplight period) ½ – half 1st; $^3/_2$ – half 3rd; Lu – Luggage; G – Guard/Brake.

Category	Diagram Number	Length & Type	Compartment Arrangement	Seats 1st	Seats 3rd
First Class	121	28ft(A)	1111	24	
	120	28ft(A)	1111	32	
	118	30ft(E)	1111	32	
	116	45ft(A)	111111	36	
	114	50ft(A)	1111111	46	
	113	50ft(A)	1111111	56	
	112	50ft(A)	1111111	42	
	111	50ft(A)	1111111	42	
	115	50ft(C)	1111111	42	
	110	50ft(C)	1111111	56	
	109	50ft(T)	1111111	56	
	108	54ft(T)	½111½111	56	
	107	57ft(T)	11111111	64	
Composite	200	28ft(A)	3111	18	10
	199	28ft(A)	1133	16	20
	198	28ft(A)	1133	12	20
	197A	30ft(A)	3113$^3/_2$	12	25
	197	30ft(A)	31Lu33	6	30
	196	30ft(A)	31Lu13	12	20
	195A	32ft(A)	33113	12	30
	195B	32ft(A)	31113	18	20
	195	32ft(A)	33Lu11	12	20
	194	32ft(A)	3113	12	20
	193	32ft(A)	1113	18	10
	192	32ft(A)	31Lu33	6	30
	191	32ft(A)	31Lu13	12	20
	190	42ft(A)	3333311	12	50
	189	50ft(A)	11333333	12	60
	188	50ft(A)	11133333	18	50
	186A	50ft(A)	3333111	18	40
	187	50ft(A)	3331111	24	30
	186	50ft(C)	3333111	18	40
	185	50ft(C)	3331111	24	30
	181	50ft(C)	3331111	32	36
	182	50ft(C)	1111133	40	24
	183	50ft(C)	3111113	40	24
	180	50ft(E)	1111133	40	24
	179	50ft(E)	1111333	32	36
	178	50ft(E)	1113333	24	48
	177	50ft(E)	3111113	40	24
	184	50ft(E)	1111133	30	20
	176A	56ft(A)	11111133	48	20
	176B	56ft(A)	11111133	48	20
	176	57ft(T)	333111333	24	72
	175	57ft(T)	33311111	40	36
Composite Brake	236	30ft(A)	31G3	6	20
	235	42ft(A)	3313G	6	30
	234	45ft(A)	1333G	6	30
	233	50ft(C)	11333G	12	30

Category	Diagram Number	Length & Type	Compartment Arrangement	Seats 1st	Seats 3rd
Third Class	300	28ft(A)	33333		50
	297	30ft(A)	33333		50
	299	30ft(E)	33333		60
	296	32ft(A)	33333		50
	295	32ft(A)	33Lu33		40
	292	42ft(A)	3333333		70
	293	42ft(A)	333Lu333		60
	291	45ft(A)	3333333		70
	290	50ft(A)	3333333		70
	289	50ft(A)	33333333		80
	285	50ft(C)	33333333		96
	286	50ft(C)	3333333		84
	288	50ft(C)	33333333		80
	286A	50ft(E)	3333333		84
	287	50ft(E)	33333333		80
	284	50ft(E)	33333333		96
	283	57ft(T)	333333333		108
	283A	56ft(A)	3333333333		100
	282	60ft(A)	3333333333		100
Third Class Brake	365	28ft(A)	333G		30
	364	28ft(A)	33G		20
	363	28ft(A)	33G		20
	361	30ft(A)	333G		30
	360	30ft(A)	33G		20
	359	30ft(A)	33G3		30
	362	30ft(E)	333G		36
	358	30ft(A)	3333G		40
	356	32ft(A)	33G3		30
	355	32ft(A)	33G33		40
	354	42ft(A)	33G33		40
	352	42ft(A)	3333G		40
	350	45ft(A)	3333G		40
	349	50ft(A)	3333G		40
	347	50ft(A)	33333G		50
	345	50ft(A)	333333G		60
	342	50ft(A)	3333333G		70
	343	50ft(A)	3333333G		70
	348	50ft(C)	3333G		40
	346	50ft(C)	33333G		50
	344	50ft(C)	333333G		60
	336	50ft(C)	333333G		72
	338	50ft(C)	33333G		60
	340	50ft(C)	33G333		60
	341	50ft(E)	33333G		50
	339	50ft(E)	3333G		48
	337	50ft(E)	33333G		60
	335	50ft(E)	333333G		72
	334	54ft(T)	33333G		60
	333	57ft(T)	333333G		72
	333A	57ft(T)	3333G		48
	333B	56ft(A)	33333333G		80
	333C	57ft(T)	333333G		72

Note: Many of the above noted third class compartments began life as seconds. For consistency, all have been noted as third class in this table. Additional details (where known) are at Appendix I.

Plate 132 This orthodox 5½ compartment 42ft radial first class coach No 165 is a type which does not appear in the final LNWR diagram book. There is, however, a gap in diagram sequence at page 117 — see Table 3 — where this type would come; which suggests a total extinction of the type circa 1916-18, shortly after the diagram book was issued.

It cannot be denied that the essential nature of the suburban non-corridor coach makes it one of the less interesting vehicles from the point of view of the student. The basic concept, derived from the typical stage coach type of body, hardly changed for over a century. Even in our present day, a suburban compartment type coach is still, essentially, a series of stage coach type bodies fixed together and mounted on a common underframe. Mid nineteenth century Wolverton coaches were no exception.

At the start of the 1890s, suburban coaches were generally either six wheelers or radial chassis 42ft eight wheelers. The six wheel group contains both 32ft radials and 30ft non-radials, the former being generally older and fewer in number. Within all coaches, standardised facilities were offered, three a side in the firsts and five a side in the seconds and thirds. Very occasionally, four per side was provided in first and second class carriages with a single centre armrest. Six wheel coaches usually had five compartments unless the vehicle was solely for first class use in which case a four compartment layout was the norm. The 42ft coaches had seven compartments, whether third or composite and there were no 42ft full firsts (but see *Plate 132*).

Accommodation in the brake coaches was a little more variable, dependent upon the length of the van portion, but a three compartment brake was the common six wheel pattern. The much smaller number of 42ft brakes usually had four compartments but there were exceptions in both cases. It should also be mentioned that quite a number of older six wheel lavatory coaches were converted to suburban types and introduced their own subtle variations.

By the mid 1890s, the old radial coaches were falling from favour. In the case of the six wheelers, many were scrapped, but many of the 42ft coaches were mounted on bogies for further use. Even so, throughout most of the 1890s, the bulk of suburban traffic was carried by the vast array of 30ft six wheel coaches built continuously until 1900. There was also a smaller, but still considerable number of 28ft four wheel coaches built during the same period. These carried exactly the same number of passengers as the six wheelers but the compartments were more cramped between partitions. They probably had some merit where platforms were restricted in length.

Progress towards something better was very slow. The short lived 45ft phase gave a little more leg room in the few coaches which were built to this dimension, but the four and six wheel coaches were not really threatened until the adoption of the 50ft standard coach at the end of the century.

There were many diagrams issued for these 50ft coaches and this tends to obscure the fact that only three basic variants were built in the non-brake series. The full first was a seven compartment vehicle, as was the composite (four first plus three third), while the full third was an eight compartment coach. However, at a later stage, some of the composites were refitted and upgraded to all first class, retaining the old compartment sizes; while others were downgraded to all third class, also retaining the old partition widths. At or about the same time, two of the full firsts were downgraded to composite and ten of the thirds were upgraded to composite. This somewhat bewildering and at first sight unnecessary reclassification was probably related to the increasing use of fixed sets of coaches for

(Text continues on page 114)

Plate 133 This very common seven compartment radial chassis type was to D292 and many were later given bogies.

No 574 later became LNWR 0574 then LMS 4621, 04621 and. finally, LMS 13626!

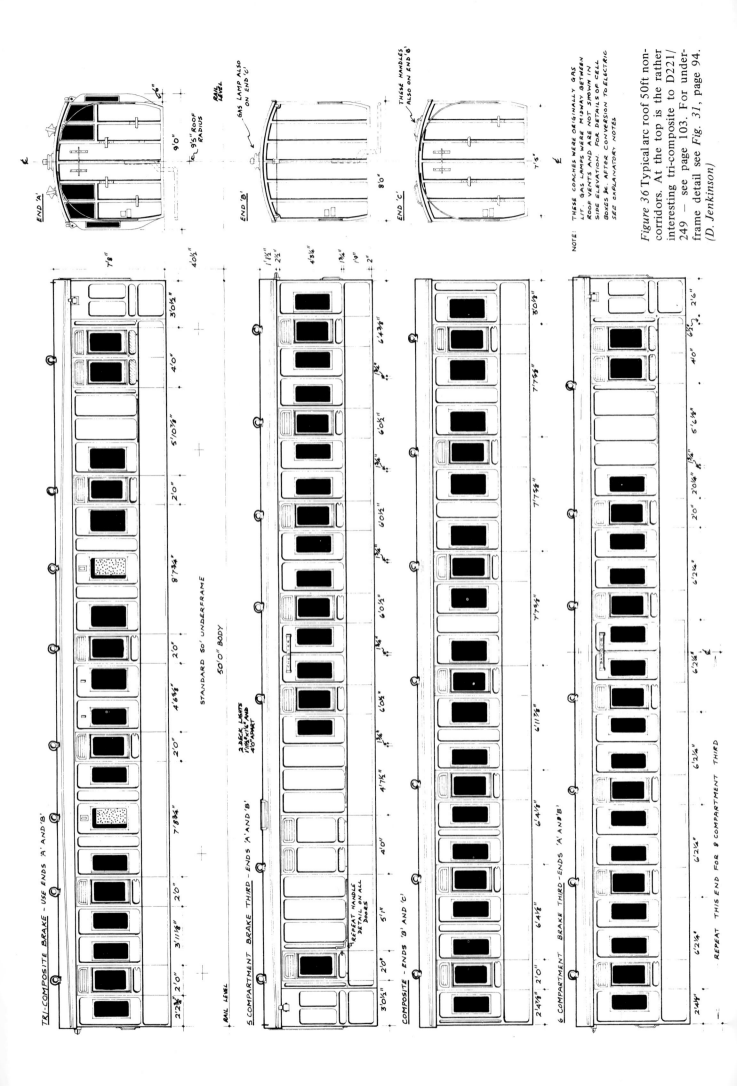

Figure 36 Typical arc roof 50ft non-corridors. At the top is the rather interesting tri-composite to D221/249 – see page 103. For under-frame detail see *Fig. 31, page 94*. (D. Jenkinson)

NOTE: THESE COACHES WERE ORIGINALLY GAS LIT. GAS LAMPS WERE MIDWAY BETWEEN ROOF VENTS AND ARE NOT SHOWN IN SIDE ELEVATION. FOR DETAILS OF CELL BOXES &c. AFTER CONVERSION TO ELECTRIC SEE EXPLANATORY NOTES

END 'A'

9'0"
9'5" ROOF RADIUS

RAIL LEVEL

GAS LAMP ALSO ON END 'C'

END 'B'

8'0"

THESE HANDLES ALSO ON END 'B'

END 'C'

7'5"

TRI-COMPOSITE BRAKE - USE ENDS 'A' AND 'B'

STANDARD 50' UNDERFRAME

50'0" BODY

RAIL LEVEL

5 COMPARTMENT BRAKE THIRD - ENDS 'A' AND 'B'

2 DECK LIGHTS 1'11⅝x5¼" AND 4'0" APART

REPEAT HANDLE DETAIL ON ALL DOORS

COMPOSITE - ENDS 'B' AND 'C'

6 COMPARTMENT BRAKE THIRD - ENDS 'A' AND'B'

REPEAT THIS END FOR 8 COMPARTMENT THIRD

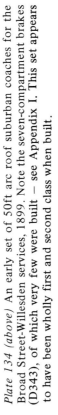

Plate 134 (above) An early set of 50ft arc roof suburban coaches for the Broad Street-Willesden services, 1899. Note the seven-compartment brakes (D343), of which very few were built – see Appendix I. This set appears to have been wholly first and second class when built.

Plate 135 (below) This World War II Emergency Office coach was converted from a 50ft non-corridor arc roof first class coach to D112.

Plate 136 (below) This quaint little four wheel brake third to D364 was a relatively late example, not being built until 1900. It is seen here as LMS 7916 on the Abergavenny service. Originally LNWR 6905, it became LMS 27521 in 1934.

(R. J. Essery's collection)

113

specific workings and was devised to ensure the correct relative proportion of seats for each particular service. It would also, of course, obviate much of the need for shunting and re-marshalling. This policy also enabled the company to make some economies when fitting electric light to the coaches. When coaches were semi-permanently marshalled into sets, it was by no means unusual for the dynamo and batteries to be fitted to only one or two coaches, the supply to the other coaches being taken to them by means of jumper cables, fitted with plugs and sockets, at the coach ends.

It was presumably the varying requirement for seats that caused the brake ended 50ft coaches also to exhibit some variety. The common standard was a five or six compartment vehicle but there were also smaller numbers of four and seven compartment brakes. It is possible that some of the latter may have been fairly cheap conversions from the standard eight compartment third class coaches. All these variations are summarised at *Table 3*.

The onset of the cove roof period saw a general expansion of coach width, thus allowing twelve seat third class compartments and eight seat firsts. The general style of coach layout closely followed the 50ft arc roof pattern except for the extra width. Of the exceptions to this general principle, most were in the nature of very small batches indeed — often single vehicles — as the summary at Appendix I indicates. However, mention ought to be made of the limited building of 8ft wide cove roof suburban coaches for specific services, in particular that which ran from Manchester (London Road) to Buxton. The sets were formed up brake third/third/first/brake third, it being highly likely that one brake third started life as a brake second. Two such sets were built.

Two quite distinct series of suburban coaches were produced during the elliptical roof period. The early coaches, exhibiting the traditional panelling, were almost wholly 50ft vehicles, while the later coaches, with exterior eaves and waist panels, were nearly all of 57ft length. In both cases, the preferred types were composites, thirds and brake thirds with only a limited number of firsts and no brake composites at all.

The 50ft coaches with traditional panelling were put into service during 1907-9 and in general, followed the styles set during the arc roof period and reinforced in the cove roof coaches — that is, seven compartment composites, eight compartment thirds and several variations within the third class brake category. Like the cove roof period, the most numerous category of brake third was a five compartment coach.

During this period, two rather interesting variations occurred. Coincidental with the building of the standard 50ft coaches, six sets of 8ft 6in wide suburbans were introduced, marshalled into four coach trains formed up as brake third/third/composite/brake thirds. These were, as far as can be deduced, the only elliptical roof suburbans to be built new to a width below the standard 9ft and the only LNWR suburban coaches of any type to have the 8ft 6in width. The brake ends had projecting lookouts in the fashion of their contemporary 8ft 6in wide corridor brakes — see page 96.

The second innovation was the introduction in 1911 of the celebrated eleven coach set of elliptical roof six-wheelers for the Birmingham-Sutton Coldfield service — *Plate 137*. The coaches involved were two brake thirds, six thirds and three firsts. Some of these coaches ran for a year or so as second class vehicles. Overall, it is difficult to see why these coaches were built. They were, oddly enough, fractionally lighter in deadweight per passenger seat than the 50ft bogie coaches but otherwise seem to have had no points in their favour. Six-wheel stock was looking distinctly old fashioned by now — even when given contemporary styling — and cannot have ridden as well. No evidence has been traced of any attempt to duplicate the set or to introduce similar coaches on other workings but it is probably worth mentioning that Wolverton did build some rather similar four wheel coaches in 1910 and 1911 for North London Railway services. These, however, are outside the scope of this book.

During the final phase of suburban coach construction, the 57ft length finally became established, along with the new style of outside panelling. As usual there were a few batches of non-typical coaches, but the characteristic 57ft suburbans of the final LNWR period were nine compartment thirds and composites and six compartment third brakes. These types were built in considerable numbers and after 1923, their layouts were adopted, unchanged, by the LMS for its own standard suburban stock. In fact, some of the LNWR designed vehicles did not actually enter service until after the grouping.

Thus, as with corridor stock so with suburban coaches, the LNWR influence on subsequent LMS carriage building was strong. The external details may have changed but the basic LNWR suburban coach layout was still being perpetuated as late as the 1950s at both Wolverton and Derby.

During the final LNWR period, the only 'non-standard' suburban coaches built new, were a few 54ft brake thirds and firsts, odd batches of 50ft and 57ft firsts and two only 57ft four compartment brakes. Some of these (undoubtedly the 54ft firsts) were rebuilds for passenger use of first world war ambulances.

Finally, mention ought to be made of the rebuilding during 1920-21 of some of the older 28ft and 30ft arc roof

Plate 137 The well known Birmingham and Sutton set of six-wheel elliptical roof coaches, built in 1911.

Plate 138 50ft cove roof brake third to D338 seen running as LMS 22375 (LNWR 7589, 1st LMS 7356). This low level view gives a good impression of the cove roof carriage profile.
(Author's collection)

Plate 139 'Toplight' period 50ft non-corridor first No M10427M (ex-LNWR 4689, 1st LMS 10114) at Birmingham New Street in 1954.
(J. E. Cull)

Plate 140 (below) The standard LNWR 57ft non-corridor vehicle of the final period is represented by this third class coach to D283 No 5426 (ex-LNWR 1683, 2nd LMS 13897), seen early in LMS days.

Plate 141 56ft arc roof brake third No M22640M at Barrow-in-Furness, 1956. This coach was constructed to D333B from two 28ft four-wheel coaches in 1921. It was the last of the batch to emerge and carried LNWR 7951 and LMS 7199 as its earlier numbers.

(F. W. Shuttleworth)

suburban coaches. This consisted of joining two old bodies together and fitting bogies to the resultant vehicle. Most of the conversions were of 28ft four-wheel coaches and gave rise to a series of 56ft composites, thirds and brake thirds. The only 30ft conversions were of ten third class coaches which re-emerged as 60ft bogie thirds.

Non-corridor Set Formations

Mention has been made of the evolution of inter district lavatory sets during the period when lavatory stock became more widespread on cross-country workings. This reflected as increasing tendency on the part of the company to marshal its coaches into set formations on a much wider scale. Such a policy reduced marshalling time and enabled more consistent seating capacity to be provided — not to mention the possibilities it afforded for economies of scale to be introduced in the carriage building programme if fewer types of coach could be produced.

It thus became fairly characteristic towards the close of the pre-group period for LNWR suburban trains and cross-country sets to present for the most part a very neat and tidy appearance, in marked contrast to the long distance express workings which were usually marshalled from a bewildering array of differently styled coaches. Lengthy analysis is not possible in the space available here but the ensuing paragraphs, based on contemporary observation, will indicate some of the trends.

It was not uncommon for stock to be built for specific services. Much of the 28ft four-wheel stock of 1892-7 went to the Outer Circle (Mansion House-Broad Street) service while the first six sets of 50ft arc roof suburban coaches were built in 1897 for the Euston-Watford trains (originally formed BS, F/S compo, F,F/T compo, T, BT). This then became a standard design of set. Known examples are few but included five for Birmingham and Sutton using five compartment brakes.

Commonly used short sets of coaches included a BTL + CL pairing (e.g. Northampton District sets) or a three coach BT + C + BT arrangement used, for example, in the Lancaster and Carlisle and the Leicester and Leamington sets. Manchester and Buxton trains often utilised specially built coaches of slightly non-standard type, including some of the rather rare 8ft wide cove roof coaches (see page 114 and Appendix I).

For general service, the basic formation was an 'Inter-District' set of which two main versions are discernible, plus many local variations formed, as required, from all sorts of vehicles. The earliest versions seem to be the cove roof BT + T + C + BT formations from Diagrams 338, 285 and 182 and the corresponding elliptical roof sets utilising Diagrams 337, 284 and 180 (apparently 20 sets) or, alternatively, Diagrams 335, 284 and 177. Later Inter-District sets were formed BT + C + C + BT from Diagrams 333 and 176, these later being reduced to three coaches by the removal of a composite. The spare composite was not infrequently then transferred to replace the third and composite from one of the earlier sets thus standardising a three coach formation.

There were also some two coach 'half' sets (BT + C), marked as 'Two coach set No. XX' and used as required for a variety of services. Finally, there should be mentioned the three coach lavatory sets (BTL + CL + BTL) which, introduced by the LNWR, were continued by the LMS utilising LMS standard coaches. In time, there was some mixing of types and in latter days it was not unusual to see LNWR composites flanked by LMS brakes — or vice versa. All told, however, there seems to have been some attempt, consciously or otherwise, to form sets from coaches of broadly similar design characteristics and, for the most part, this remained the case until withdrawal of the coaches concerned.

Chapter 6 Saloons and Special Stock

It is almost axiomatic that to the railway enthusiast and historian, the unique or the unusual .commands greater interest and attention than the commonplace. Within the realm of coaching stock, it is the saloons and special coaches which attract this particular interest and it cannot be denied that Wolverton produced its fair share of distinctive, unique or unusual coaches which will now be considered.

The trouble with this particular group of vehicles is that by their very nature, the individual types were usually built in small numbers — often one example only — and generalisation is either impossible or pointless. Furthermore, saloons rarely covered much mileage by comparison with general service stock and, as a result, remained serviceable for a very long period. Thus it is that contained within the diagram book are details of some very venerable vehicles indeed whose origins go back well before the starting date adopted for the more detailed surveys in this book. Many of these old vehicles eluded photographers or contemporary writers and failed to survive for long enough after the grouping for even their full numbering details to be discovered. Such information as is known is given for some of them in the summary table at Appendix II but their gaps will make clear how much more is missing.

Finally, to attempt to describe each and every type of saloon or special coach built, even but briefly, would be to allocate a disproportionate amount of the available space to this subject; so let it be admitted from the outset that this review of LNWR and WCJS special stock must, of necessity,

take on a more fragmented character than previous chapters. In general, such emphasis as is given will be to the later and longer lasting coaches which survived to LMS days. For convenience, the summary table for saloons and special coaches is listed separately as Appendix II. Sketch plans of the various saloons are given through this chapter.

Royal and Semi-Royal Saloons

Pride of place amongst the LNWR saloons must go to the magnificent vehicles built at Wolverton for Royal use. Happily, some of them are still in existence at the National Railway Museum at York and much detailed information is available both at first hand and from other published sources so it is not essential to go into great detail here.

The most elaborate coaches are the three genuine Royal Saloons, all preserved. Oldest by far is Queen Victoria's saloon rebuilt onto its present twelve-wheel underframe from its original twin six-wheel chassis. It is a truly remarkable vehicle both in style and finish. Built to Richard Bore's design in 1869, it predates by some considerable time the main period covered by this book. However, the pair of saloons built in 1903 for King Edward VII and Queen Alexandra are right in the mainstream of Wolverton carriage development. It is, of course, true that they carry considerably more elaboration than did the general service coaches of the day, but essentially they are genuinely representative of the elegant 9ft wide clerestory period just after the turn of the century. Words cannot really do justice to these coaches but fortunately they are not necessary since the saloons can

Plate 142 Queen Victoria's twin saloons as originally built in 1869. At that time, they were the first British railway coaches to be connected by a flexible gangway. The photograph was taken immediately prior to their being joined together on a single twelve-wheel underframe in which form they are preserved at the National Railway Museum, York.

Plates 143 & 144 Queen Victoria's Train These two pictures show Queen Victoria's LNWR Royal Train at two different phases. Above is a specially posed official picture dating from the 1880s. It is one of a series and shows the Queen's twin saloons as the sixth and seventh vehicles. The fourth vehicle is the Prince of Wales' Saloon – see also page 126. Below is a photograph taken at Ballater in 1900 when Queen Victoria used her special saloon for what is believed to be the last time. It shows the whole of the LNWR Royal Train crew. *(Plate 144 – Author's Collection)*

Plate 145 Queen Victoria's saloon as preserved at the National Railway Museum.

be seen at first hand. Few can seriously doubt that they represent the best of Wolverton's craftsmanship.

The three Royal Saloons never appeared in the LNWR diagram book, nor did they carry running numbers in pre-group days. In 1932, the LMS, tidy as ever, allocated Nos 800-1 to the clerestory pair and No. 802 to Queen Victoria's coach, but as far as is known, these numbers were never marked on the coach bodies, although 800/801 are known to have carried their numbers on the underframe in later days.

Associated with the Royal Saloons and, this time, included in the diagram book were eight more coaches of two types. Six of them were built in 1903 as semi-royals to match the new twelve-wheel saloons and these occupy place as D1 in the LNWR lists. They were 57ft clerestories, styled exactly as the 65ft 6in coaches of the time but mounted on four-wheel bogies. The summary table gives their essential details and amongst the more interesting aspects of their history is the fact that LMS No. 804 was adapted for use during World War II as the Prime Minister's private saloon which formed the essential ingredient of the rather interesting train assembled by the LMS for Winston Churchill's use.

These semi-royals had a long history. For many years they could be hired by any individual (who had sufficient money) for private use – the ultimate in family saloons as it were. It is believed that the hire fee was something in the order of two dozen first class fares for the journey in question. The saloons survived into the 1950s before scrapping started and the last one did not go until 1968 and has been privately preserved. Some idea of the original nature of these coaches can be gained by examining the somewhat similar private saloon built at Wolverton for the Duke of Sutherland, which coach is preserved in the national collection. Most sources seem to think that this coach was regarded by Wolverton as a 'try-out' for the new Royal and semi-royal saloons.

The other two coaches in the 'Royal' group were 42ft radial saloons to D4. Classified as 'Special Saloons', they were designed for the Prince of Wales (afterwards King Edward VII) and his equerries. They formed part of the old nineteenth century LNWR Royal train, along with Queen Victoria's coach and were withdrawn before the grouping. During their later days they ran on bogie underframes and in terms of styling, they exhibited the traditional type of panelling with cove roofs of the type adopted for the early radial chassis sleeping cars. The diagram book also indicates the presence of a clerestory.

(There follow eight pages of drawings and pictures relating to the Royal Saloons. The main text continues on page 128).

Figure 37 Sketch plans of Royal and Departmental saloons. *(D. Jenkinson)*

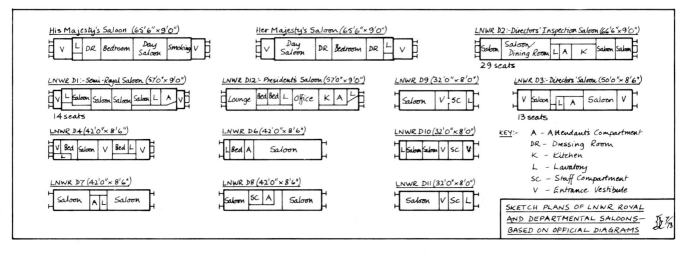

119

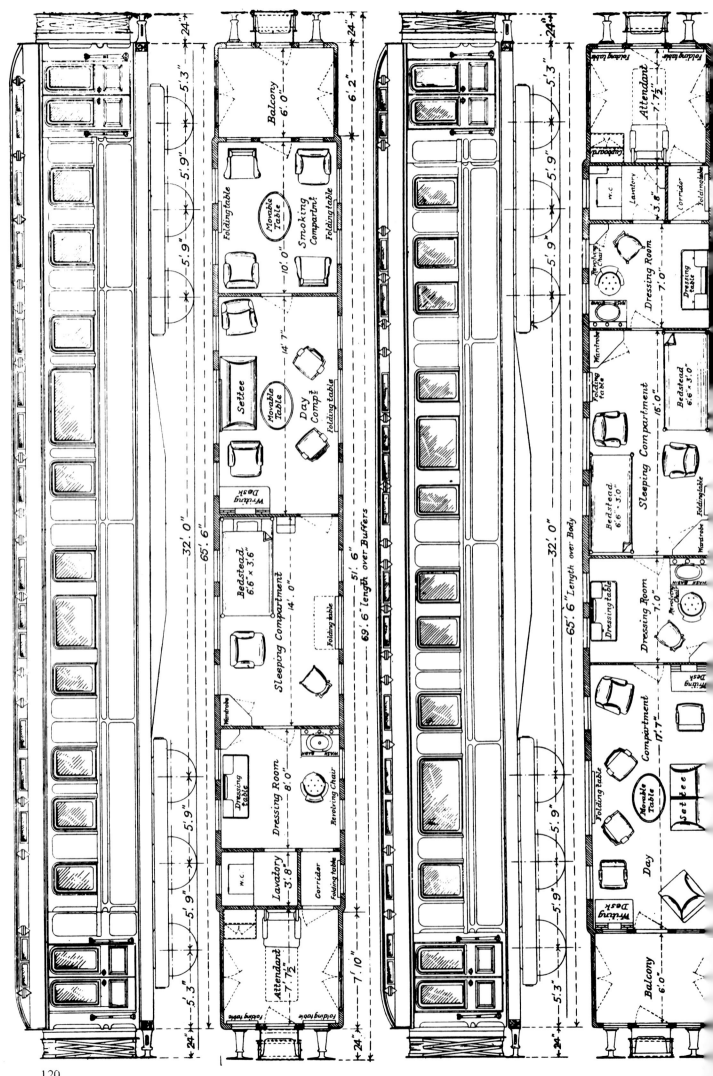

On this page are depicted what could well claim to be the finest pair of railway carriages ever built in Britain – the LNWR Royal Saloons of 1903. *Figure 38 (opposite)* shows elevations and plans of the two vehicles, the King's Saloon being uppermost. An end elevation is given on page 124. On this page, *Plate 146 (above)* shows the two saloons as built, the King's saloon being nearer the camera, while *Plate 147 (below)* shows a posed 'Royal Train' formation consisting of two full brakes, the two Royal Saloons and four matching semi-royals to LNWR D1 – see page 124. It is unlikely that the Royal Train ever ran to this formation.

(Drawing: 'Railway Engineer', courtesy National Railway Museum)

Plate 148 King Edward VII's day compartment as originally finished.

Plate 149 The King's smoking compartment as originally finished.

Plate 150 Queen Alexandra's day compartment.

Plate 151 Queen Alexandra's sleeping compartment as originally furnished with canopies over the beds.

Plate 152 The Queen's dressing room as first altered to a bathroom.

Plate 153 The Queen's bedroom as altered to meet the wishes of Queen Mary. Note the 'M' monogram on the bedstead.

123

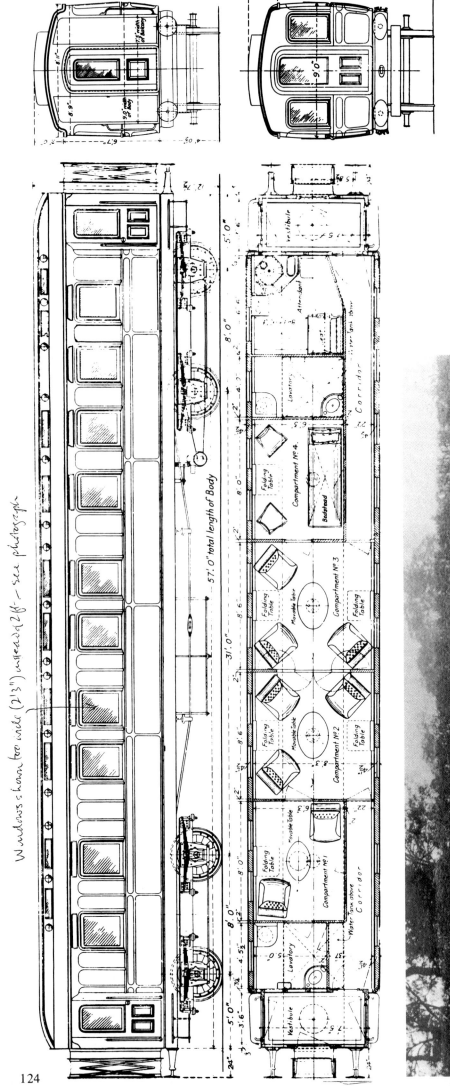

Windows shown too wide (2'3") instead of 2ft – see photograph

57'.0" total length of Body

Figure 39 Elevations and plan of the 57ft clerestory Semi-Royal Saloons to LNWR D1, together with an end elevation of the Royal Saloons at page 120. The photograph shows saloon 75, later 5075 (LMS 10507, later 807) from the corridor side. A view of the other side of these coaches (the window arrangement was not identical on both sides) is given at *Plate 155* (opposite). (*Drawing: 'Railway Engineer', courtesy National Railway Museum*)

124

Plate 154 Interior view of LMS Saloon 803 (ex-LNWR 71/5071, 1st LMS 10503) as used in the Prime Minister's train during World War II. This saloon was the only vehicle of the six to LNWR D1 which remained substantially as built during its whole life.

Plate 155 LMS Saloons Nos 804 (nearer the camera) and 803 at Wolverton 1956. Saloon 804 remains as altered for Winston Churchill's use. Note the air duct along the clerestory.

(F. W. Shuttleworth)

Plate 157 The Prime Minister's lounge in Saloon No 804. The Study/Office can be seen through the open door.

Plate 156 The Prime Minister's bedroom in Saloon No 804.

Plate 158 Special Saloon 153, later 5153, to LNWR D4. Two identical vehicles were built to this diagram for the Prince of Wales (later King Edward VII) and his equerries. Saloon 153 was the coach officially designated for the equerries' use.

Plate 159 Apart from the replacement of the principal Royal Saloons in 1941 (for reasons of safety in the event of air attack on a wooden bodied coach), the old LNWR Royal Train remained intact until the mid-1950s. A typical early BR view is given here.

Plates 160 & 161 Two interior views of the Special Saloons to D4 *(opposite)*. The vehicle is not identified but was probably the same coach (153). Note the reflection of the huge plate camera used for taking these pictures in the mirror of the door.

Departmental Saloons

Most of the departmental saloons listed in the LNWR diagram book were classified as Inspection saloons and most of the relevant details can be gathered from the accompanying sketch plans and the summary tables. From these summaries it can be seen that the coaches form three main groups. First were the three VIP type saloons to D2, D3 and D12; next in importance were the 42ft vehicles to D6-8 and finally were the residual 32ft saloons (D9-11) about which relatively little is known.

Pride of place amongst the departmental saloons was held by the Chairman's Saloon (D12), a distinctive 57ft elliptical roof coach with non-standard panelling — neither traditional Wolverton or 'twelve-wheel'. It approximated to the toplight style but did not quite match even this period of coach decoration. Designated by the LMS as the 'President's Saloon', the vehicle is still in existence as No. 45000 (now mounted on BR 100 mph bogies) and is not infrequently to be seen marshalled in the Royal Train. Even bigger than this coach was the massive twelve-wheel 66ft 6in saloon to D2. This coach was for the LNWR directors' use and although styled in somewhat similar fashion to the final twelve-wheel elliptical sleepers and diners, it had outside doors flush with the exterior side panelling and considerably less outside ornamentation than the typical twelve wheel coach.

The last of this group of three major saloons was the 50ft saloon to D3. This was an older saloon than D2 but still classified for the Directors' use. It was a much more traditional Wolverton coach and the LMS reclassified it as an Inspection Saloon in 1937 — *Plate 166.*

The group of 42ft inspection saloons all seem to have originated from other types of vehicle. Diagrams 6 and 7 were very similar in external appearance and seem to have been converted from redundant sleeping cars of pre-twelve-wheel vintage. Their external panelling was certainly of this type, as was the roof profile, but their exact origins have not been confirmed. Little is known of the saloon to D8. It did not reach the LMS and appears to have been a conversion from a 42ft day saloon — see summary table.

The 32ft departmental coaches also seem to have been conversions from older coaches but once again, too little information has survived to enable positive identification to be made. The coaches lasted quite well and were occasionally photographed, but it has not been possible to verify origin beyond that which is included in the table. From their appearance, some of them may well have started life as 32ft sleeping cars.

Finally, mention should be made of three 45ft clerestory inspection saloons (LMS 45031-3) which were not issued with a separate diagram. These were conversions from WCJS family saloons (WCJS D13) and their full history is considered on page 141.

Plates 162 & 163 Two views of the LNWR Chairman's Saloon to D12. Above, it is seen as LMS 45000 in an unusual, probably unique, Crimson Lake and cream livery, received for a short time in the early 1930s when given LMS bogies. It is not known whether the LMS was seriously contemplating adopting this rather attractive livery for all stock, but fairly soon, No 45000 received the orthodox fully lined all-crimson LMS colours *(lower view)* which it retained for 29 years after nationalisation! This picture was taken in 1956 when the LMS emblems had been removed. The saloon was finally repainted in Royal Train colours in 1977, losing its elaborate lining in the process.

(Plate 163 — F. W. Shuttleworth)

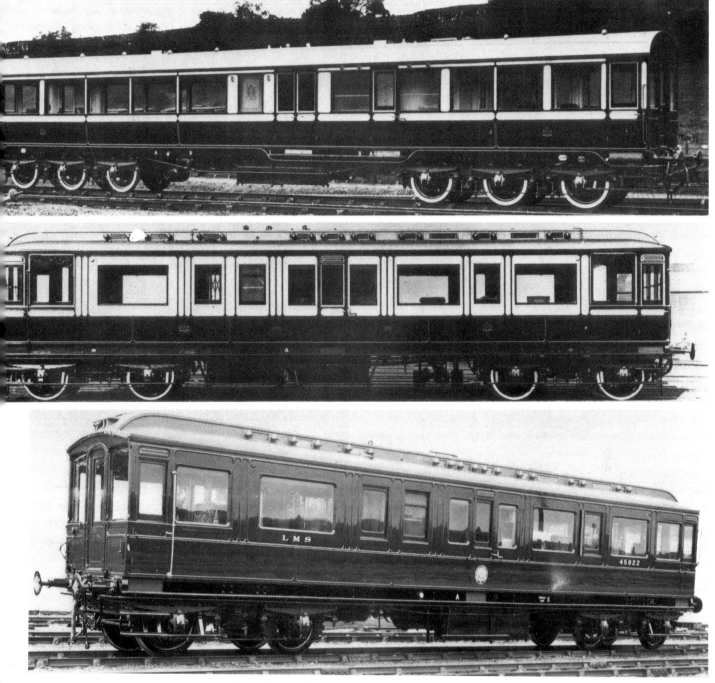

Plate 164 (above top) LNWR Directors' Inspection Saloon No 5318 to D2.

Plates 165 & 166 (above, centre and lower) This rather elegant 50ft clerestory saloon was to LNWR D3. Numbered 5201 it was, like D2, for the Directors' use and apparently kept its LNWR colours for many years after the grouping. The upper view shows it as built and the lower picture shows it modified in 1937 by the LMS as Inspection Saloon 45022. The main change was to replace the folding side windows of the end verandahs with conventional fixed windows.

Plate 167 (below) Inspection Saloon 5179 was to D6, one of several diagrams of markedly similar saloons. It became LMS 10683, later 45013 and was probably converted from a 42ft sleeping car, whose body style it shared — see Fig.1, Plate 43.

Special Corridor Stock

It has been remarked elsewhere that the LNWR tended not to favour the building of special sets of coaches for its corridor trains and even on the WCJS side, sets were not common. A few coaches were clearly designed (originally) for working in sets (e.g. the pioneer 1893 corridor sets, the 1897 WCJS 50ft sets and the 1913 elliptical roof sets for certain Anglo-Scottish workings) but these were of essentially standard type vehicles and could be readily interchanged with or supplemented by other coaches. However, two distinctive sets of vehicles built in 1908 stand right outside the main trends of LNWR and WCJS corridor coaches and merit special attention. These coaches were, of course, the elegant vehicles built for the 2 pm Euston-Scotland service (the famous 'Corridor') and the similarly styled coaches constructed for the Euston-Liverpool (Riverside) boat trains for the North American ocean liner trade.

The '2 pm' and 'American Special' stock was all built to a common elliptical roof style with exterior panelling and decoration matching that of the by now familiar twelve-wheel sleeping and dining cars. All told, only 48 coaches were built for the two services but to no fewer than thirteen diagrams — and even then, the '2 pm' had to make do with older dining cars. The history of the coaches concerned is very well documented and full details are given in the summary table. Plans of the twelve-wheel coaches are appended at *Fig. 41*.

The '2 pm' coaches were designed to operate as the main passenger carrying portion of fixed eight coach formations, marshalled as shown at *Fig. 41*. It will be noted that because of the handing of the brake coaches, it was possible to assemble the train with the corridor entirely on one side — apparently a desirable feature. No matching dining cars were provided so each train was completed by two of the clerestory coaches to WCJS D9, described on page 59. Although these coaches were only a few years old, their clerestories broke the symmetry of the train and it is a little surprising that some of the later elliptical roof diners were not built to WCJS order and used as replacements.

Unlike many LNWR (and later LMS) special sets, the coaches were not supplied in exact multiples of three, although there were six spare coaches — see summary table. These coaches could have been formed into a spare set, with slightly different seating capacity, but whether or not this was ever done cannot be stated. It would have caused problems with seat reservation and the leading brake third would have been wrong handed. Be that as it may, however, the coaches themselves remained rostered on the 'Corridor' (renamed the *'Mid-day Scot'* by the LMS) until about 1930 when they were finally considered too old and were relegated to less important tasks, usually working as single vehicles.

Plate 168 First class compartment interior of the '2 pm' stock.

The '2 pm' was a supremely comfortable train and there is no doubt that it brought great prestige to the West Coast Route. It is arguable that in its day it was without peer and certainly to have travelled in it was to have experienced probably the finest form of rail travel available anywhere in Europe to passengers not paying some form of supplementary fare. So popular was the train that it is clear, from photographic evidence, that the standard set rarely sufficed to cater for the number of people who wished to use it. Somewhat surprisingly, as far as can be seen, the spare twelve-wheelers were not often used to augment the train and it was usually enlarged by the addition of the inevitable mixture of LNWR coach styles then available — to the detriment of its appearance.

(Text continues on page 135)

Plate 169 Four compartment third class brake No 395 to WCJS D64 (LMS 6466, later 6388). This was one of the two brakes built for the Edinburgh portion of the '2pm' train. An interesting style variation, unique to these Edinburgh brakes, was the vertical panel dividing strips below the waist set centrally below the windows. All other '2pm' coaches had the panel dividers between the windows.

Plate 170 (above) The '2pm' ready to leave Platform 6 at Euston c. 1909. The vehicle in the foreground is the third brake at the end of the Glasgow section and the other coaches in the distance are for Edinburgh.

Plate 171 (below) The northbound '2pm' near Bletchley behind a Prince of Wales Class 4-6-0. There were only seven of the twelve-wheelers on this particular occasion — the Aberdeen brake composite being absent — and the train was augmented by several 50ft arc roof coaches.

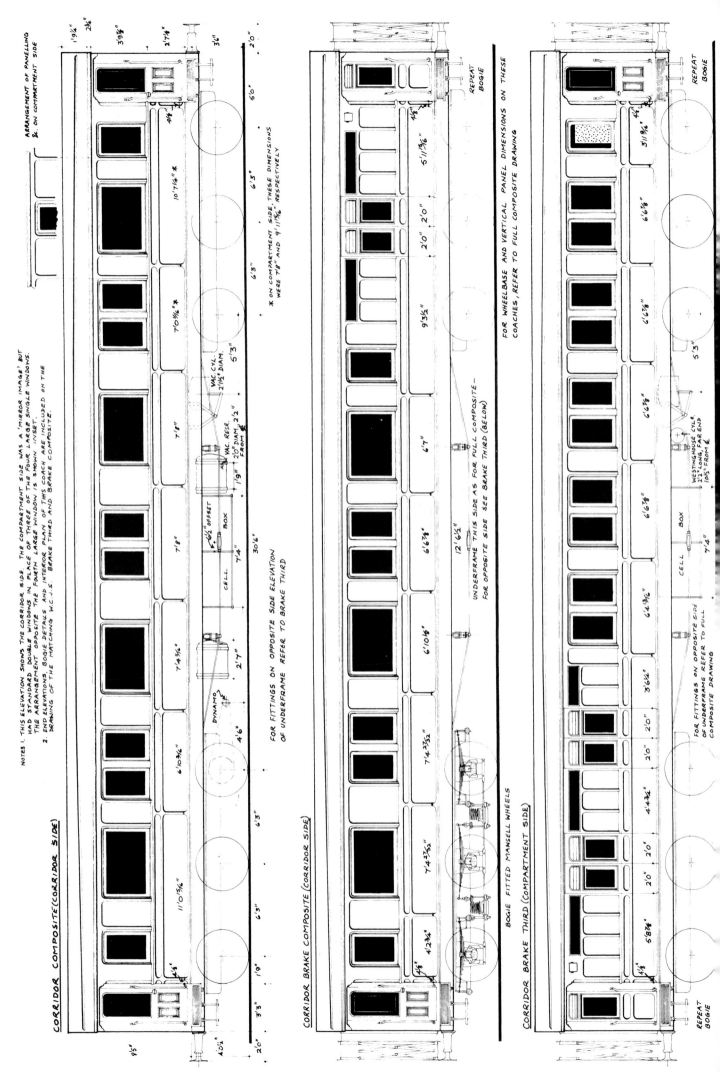

NOTES 1. THIS ELEVATION SHOWS THE CORRIDOR SIDE. THE COMPARTMENT SIDE WAS A 'MIRROR IMAGE' BUT HAD STANDARD DOUBLE WINDOWS IN PLACE OF THREE OF THE FOUR LARGE SINGLE WINDOWS. THE ARRANGEMENT OPPOSITE THE FOURTH LARGE WINDOW IS SHOWN INSET.

2. END ELEVATIONS, BOGIE DETAILS AND INTERIOR PLAN OF THIS COACH ARE INCLUDED ON THE DRAWING OF THE MATCHING W.C.J.S. BRAKE THIRD AND BRAKE COMPOSITE.

ARRANGEMENT OF PANELLING
2. ON COMPARTMENT SIDE

CORRIDOR COMPOSITE (CORRIDOR SIDE)

FOR FITTINGS ON OPPOSITE SIDE ELEVATION
OF UNDERFRAME REFER TO BRAKE THIRD

* ON COMPARTMENT SIDE, THESE DIMENSIONS
WERE 7'8" AND 9'11⅝" RESPECTIVELY

CORRIDOR BRAKE COMPOSITE (CORRIDOR SIDE)

UNDERFRAME THIS SIDE AS FOR FULL COMPOSITE -
FOR OPPOSITE SIDE SEE BRAKE THIRD (BELOW)

BOGIE FITTED MANSELL WHEELS

FOR WHEELBASE AND VERTICAL PANEL DIMENSIONS ON THESE
COACHES, REFER TO FULL COMPOSITE DRAWING

CORRIDOR BRAKE THIRD (COMPARTMENT SIDE)

FOR FITTINGS ON OPPOSITE SIDE
OF UNDERFRAME REFER TO FULL
COMPOSITE DRAWING

132

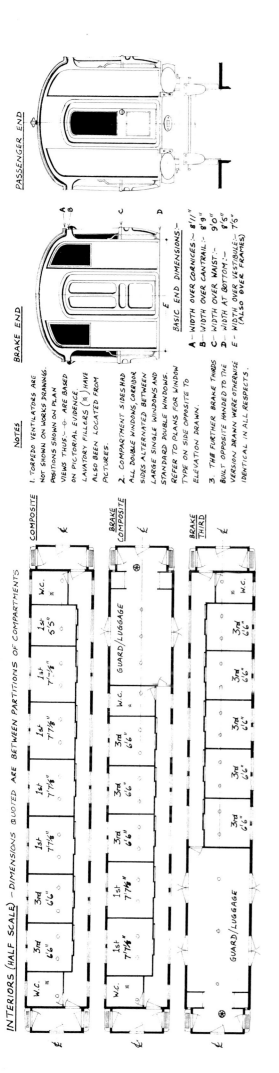

PASSENGER END

BRAKE END

NOTES

BASIC END DIMENSIONS:-

A — WIDTH OVER CORNICES:- 8'11"
B — WIDTH OVER CANTRAIL:- 8'9"
C — WIDTH OVER WAIST:- 9'0"
D — WIDTH AT BOTTOM:- 8'5"
E — WIDTH OVER VESTIBULE:- 7'5" (ALSO OVER FRAMES).

1. TORPEDO VENTILATORS ARE NOT SHOWN ON WORKS DRAWINGS. POSITIONS SHOWN ON PLAN VIEWS THUS:- ⊕ ARE BASED ON PICTORIAL EVIDENCE. LAVATORY FILLERS (⊠) HAVE ALSO BEEN LOCATED FROM PICTURES.

2. COMPARTMENT SIDES HAD ALL DOUBLE WINDOWS, CORRIDOR SIDES ALTERNATED BETWEEN LARGE SINGLE WINDOWS AND STANDARD DOUBLE WINDOWS. REFER TO PLANS FOR WINDOW TYPE ON SIDE OPPOSITE TO ELEVATION DRAWN.

3. THE FURTHER BRAKE THIRDS BUILT OPPOSITE HANDED TO THE VERSION DRAWN WERE OTHERWISE IDENTICAL IN ALL RESPECTS.

INTERIORS (HALF SCALE) - DIMENSIONS QUOTED ARE BETWEEN PARTITIONS OF COMPARTMENTS

COMPOSITE

| W.C. | 3rd 6'6" | 1st 7'7⅛" | 3rd 6'6" | 1st 7'7⅛" | 1st 7'7⅛" | 1st 7'7⅛" | 1st 7'–½" | 1st 5'5" | W.C. |

BRAKE COMPOSITE

GUARD/LUGGAGE | W.C. | 1st 7'7⅛" | 1st 7'7⅛" | 3rd 6'6" | 3rd 6'6" | W.C.

BRAKE THIRD

GUARD/LUGGAGE | 3rd 6'6" | 3rd 6'6" | 3rd 6'6" | 3rd 6'6" | W.C.

Figure 40 Elevations and plans of three varieties of '2pm' stock, the omitted types being the 'Edinburgh' brake third and composite coaches. The picture shows 'Glasgow' composite 381 (LMS 7987, later 4782) from the opposite side to the upper elevation on the page opposite. (Drawings: D. Jenkinson)

133

Plate 172 (above) Seven coaches of one of the '2pm' sets seen at Wolverton. The four coaches on the left form the Glasgow portion, the three on the right the Edinburgh section.

Plate 173 (below) American Special first class dining car No 309, later 5309 (LMS 10392, later 7556).

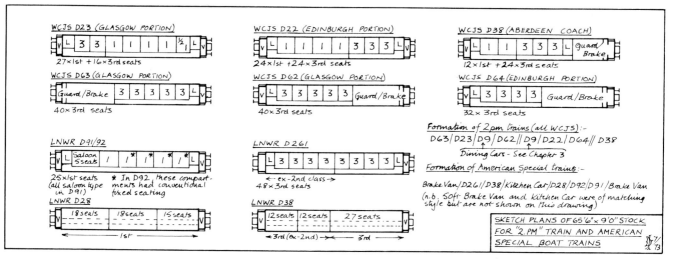

Figure 41 Sketch plans of special corridor stock.
(D. Jenkinson)

The American Specials were much tidier sets of coaches. In this case, three genuine matching sets were provided, each of eight coaches and marshalled as shown in *Fig. 41*. The use of a separate kitchen car was unusual as was the building of matching brake vans to keep the profile consistent. These two varieties of coach were 50ft eight-wheel vehicles. The trains were clearly intended to impress the overseas visitors and must have succeeded, for in 1913, six additional corridor firsts were built to increase the formation to ten coaches.

As with the '2 pm', the American Specials remained rostered on their original duties well into LMS days and the coaches themselves were not generally scrapped until the 1950s. During the 1920s, two of the corridor firsts were refitted for use as Club Saloons — see below — and this may possibly have reflected the start of a decline in boat train traffic in face of competition from the big ocean liners now beginning to use Southampton as their terminal port. There were also one or two instances of the occasional use of the odd American Special coach in the Royal Train.

The interior finishing of both the '2 pm' and American Special trains was very similar. Although very opulently furnished — as the illustrations in this chapter indicate, the overall style was that which had become very familiar in most twelve-wheel coaches by this period. First class compartment upholstery was of the favourite green Blenheim moquette while thirds were finished in crimson and black velvet. Second class compartments in the American sets were also upholstered in a patterned material but its colour is not known. Curtains, blinds and wood finishes were all of the customary high standard. The main difference between the two sets of coaches was to be found in the first class compartments of the American sets. In

Plate 174 Third class compartment interior of a '2pm' coach.

Plate 175 Second and third class corridor coach No 1920 (LMS number correlation not known) from the 'American Special'.

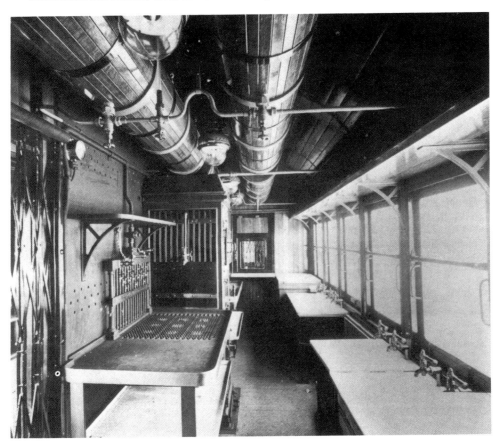

Plates 176 & 177 Exterior and interior views of kitchen car 315, later 5315, built for the American Train. The coach later became LMS 3202, finally 30197.

these trains, several compartments were equipped with a mixture of movable armchairs and fixed settees whereas the WCJS coaches all had the traditional fixed seats. Furthermore, even the fixed seat compartments in the American trains only seated four passengers, whereas the '2 pm' firsts had the conventional three per side seating. Finally in the American trains, one compartment in each first class coach was rather larger than the remainder and was fitted out rather like a miniature saloon for five passengers.

The open dining cars for the boat trains were conventional twelve-wheelers, each seating 51 passengers in eight and a half bays. The proportions of the individual saloons within each type are indicated at *Fig. 41*. Externally, the two types of coach were all but indistinguishable and after 1911, the composites became all third. Inside the coaches, the dining seats were in the form of individual armchairs and it is interesting to note that this style of furnishing followed that which had been introduced only a few years beforehand in the WCJS clerestory dining cars which ran with the '2 pm' sets — so the dining cars on the two services were more alike than outward appearance might suggest. It is to be hoped that the comfort of the 'loose' armchair seats belied their rather spartan appearance — *Plate 179* — which contrasted ill with the generally lavish fittings given to these sets of coaches. An interesting piece of Edwardian class distinction in the American diners was the considerably more restrained use of lincrusta panelling on the ceilings of the composites. During the LMS period, these coaches were quoted as 48 seat cars, the end half bay of seats having, apparently, been appropriated for other purposes.

Plates 178 & 179 Above is the second and third class dining saloon 312, later 5312 (LMS 10478, later 9584) while below is the interior of first class car 309, also seen at *Plate 173*. Both inside and out, the two types were all but identical.

Plate 180 Interior view of corridor first class coach No 126 (later number correlation not known) of the 'American Special' sets.

Plate 181 Second class compartment interior of coach No 1920.

Day, Invalid and Family Saloons

This group of vehicles again contained some very elderly representatives about which little more can be said than is given in the sketch plans and summary tables. From these it will be seen that the so-called 'Day Saloon' had clearly fallen from favour in late LNWR days and that the need for Invalid Saloons was relatively small. However, there was a much more widespread distribution of family saloons and many of these reached the LMS.

None of the day saloons survived to reach the LMS in that form, if at all – but the coaches to D52 and D53 were quite interesting. They were originally built as pairs of saloons, one to each diagram and ran on 42ft radial underframes. They were later rebuilt with cove roofs and bogies and are shown in their original guise on pages 6-7. One known utilisation of these coaches, which were furnished something in the manner of a cross between a dining car and a compartment first, was on the American boat trains and one of them can be seen in the background of the picture at *Plate 182*. It is possible, but not confirmed, that some of them could have gone into departmental service at a later date, but the only reasonably certain example is LNWR No. 5121 which is believed to have been the vehicle converted to LNWR D8 (above).

The 32ft day saloons to D54 were orthodox six wheel radial coaches and internally they were finished in fairly conventional manner. The diagram indicates that some of the seats could be drawn out to form beds so they were probably related to, if not derived from, the early 32ft sleeping saloons. Two were withdrawn quite early but one of them was subsequently modified and became an inspection saloon to D9. Its subsequent disposal is not known.

The few invalid saloons listed in the diagram book were quite interesting examples of the age they represented. The three short saloons (D57-D59) were all substantially similar and the 32ft examples are described in contemporary accounts as not differing much from the normal LNWR style of coach; but they did include sofas and comfortable corner seats, not to mention the bed itself, so they were more than adequately furnished – see *Figure 42*.

The 50ft invalid saloons were distinctly more lavish and the elliptical roof coaches to D56 were undoubtedly finished in luxury style. Although designed for invalids and given double doors wide enough to admit a bath chair, they were also capable of being used as family saloons. If required, green tapestry curtains could screen the bed area from the entrance to the main saloon. In this area, the coach was equipped with two armchairs and a settee in addition to the bed. The rest of the coach contained two conventional first class compartments (with four corner seats and a central gangway), three lavatories and a large luggage compartment. Upholstery was in the favoured green Blenheim moquette – an almost universal Wolverton finishing in first class carriages of the period – and wall panelling was in American walnut and sycamore. Floors were, of course, carpeted and the windows were fitted with gold tapestry blinds similar to those used in the contemporary sleeping cars. Ceilings were gold on white lincrusta and the conventional compartments were convertible for night use if necessary. The other 50ft invalid saloon to D55, a cove roof coach converted from a first world war ambulance vehicle, had similar facilities to the elliptical roof coaches but arranged in a rather different way – see

(Text continues on page 141)

Plate 182 Although heavily retouched by the LNWR studios, this picture of an American boat train at Riverside station, gives a good impression of late nineteenth century travel. The coach in the foreground is one of the twin 34ft diners – see Chapter 3 – while in the distance can be seen a day saloon to D52 or D53.

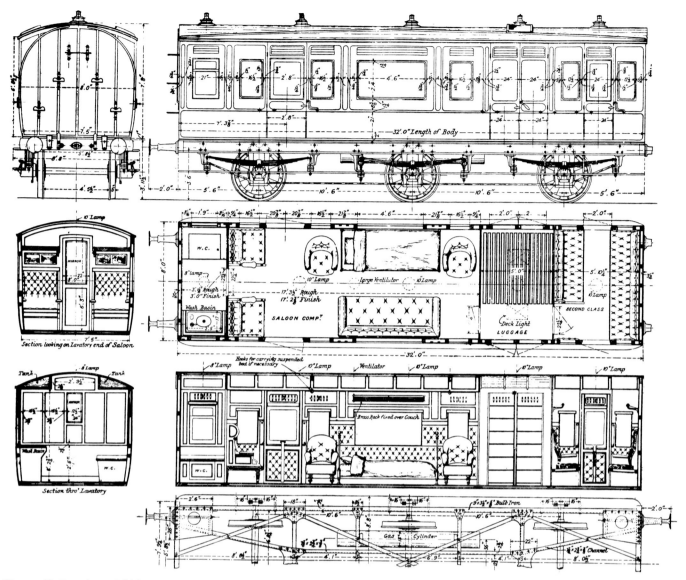

Figure 42 Drawing of 32ft Invalid Saloon to LNWR D57. Only one example is listed in the final diagram book, 5208, but the design is highly typical of most of these vehicles. (*'Railway Engineer', courtesy National Railway Museum*)

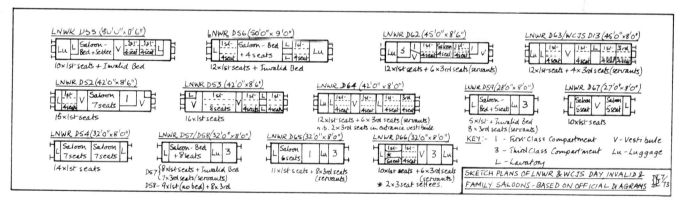

Figure 43 Sketch plans of day, invalid and family saloons. (*D. Jenkinson*)

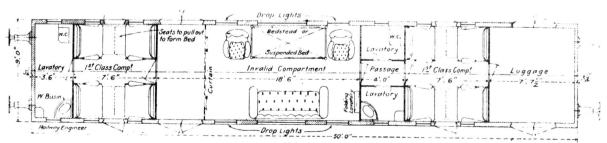

Figure 44 Detailed plan of Invalid Saloon to D56, pictures of which are overleaf.

('*Railway Engineer*',
courtesy National Railway Museum)

Plates 183-6 Exterior and interior views of the D56 invalid saloon No 27, later 5207 (LMS 10509, 811) both before and after the grouping. Apart from the change of livery, the most obvious LMS alteration is the fitting of gangways and the re-trimming of the interior. Note that in LMS days, the practice of picking out the ceiling detail in gilt was suppressed in favour of a plain paint finish.

sketch plans. Its upholstery and finishing details are not known.

The elaborate finishing of these later invalid saloons was closely derived from that adopted in the more orthodox family saloon type of coach. These coaches were quite numerous in LNWR days and several different designs were built as the sketch plans and summary table show. The essential difference which distinguished a family saloon from its contemporary day and invalid saloons seems to have been the presence of a servants' compartment, universally provided in family saloons. Of the family saloons, the most noteworthy and numerous examples were the handsome 45ft clerestory coaches to LNWR D63 and WCJS D13. Built at the turn of the century, these coaches were lavishly equipped and provided all the facilities for the well to do family man to move his whole household, including many servants and a vast quantity of luggage, on the annual pilgrimage to the grouse moors — or whatever.

The interior finishing was to the highest standard of the day. Wood panelling was standard 'Wolverton', extensive use being made of American walnut framing and fumed mahogany panels in the saloons with polished oak in the vestibules and alcoves. The servants' compartment was finished in teak with oak panels and mouldings. Ceilings were cream on gold ground floral flockpaper in the saloons and cream lincrusta with gilt mouldings in the servants' compartment. Gold tapestry sprung blinds were fitted to the windows.

Upholstery and floor coverings were also to the standard styles. First class areas had figured crimson and brown saladin moquette seat coverings with matching crimson laces and Wilton carpets on the floors, while the servants'

area was upholstered in crimson figured velvet with linoleum floor coverings. Within the smoking vestibule, two revolving cane seat chairs and two sprung folding seats were provided. Later drawings show these areas fitted out exclusively with individual chairs.

In a sense, these saloons, plus the 50ft invalid coaches already described, marked the end of a somewhat unique phase in British rail travel and their decline was clearly the first manifestation of the effect of the motor car on railway travelling habits. After all, it was the rich who could first afford to buy motor cars.

The clerestory saloons survived in their original form until well into the 1920s, but thereafter, their fate was mixed. The majority were relegated to picnic saloons, two went to the Royal Train, one of them had a short run as a first class club saloon, one became a motor fitted saloon for push-pull working and three were converted to Inspection saloons, far outliving the rest in the process.

The remaining family saloons were much fewer in number than the 45ft clerestory coaches but the six carriages to D62 are worthy of more than passing mention. These dated from the middle 1890s and had a semi-corridor interior arrangement — see plans at *Fig. 43*. However, their main interest is in the exterior treatment adopted. They were given body panelling of quasi-twelve-wheel style and one wonders if, at this time, Wolverton may have been considering a more universal change of exterior treatment than in the event took place. No other examples of this type of exterior treatment have come to light. Like most of the family saloons which were not scrapped at an early stage, these coaches were converted to picnic saloons during LMS days *(Plate 24)*.

Plates 187 & 188 These views show the 45ft clerestory family saloons in early and late guise. Both are examples from WCJS D13. Saloon 357 *(below)* is shown as built, it later became LMS 10552 and 979. To the right is Engineers' Saloon 45031, converted from WCJS 353, 1st LMS 10548.

(Plate 187 – R. J. Essery's collection)

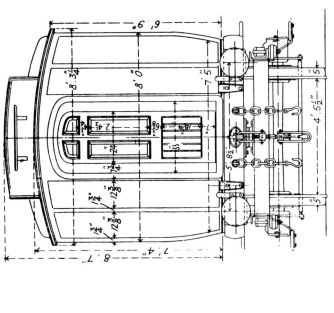

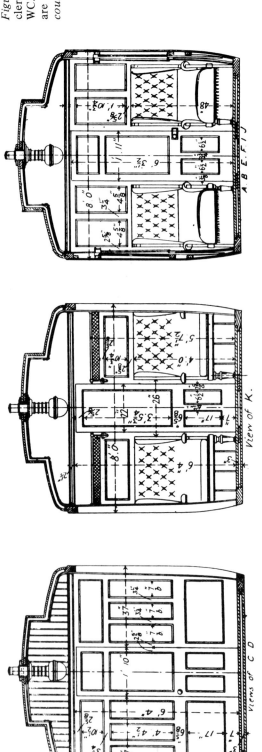

Figure 45 These drawings show the 45ft clerestory family saloon to LNWR D63 and WCJS D13 as built. Photographs of this design are on the previous page. ('*Railway Engineer*', courtesy *National Railway Museum*)

Plate 189 Ex-American Special corridor first seen at Abergele in 1937 converted into a club car to D69 (LMS 816) for use between Manchester and Llandudno.
(J. P. Richards)

Club and similar Saloons

The travelling club, wherein each member had his own designated seat within a specially equipped saloon, was an interesting feature of train working in the earlier part of the twentieth century. The idea was aimed particularly at well to do business commuters who were travelling quite long distances and the saloons were usually brought into use with one particular service in mind. In consequence, many different designs existed and their main features are indicated in the sketch plans and summary table. Little needs to be added to this information which is, by way of a change, largely complete.

The saloons themselves were a mixture of purpose built coaches such as D70 and D71 (picture — p. 19) and vehicles which had seen previous service in other forms. Of the latter, perhaps the most interesting were the LMS conversions of two of the American Special coaches for the Manchester and North Wales services. Two corridor firsts were concerned and the conversion took the form of removing most of the interior partitions to open up the coach into large saloon areas. In both cases, some of the original compartments and lavatories were retained — see plans. These coaches, like most travelling clubs, were for the use of first class passengers but D71B was an attempt to attract the third class traveller. This coach was a fairly straightforward conversion of one of the 42ft arc roof picnic saloons — see below — and is illustrated at *Plate 190*. The service for which it was built is not known, nor whether the idea was a success.

Of somewhat similar type to the genuine club saloons were a few other vehicles which are not easily classified (D100A, later D100B; D103; D103A). The LNWR diagram book puts them amongst the first class non-corridor lavatory coaches but two of the three types were gangwayed and all three had rather more elaborate interiors than the coaches considered in Chapter 5. Essentially they were what, in modern days, we would call 'open firsts'. Even the LMS had some difficulty in classifying them as can be seen from the second LMS numbers. Two were numbered in the first class corridor series, several were given genuine saloon numbers and one was put amongst the non-corridor lavatory coaches.

The largest of the three designs was D100A which, in original form, was not unduly different from an orthodox lavatory first but it did have one rather large saloon and an attendant's compartment which rendered it a little out of the ordinary. It was a 54ft cove roof vehicle and in 1924 was altered to D100B by opening up the whole central area into a large single saloon. In this form, it was used as a genuine club saloon between Manchester and Windermere.

The other two designs in this group were both 50ft arc roof gangwayed vehicles whose interior partition arrangement was identical. In essence, these coaches were centre gangwayed open firsts with the coach divided into a series of saloon type areas. Some seats were of the fixed type and others were cane bottom armchairs. The only difference between the two designs was that in D103A, a two seat settee was substituted in one of the saloons in place of the armchair and small table in the same area of D103. The services for which these six coaches were built is not known, but they were certainly used on the American boat trains at one time.

Plate 190 Third class club car to D71B No 5238, converted in 1913 from 42ft picnic saloon to D77 — see page 146. It later became LMS 10577.

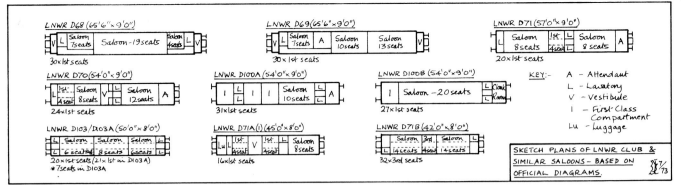

Figure 46 (top) Sketch plans of club and similar saloons. *(D. Jenkinson)*

Plates 191 & 192 Two views of the unique 54ft cove roof club car to D70 (LNWR 5068, LMS 10573, later 813). Above, it is seen in original LNWR colours while to the left is a view taken at Aberdovey in July 1956 when the car formed part of the Cambrian Radio Cruise Train.

(Plate 192 – F. W. Shuttleworth)

Plate 193 Interior view of first class coach to LNWR D103.
(Original LNWR postcard from F. W. Shuttleworth's collection)

144

Plate 194 Interior view of 42ft picnic saloon to D77. Exterior view and drawings of this type are given overleaf.

Picnic Saloons

In the days before universal car ownership and widespread motor coach touring, it was not unusual for groups of people to hire a picnic saloon for day outings. In consequence, the LNWR diagram book contains a considerable number of such vehicles of widely differing styles, sizes and origins. Many were built new for the job but many others were conversions from other types of coach. Unlike the family saloon, the picnic saloon seems to have managed to hold its own as a type for much longer and during the early LMS period, several new picnic saloons were created from redundant family saloons.

The picnic saloon was invariably a third class coach and furnished in a somewhat basic, though not necessarily austere manner. The seating was almost invariably arranged longitudinally down the sides of the coach sometimes with extra corner seats and the central area was equally commonly fitted out with a large table or series of tables. Of the many designs which were put into service and which are summarised at Appendix II, the biggest single group — and in many ways the most typical — were the 42ft arc roof coaches to D77.

As first built, these coaches were equipped with long couches upholstered with figured moquette or brown and gold combination rep. The seats themselves were framed with brown oak while the interior panelling was inlaid

brown oak framed in teak with polished mouldings. Ceilings were covered in flock paper enamelled white with the floral pattern picked out in terra cotta. Floors were linoleum covered. Small luggage and parcels racks were provided at the sides and ends of the saloons, while movable tables were made of pitch pine with teak tops. There were the usual framed pictures of the LNWR system inside the coach and the two interior saloon areas were entered via sliding doors with brass fittings. Windows were fitted with gold colour tapestry spring blinds. It was one of these coaches which was altered to a third class club saloon (above).

Other numerous groups of picnic saloons were the 45ft ex-family saloons already mentioned. These conversions (to D71A(2); D78; D78A) took place in the 1920s and the coaches were given new interior fittings basically along the lines of the 42ft coaches already described.

These larger picnic saloons themselves evolved from the older, generally six-wheel coaches which had been built during the nineteenth century. Naturally enough, these coaches were fairly early withdrawals, many failing to reach the LMS, but in general, reasonably comprehensive details have survived and are summarised in the sketch plans and summary tables. As a type, the picnic saloon lasted quite well and the final withdrawals did not take place until after the second world war.

Plate 195 LMS picnic saloon No 10632 to D80. Originally a family saloon, its LNWR number was 5004 and it ended its life as LMS 944.

(S. H. P. Higgins, courtesy F. W. Shuttleworth)

145

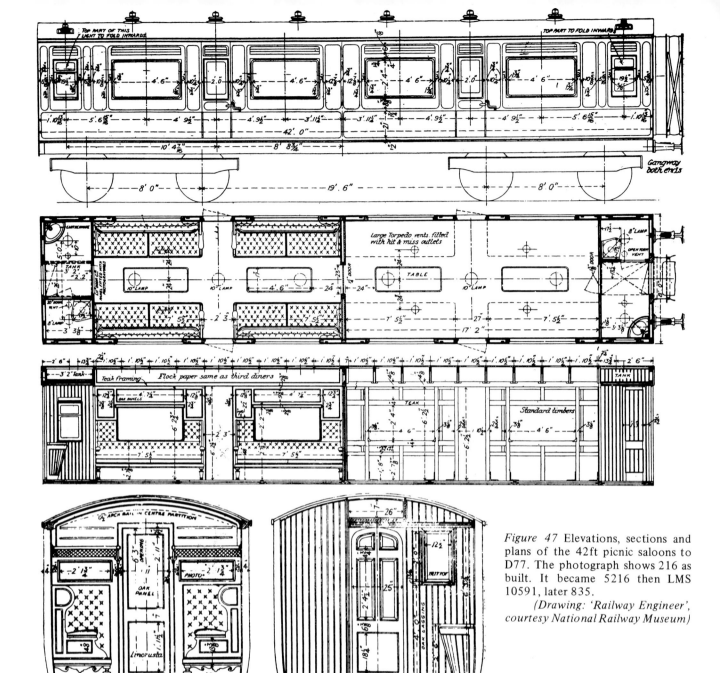

Figure 47 Elevations, sections and plans of the 42ft picnic saloons to D77. The photograph shows 216 as built. It became 5216 then LMS 10591, later 835.

(Drawing: 'Railway Engineer', courtesy National Railway Museum)

Figure 48 (bottom) Sketch plans of picnic saloons. *(D. Jenkinson)*

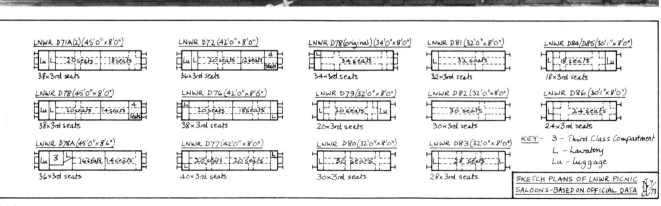

146

Chapter 7   Motor Fitted Stock

Introduction

Motor fitted coaches which, together with their prime movers, were variously described as auto-trains, motor trains or push-pull trains were an important part of the railway's attempt not only to fight the growing competition from road vehicles but also to economise on the operation of branch line minor services. In this type of working, the LNWR was well to the fore and its motor fitted stock represents an important, albeit numerically small aspect of the company passenger stock. However, in complexity of types and styles, the LNWR motor fitted vehicles were a somewhat bewildering group of coaches, additionally complicated by the fact that re-building of former locomotive hauled stock continued well after the 1923 grouping.

Table 4 attempts to summarise the basic categories of coaches as listed in the diagram book. As can be seen, thirteen types of vehicle can be identified, not to mention the various styles of coach-building represented. When it is realised that in addition to the variety obvious from the tabular summary, no fewer than 68 separate diagrams of motor fitted vehicles were issued, half of which covered but one vehicle each, the impossibility of making broad generalisations can be appreciated. For this reason, as in the case of the special saloons, the tabular summary of motor fitted coaches has been separated from the main bulk of the vehicles in the LNWR list and will be found at Appendix III. It is logical to seek an explanation for this high degree of variety since the LNWR was, in most essentials, a highly standardised company, building its locomotives and rolling stock in large batches of broadly similar types. One can, of course, never be absolutely certain in these matters but, parodoxically, the main reason for the variety could well

have been the high degree of standardisation achieved elsewhere. By the time that motor fitted working began to assume importance (broadly speaking from about 1910 onwards), the company had a large collection of standardised locomotive hauled coaches which would, to some extent, become redundant if a new mode of operation was to be adopted. It doubtless seemed more economical to make relatively cheap conversions of existing stock than to build new vehicles especially if, as was often the case, the locomotive hauled stock was not life expired.

On examination, therefore, the motor fitted vehicles can often be seen to be relatively simple conversions of standard general service vehicles. Since conversion of stock did not take place all at one time but was generally undertaken only when specific need arose for motor coaches, it can also be appreciated why the individual number of vehicles involved was often very small — hence the large number of separate diagrams raised.

Nevertheless, the LNWR did experiment with new construction for this mode of working and the small number of vehicles concerned, mostly open stock, added to the variety to be observed. In fact, it may even have been that experience with purpose built stock influenced the subsequent decision to concentrate on rebuilding older coaches on the grounds of economy.

As with special saloons, detailed descriptions of each and every design would occupy too much space, but a reasonable amount of detail has been included at Appendix III. In this chapter, attention will be concentrated on the general trends of LNWR motor fitted coach design.

TABLE 4 SUMMARY OF LNWR MOTOR-FITTED COACHES
The information tabulated is taken from the final version of the LNWR motor diagram book. Although all coaches listed are of LNWR origin, some conversions did not take place until after the 1923 railway grouping.

TYPE / STYLE	ARC ROOF 42'	ARC ROOF 50'	COVE ROOF 42'	COVE ROOF 50'	COVE ROOF 57'	ELLIPTICAL* 50'	ELLIPTICAL* 57'	ELLIPTICAL* 60'	OTHERS 57'	OTHERS 45'	OTHERS 42'	Totals
Third Class Saloon			1									1
Third Class Saloon (Driving)	2		1							1		4
Third Class Steam Railmotor							6	1				7
Open Composite						1			3			4
Open Composite (Driving)							4					4
Compartment Composite		3		5		4	5					17
Compartment Composite (Driving)		12		9		2						23
Open Third							4					4
Open Third (Driving)		6					12	1			1+	20
Compartment Third		18		9		4	1					32
Compartment Third (Driving) ≠		8		13		4	4					29
Corridor Third					3		13					16
Corridor Third (Driving)						4						4
Totals	2	47	2	36	3	18	50	2	3	1	1	165

*   In this category it is not readily possible to distinguish between standard and toplight designs since there were so many style variations
+   Actually a 41 ft 7 in coach
≠   Some of these classified as brake third in the diagram book

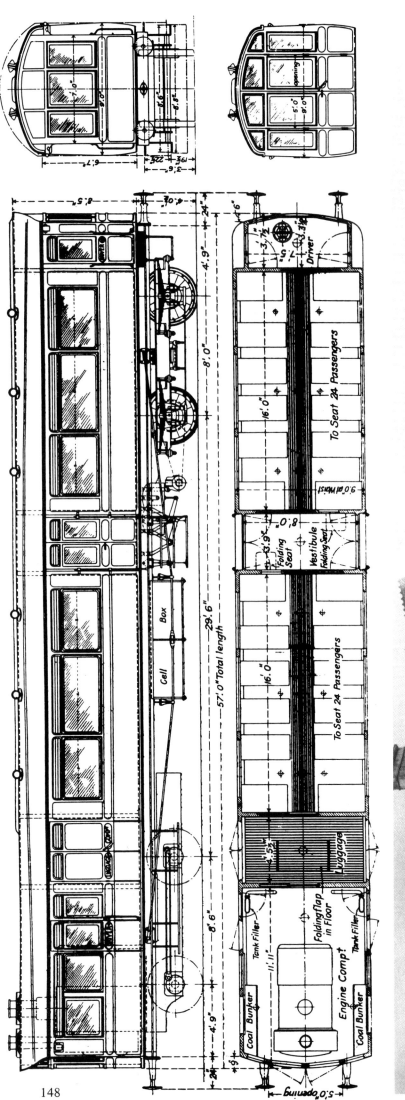

Figure 49 Elevations and plan of 57ft steam railmotor to Diagram M7. The picture to the left shows railmotor No. 3; that above shows the pioneer car No. 1. Other views are given opposite.

Plate 196 Close-up view of the open doors of the engine compartment of LNWR Steam Railmotor No 1.

Plate 197 LNWR Steam Railmotor No 3, later 5503 and LMS 10696 seen at Bicester on the Oxford branch. The engine compartment is at the far end in this view.

Purpose Built Open Stock

As far as can be determined, the first purpose built stock for motor fitted train working on the LNWR took the form of the six steam railmotors of 1905/6 (Diagram M7 – *Plate 196-7*). These were 57ft long and among the first, if not the very first LNWR passenger vehicles to incorporate a high elliptical roof. Like all steam railmotors of the period, the LNWR examples all suffered from lack of power in the self-contained locomotive portion. Augmentation of the railmotor by even one vehicle tended to overtax the engine portion and the vehicles were thus somewhat inflexible in operation if large numbers of extra passengers occasionally presented themselves. The LNWR built but one further steam railmotor (Diagram M6) in 1910, a 60ft derivative of the previous design. It seems to have been paired with a matching 60ft trailer (Diagram M44).

All but one of the railmotors had gone by 1931 but in that year, the sole survivor (LMS 10697, later 29988) was sent by the LMS to work the Moffat branch of the former Caledonian Railway – a service it continued to perform until 1948.

The push-pull type of train, with its separate locomotive rapidly superseded the self-contained railmotor designs on many of the British railway systems and the LNWR was no exception. This type of working was much more satisfactory since, within the limits imposed by engine power, quite a degree of augmentation was possible at busy times. Furthermore, the engine itself could be used for other purposes when not needed for push-pull working.

To work some of the early push-pull services, the LNWR introduced a whole series of somewhat experimental saloons during the years 1910-14, with an odd later example in 1916. These were either composites (Diagram M11-18 inclusive) or third class (Diagrams M44-50 inclusive). All of the composites and four of the third class diagrams were for single vehicles and only three of the third class diagrams were built in any number. Even so, the largest single batch was only six strong (the driving trailers to Diagram M49). Plans of the various types are given at *Figure 50*.

In stylistic terms, most of these open coaches, whether fitted with driving equipment or not, exhibited large areas of window and generally bore a family resemblance both to the toplight series of general service coaches and to the preceding steam railmotors. There were, however, a few experimental innovations. Some were built with intermediate gangways at one end only – to facilitate movement within a two coach set – and all were entered via separate entrance

Figure 50 Sketch plans of motor fitted open stock.

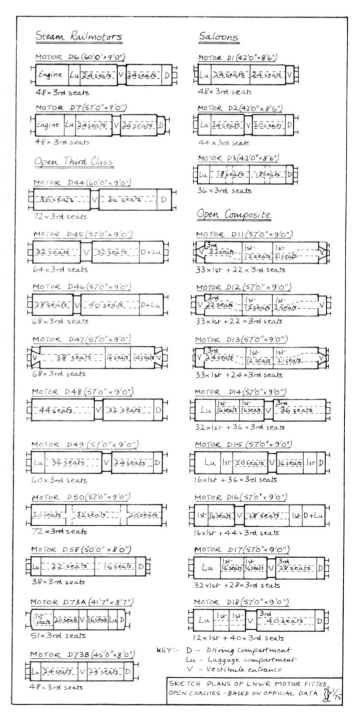

Plate 198 Open composite driving trailer No M15846M, by now downgraded to all third at Delph in 1955. This vehicle, to Diagram M15, was reasonably typical in visual terms of much of the purpose built LNWR motor fitted open stock.

(J. E. Cull)

Plates 199 & 200 (above) Open composite 3751 (LMS 9526, later 3426) to Diagram M13 at two stages in the life of the vehicle. The upper view is believed to be the earlier one. Note the deeply recessed doors at the first class end which appear to be angled the opposite way to that shown on the diagram and given at *Fig. 50*.

Plate 201 (below) LNWR observation car to Diagram M50 in service as LMS 5316 in 1926. The service in question was between Llandudno Junction and Blaenau Ffestiniog and the vehicle itself is now preserved on the Bluebell Railway.

vestibules (located at the ends or in the centre) rather than by conventional side doors of compartment pattern. Seating was usually in pairs on each side of a centre aisle being somewhat reminiscent of contemporary tramcar practice.

Most of these saloons had a full height roof but a few of the composites (Diagrams M11-13) had a roof profile somewhat intermediate between the cove roof and the full elliptical roof. Externally, these vehicles bore more than a passing resemblance, including the deeply set back end entrance doors, to the Siemens and Oerlikon multiple unit electric stock of broadly similar vintage built for the London suburban area. It is tempting to infer some connection between the two events but no conclusive evidence has been found. One of the contemporary open third designs (Diagram M47) also had the deeply recessed entrance doors but with a full height roof.

Another interesting group during this period were the three third class coaches to Diagram M50. Built during 1912-13, these vehicles had even more glass area than normal, including fully glazed ends, and formed the well known observation saloons of which the final example (LMS 15843) was sold in 1962 to the Bluebell Railway for preservation.

The LNWR purpose built open push-pull stock, unlike the steam railmotors, had a high survival rate. There were odd early withdrawals, but most of them lasted until the middle 1950s, the last survivor being the above mentioned observation saloon.

Converted Open Stock

The building of new open stock for push-pull working may have been connected in some way with a few interesting motor fitted conversions of erstwhile, locomotive hauled saloons of various types. In this group it is difficult to differentiate between coaches officially regarded as saloons and those labelled as being of lesser status. They will be considered together in this survey.

Officially described as 'saloons' were the three diagrams M1-3. The first two, illustrated at *Plate 203*, were respectively the trailing and driving saloon for the Redwharf Bay service. They were also listed in the main LNWR diagram book as D73 and D74 but are thought to have started life earlier as 42ft sleeping cars. Certainly their 8ft 6in wide, cove roof style was entirely that of the pre-12 wheel sleeping saloons. They were withdrawn before 1933.

The other 'saloon' diagram was M3. This covered a pair of 42ft arc roof ex-picnic saloons from LNWR D77. Both had driving ends and were designed for the Holywell Town service. They lasted until 1935.

The largest group of converted open coaches to be motor fitted were the six vehicles of Diagram M58. All of them were 50ft arc roof coaches with a combination of doors/quarterlights and long lights along the passenger saloons. It is not known whether they were built as motor fitted coaches but it is thought unlikely. Their original building date was 1900 and they may have originally been intended for some form of special working – c.f. D103/103A, page 143.

The final converted open coaches were a pair of oddities (Diagrams M73A/73B). The latter was a 1930 conversion of one of the familiar ex-WCJS 45ft clerestory family saloons (see page 141) and survived until 1938 while M73A was a conversion in 1926 of an experimental petrol electric railcar. It served on the Bletchley-Buckingham branch in 1937.

Plate 202 (right) Driving trailer to Diagram M58 No M3404M (ex-LNWR 2333, 1st LMS 5218), by a long margin the last of this type to survive, not being withdrawn until 1958.   *(R. J. Essery's collection)*

Plate 203 (below) The Redwharf Bay pair of motor fitted 42ft open saloons to Diagrams M1 and M2. The general style of these coaches is similar to that of the 42ft sleeping saloons of the 1880s and 1890s and it is more than possible that these vehicles started life as sleeping saloons.

Compartment and Corridor Stock

By far the bulk of motor fitted coaches of LNWR origin were converted from conventional general service vehicles, most styles of LNWR carriage 'architecture' being, eventually, represented. Third class coaches were numerically the most common, representing some two thirds of the total. The rest were composites. As with the open vehicles, numerous diagrams were issued, many for only one vehicle and the full details are given at Appendix III. The arrangement of the compartments in the various non-corridor types is listed at Table 5.

Essentially, if one ignores the actual styling of the vehicle exterior, LNWR motor fitted vehicles were converted from four basic types of coach namely non-corridor third class brakes, orthodox non-corridor thirds and composites and corridor thirds. The largest single group were the non-corridor coaches (Composite Diagrams M20-39 and Third Class Diagrams M53-64/72-4). Diagrams M70/71/78 were ex-third class brakes and Diagrams M52/75-7 were ex-corridor coaches. The appendix lists them in these categories although is should be remarked that, confusing the issue, some of the coaches of non-brake origin were classified as brakes after conversion (M72/73). As far as can be ascertained, only four, compartment type coaches (Diagrams M19/M51) were built new for motor train working. They were orthodox late period non-corridors and are illustrated at *Plate 205*.

In most of the converted coaches, relatively little structural alteration was made. In the case of coaches fitted with a driving compartment, the arrangement was either to place this at the brake van end of brake coaches or to convert one or two compartments (usually only one) of a non-brake coach for the driver's use. Quite a number of coaches were simply appropriated as non-driving trailers and were, externally, all but indistinguishable from their conventional equivalents. Apart from the fitting of driving compartments to many coaches, the most common alteration was the reclassification of compartments in the composite series. In some cases, the conversions were quite logical, erstwhile first class compartments being downgraded; but one or two examples could be observed where former third class compartments were re-upholstered to first class standard — but with no change in compartment size (e.g. Diagrams M21/M25).

Plate 204 50ft arc roof composite (ex-D187) No M17985M at Birmingham New Street in 1954. The vehicle was converted for motor train working to Diagram M36 during LMS days and is seen here in this form, almost unaltered from the original. It was originally LNWR No 3175, 1st LMS 9515. *(J. E. Cull)*

Key to coach types: A – Arc Roof; C – Cove Roof;
E – Elliptical Roof; T – Elliptical Roof (Toplight Period)

Key to symbols: 1 – First Class; 3 – Third Class;
D – Driving compartment; Lu – Luggage compartment

Category	Diagram Number	Length & Type	Compartment Arrangements	Seats 1st	Seats 3rd
Composite	M19	57ft(T)	333333311	16	84
	M19B	57ft(T)	33333111	24	60
	M22	50ft(E)	3333111	24	48
	M23	50ft(E)	3333111	24	48
	M29	50ft(C)	3311111	40	24
	M30	50ft(C)	3331111	32	36
	M36	50ft(A)	3331111	24	30
	M37	50ft(A)	3333111	18	40
	M38	50ft(E)	3331111	32	36
	M39	57ft(T)	333111333	24	72
Composite (Driving)	M20	50ft(E)	333111Lu+D	24	36
	M21	50ft(E)	3333311Lu+D	16	60
	M24	50ft(C)	331111Lu+D	32	24
	M25 / M26	50ft(C)	333311Lu+D	16	48
	M27	50ft(C)	3333113Lu+D	16	60
	M28	50ft(C)	3333313Lu+D	8	72
	M31	50ft(A)	3333111Lu+D	24	40
	M32	50ft(A)	333111Lu+D	24	30
	M33	50ft(A)	111333Lu+D	18	30
	M34	50ft(A)	333311Lu+D	16	40
	M35	50ft(A)	333331Lu+D	6	50
Third	M55	50ft(E)	33333333	–	96
	M57	50ft(C)	33333333	–	96
	M61	50ft(A)	3333333	–	70
	M62 / M63	50ft(A)	33333333	–	80
	M74	57ft(T)	333333333	–	108
Third (Driving)	M51	57ft(T)	333333Lu+D	–	72
	M53 / M54	50ft(E)	333333Lu+D	–	72
	M56	50ft(C)	333333Lu+D	–	72
	M59	50ft(A)	333333Lu+D	–	60
	M60	50ft(A)	3333333Lu+D	–	70
	M64	50ft(C)	3333333Lu+D	–	84
	M70*	50ft(E)	33333Lu+D	–	60
	M71*	50ft(C)	33333Lu+D	–	60
	M72*	50ft(A)	3333333Lu+D	–	70
	M73*	50ft(A)	333333Lu+D	–	60
	M78*	57ft(T)	333333Lu+D	–	72

* These coaches officially listed as third brakes in the diagram book

Plate 205 This pair of coaches represent the only type of LNWR compartment vehicles to be specifically built for motor train working. They are third class driving trailer No 243 (LMS 5318, later 15848) and composite trailer No 3729 (LMS 9525, later 7992).

Plate 206 Unidentified cove roof driving trailer third, coupled to a non-driving trailer to Diagram M36. The driving trailer is probably an example from Diagram M56 but the position of the luggage door is not as shown on this diagram. The other alternative is a downgraded example of Diagram M26.

(F. W. Shuttleworth's collection)

Plate 207 Typical motor fitted conversions of previous locomotive hauled arc roof coaches. Leading is a composite driving trailer to Diagram M33, almost certainly converted from D187.

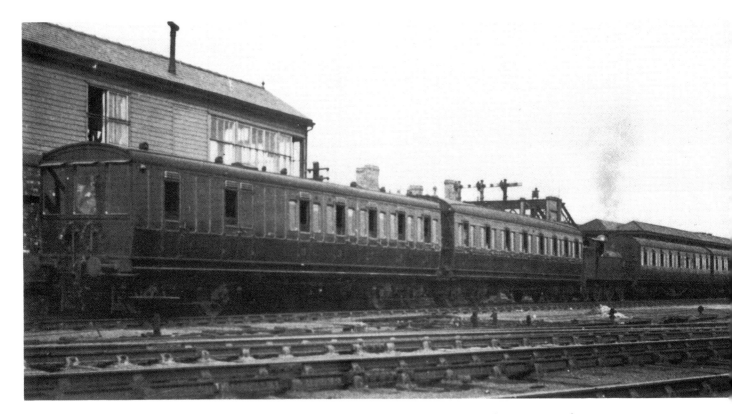

Plate 208 LMS motor fitted train leaving Bescot station in 1934. The leading coach is a cove roof third class driving trailer to Diagram M71 and is believed to be ex-LNWR 6942 (see Appendix III). The elliptical roof composite coupled to the bunker of the locomotive is the unique Diagram M19B which later operated on the Leighton Buzzard-Dunstable service.

(W. A. Camwell, courtesy J. E. Cull)

The corridor coaches were an interesting group of vehicles and were divided into two categories, 50ft and 57ft long respectively. The 50ft vehicles (Diagram M52) originated in 1913 and were very similar to the matching corridor thirds to D267 – page 95. They may have been conversions from D267 and were certainly used for push-pull work before 1923. They had driving compartments and were the only side corridor vehicles thus equipped. The driving compartment replaced one of the end lavatories in the vehicle, the other end lavatory being replaced by an entrance vestibule.

The 57ft corridor coaches, all used as non-driving trailers, were mostly LMS conversions and all but three had started life as D265, the standard 8ft 6in wide corridor third of the 1908-10 period (page 93). These coaches seem to have been converted in two phases. Initially, they retained their eight compartments and in some of them, one lavatory was replaced by a small luggage compartment. The later stage of conversion, to which all eventually conformed, was with an enlarged luggage space at one end (utilising the area of the lavatory and one compartment), but retaining the lavatory at the other end. The three remaining corridor coaches were conversions from the spacious cove roof D264 (page 79) and retained both lavatories.

All the ex-LNWR motor fitted coaches had a long life, survival being generally until the mid 1950s when branch line closures and the introduction of DMU working caused the onset of large scale withdrawals. They represented an interesting phase of railway history and it is rather regrettable that no examples have survived for posterity, other than the observation saloon – not exactly the most typical of the collection.

Plate 209 50ft third class corridor driving trailer to Diagram M52 No 514 (LMS 5213, later 3409). These vehicles may have been converted from D267 (page 95) but, unlike D267, they displayed round corners to all panelling and may, therefore have been built motor fitted from the start at a slightly later date.

154

Chapter 8   Non-Passenger Coaching Stock

Apart from the full brakes, outlined in Chapter 4, Wolverton also built a great variety of non-passenger carrying vehicles which were designed to be operated at passenger train speeds. The various types listed in the diagram books are summarised at Table 6 (page 158). To describe all these varieties in the same detail as for the passenger carrying vehicles would allocate these vehicles a disproportionate amount of space; yet they should not be omitted from a survey of LNWR/WCJS carriage stock. Fortunately, if Table 6 is examined in detail, it can be seen that most of the designs represent but few actual vehicles and that only seven of the 80 odd types represented were built to the tune of 100 or more units. It therefore seemed reasonable to compile this section on a slightly different basis and it will take the form of a series of pictures of some of the more interesting varieties, with extended captions replacing the running text. For convenience, the non-passenger vehicles have been subdivided into their principal categories.

Post Office and Allied Vehicles
These vehicles constitute the largest single section of the non-passenger diagrams in terms of types built, but in numerical terms, the actual quantity of vehicles is small. For obvious reasons, many of these designs were in the WCJS lists.

Plates 210 & 211 Two views of a typical Wolverton six-wheel TPO, WCJS 348. This coach was built as a non-radial coach to Diagram W89 in 1886. It became LMS 3253 after 1923 but did not last much longer. It was from vehicles similar to this (but not this example) that the unique 64ft TPOs were built which are featured on the next page.

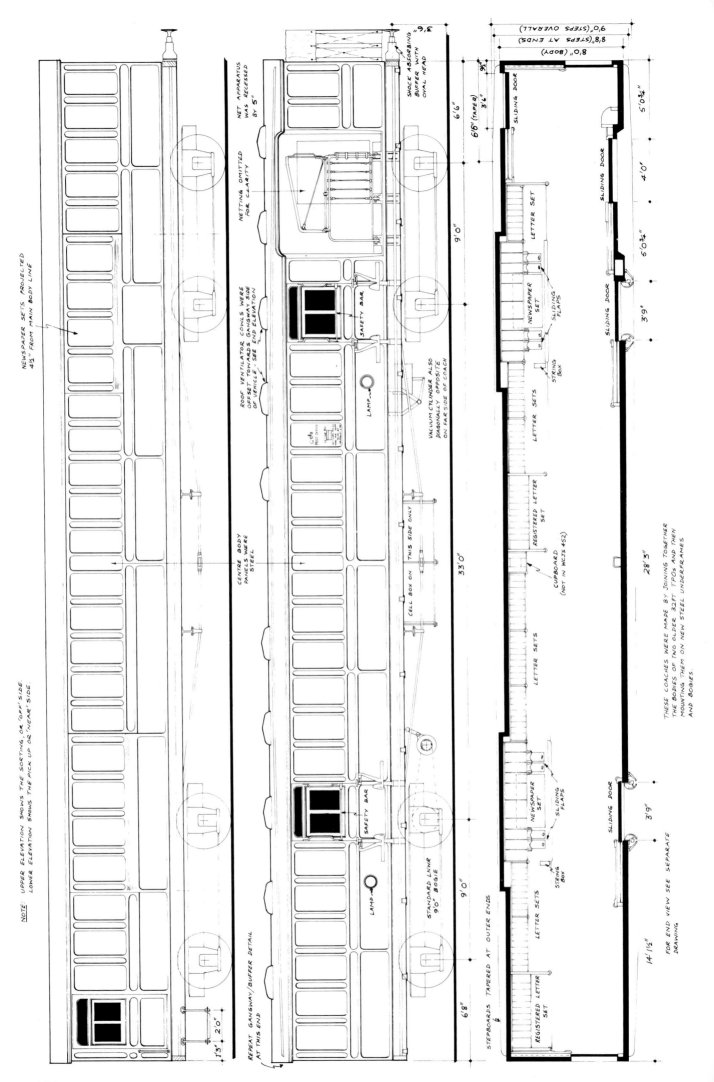

NOTE: UPPER ELEVATION SHOWS THE SORTING, OR 'OFF' SIDE.
LOWER ELEVATION SHOWS THE PICK UP OR 'NEAR' SIDE

NEWSPAPER SETS PROJECTED
4½" FROM MAIN BODY LINE

CENTRE BODY
PANELS WERE
STEEL

REPEAT GANGWAY/BUFFER DETAIL
AT THIS END

NET APPARATUS
WAS RECESSED
BY 5"

NETTING OMITTED
FOR CLARITY

ROOF VENTILATOR COWLS WERE
OFFSET TOWARDS GANGWAY SIDE
OF VEHICLE - SEE END ELEVATION

SAFETY BAR

LAMP

VACUUM CYLINDER ALSO
DIAGONALLY OPPOSITE
ON FAR SIDE OF COACH

CELL BOX ON THIS SIDE ONLY

SAFETY BAR

LAMP

STANDARD LNWR
9'0" BOGIE

STEPBOARDS TAPERED AT OUTER ENDS

SHOCK ABSORBING
BUFFER WITH
OVAL HEAD

3'6"

6'6"

6'6" (TAPER)

9'0"

33'0"

9'0"

6'8"

13'   2'0"

8'0" (BODY)

8'8" (STEPS AT ENDS)

9'0" (STEPS OVERALL)

3'6"

9½"

5'0¾"

4'0"

5'0¾"

3'9"

28'3"

3'9"

14'1½"

LETTER SET

NEWSPAPER
SET

SLIDING
FLAPS

STRING
BOX

LETTER SETS

REGISTERED LETTER
SET

CUPBOARD
(NOT IN WCJS 452)

LETTER SETS

SLIDING DOOR

SLIDING DOOR

SLIDING DOOR

SLIDING DOOR

NEWSPAPER
SET

SLIDING
FLAPS

STRING
BOX

LETTER SETS

REGISTERED LETTER
SET

THESE COACHES WERE MADE BY JOINING TOGETHER
THE BODIES OF TWO OLDER 32FT TPOs AND THEN
MOUNTING THEM ON NEW STEEL UNDERFRAMES
AND BOGIES.

FOR END VIEW SEE SEPARATE
DRAWING

G.R.
POST OFFICE

156

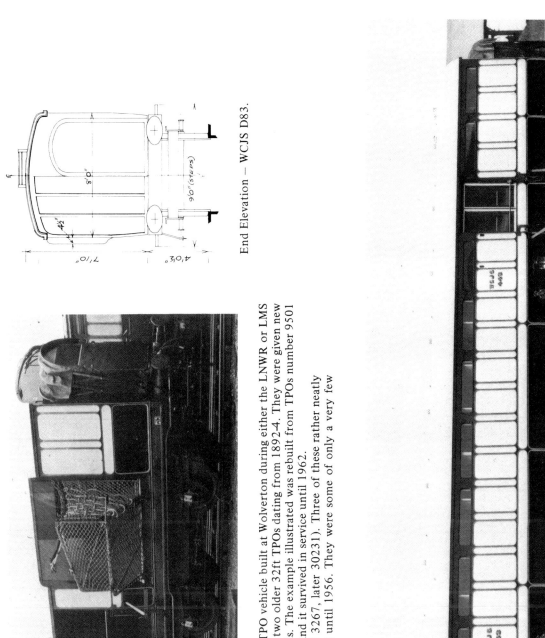

End Elevation — WCJS D83.

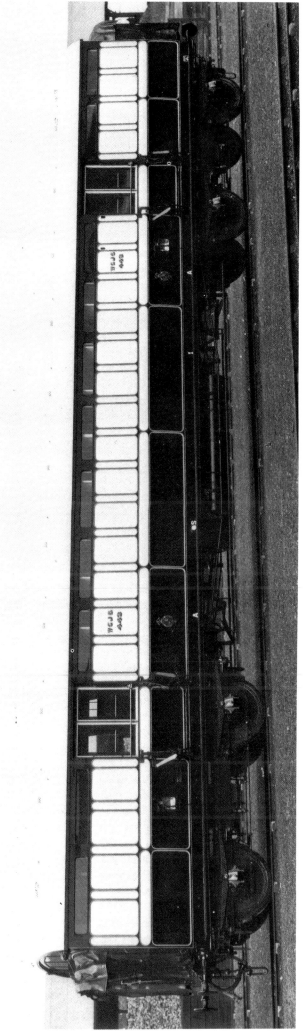

Figure 51 (above) This rather unusual TPO to WCJS D83 was the longest TPO vehicle built at Wolverton during either the LNWR or LMS period. Three were constructed in 1917 and were, in fact, each rebuilt from two older 32ft TPOs dating from 1892-4. They were given new underframes on rebuilding with the bogies set well in from the vehicle ends. The example illustrated was rebuilt from TPOs number 9501 and 9508 and became WCJS 452. The LMS numbered it 3210, later 30207 and it survived in service until 1962.

Plate 212 (below) 57ft parcel sorting carriage to WCJS D93 No 443 (LMS 3267, later 30231). Three of these rather neatly designed coaches were built in 1910 and the example illustrated survived until 1956. They were some of only a very few elliptical roof TPOs built at Wolverton prior to 1923.

TABLE 6 OUTLINE SUMMARY OF NON-PASSENGER COACHING STOCK

Diagram No(s)	Official Description	Length x Width	Body Style[1]	No. of Types[2]	No. of Vehicles[2]
W83	Post Office	64' x 8' 0"	C	1	3[3]
W84	Letter Sorting Carriage	57' x 8' 6"	E	1	4
W85	Post Office	57' x 8' 6"	E	1	3
391	Post Office	50' x 8' 6"	E	1	2
392	Post Office	50' x 8' 0"	C	1	4
W86	Post Office	50' x 8' 0"	C	1	7
393	Post Office	42' x 8' 0"	A	1	2
394	Post Office	42' x 8' 0"	CL	1	1
W87/8	Post Office	42' x 8' 0"	C	2	7
395-404	Post Office	32' x 8' 0"	C	10	25[4]
W89-92	Post Office	32' x 8' 0"	C	4	9
406/406A	Postal Brake Van	57' x 9' 0"	E	2	3[5]
407	Postal Sorting Van	50' x 8' 6"	E	1	3
408	Parcel Sorting Van	50' x 8' 0"	C	1	1
W103	Parcel Sorting Van	30' x 8' 0"	A	1	8
W96/7	Parcel Post Van	42' x 8' 0"	A	2	7
410	Parcel Post Van	32' x 8' 0"	A	1	1
411	Parcel Post Van	30' x 8' 0"	A	1	1
412	Parcel Post Van	27' 6" x 8' 0"	A	1	1
W93	Parcel Sorting Carriage	57' x 8' 6"	E	1	3
415	Parcel Sorting Van	45' x 8' 0"	CL	1	25[6]
416	Parcel Sorting Van	35' x 8' 0"	A	1	8
417/8	Parcel Sorting Van	32' x 8' 0"	A	2	27
419	Parcel Sorting Van	30' x 8' 0"	A	1	18
W94/5	Letter and Parcel Van	42' x 8' 0"	A	2	3
424	Parcel Van	32' x 7' 9"	A	1	10
425	Parcel Van	30' x 8' 0"	A	1	59
426	Parcel Van	25' x 8' 0"	A	1	1
427	Newspaper Van	45' x 8' 0"	A	3	3
430	Bicycle Van	45' x 8' 0"	CL	1	20[7]
431	Bullion Van	50' x 8' 0"	E	1	4
435	Double Horse Box	30' x 8' 0"	N/S	1	1
436	Horse Box	21' x 8' 0"	N/S	1	694
438	Horse Box	19' 6" x 7' 10"	N/S	1	88
440/1	Covered Scenery Truck	50' x 8' 6"	E	2	12
442	Covered Scenery Truck	50' x 8' 0"	E	1	5[8]
443	Covered Fourgon Truck	30' x 8' 0"	N/S	1	1
444	Combination Truck	30' x 8' 0"	N/S	1	132
444A	Combination Truck	30' x 8' 6"	N/S	1	64[9]
445	Combination Truck	21' x 8' 0"	N/S	1	248
445A	Combination Truck	21' x 8' 0"	N/S	1	c.94[10]
446	Covered Truck (Motor Car)	27' x 8' 0"	N/S	1	6
447	Covered Carriage Truck	25' x 8' 0"	N/S	1	4
448	Covered Carriage Truck	21' x 8' 0"	N/S	1	22
454	Fruit Van	30' x 8' 0"	N/S	1	25
456	Covered Fish Van	30' x 8' 0"	A	1	8
W106	Fish Van	30' x 8' 0"	A	1	6
W107	Fish Van	30' x 8' 0"	C	1	102
W108	Fish Van	25' x 8' 0"	A	1	33
457	Fruit and Fish Truck	16' x 8' 0"	A	1	100
461	Open Scenery Truck	50' x 8' 0"	N/S	1	6
461A/B	Open Truck (with Parcel Containers)	45' x 8' 0"	N/S	2	5[11]
462	Open Scenery Truck	45' x 8' 0"	N/S	1	27
462A	Omnibus Truck	24' x 7' 10"	N/S	1	10
463	Open Carriage Truck	25' x 8' 0"	N/S	1	13
464-6	Open Carriage Truck	21' x 8' 0"	N/S	3	375
468	Open Fish Truck	21' x 7' 10"	N/S	1	231

Plates 213 & 214 These two views of TPO No 437 to WCJS D84 show the most numerous variety of elliptical roof post office coach built at Wolverton during the pre-grouping period. Even so, only four were built. Utilising a standard 57ft chassis, they were the fore-runners of many more elliptical roof TPOs built during LMS days. WCJS 437 became LMS 3213, later 30200 and was withdrawn in 1951.

Footnotes

1   Symbols as follows: A   Arc Roof
                         C   Cove Roof   These styles match, in all essentials,
                         CL Clerestory Roof   those of the passenger carrying coaches.
                         E   Elliptical Roof
                         N/S Non-standard body style
2   Refers to the number of separate diagrams within the same dimension/style category and the number of vehicles shown in the diagram book.
3   Each example converted from two 32ft vehicles.
4   Some later transferred to WCJS.
5   See also D370B (Brake Van) in Appendix I.
6   Later to D381A (Brake Van) – see Appendix I.
7   Later to D381B (Brake Van) – see Appendix I.
8   Non-standard Elliptical roof c. 4in taller than standard form.
9   Some possibly converted or rebuilt from D444.
10 Conversions ex-D445 with modified roof profile.
11 Ex-D462.

Plates 215-17 LNWR TPO No 35, later 9535 was built to D392 in 1900 as one of a batch of four coaches, all 50ft long. These views include a close-up of the extended net and the interior arrangements. The coach became LMS 3231, later 30252 and was withdrawn in 1937, rather prematurely compared with others of the same batch — see *Plate 218, below.*

Plate 218 This view, taken at Workington in 1954, shows the final version of LNWR D392. The vehicle is seen running without its pick-up nets and in plain BR red livery as M30243M. It was the last example of D392 to be built (LNWR 9235; 1st LMS 3232). A surprising amount of the original panelling survived intact on this vehicle.

(F. W. Shuttleworth)

Plate 219 (above) WCJS TPO No 195 was built to WCJS D86 as one of seven coaches all but identical to LNWR D392. The main difference was the dual fitted underframe. It is also carrying side lights below the waist, not present on LNWR No 35 (Plate 215). WCJS 195 became LMS 3223, later 30312 and was fitted with a lavatory in 1930. It was withdrawn in 1937.

Plates 220 & 221 (right, centre) The distinctive form of panelling adopted on nearly all the Wolverton pre-group TPOs may still be seen on WCJS No 186, for this vehicle is preserved at the National Railway Museum. It is a 42ft radial design to Diagram W87. Several 42ft radial TPOs were built and many (probably all) of them were later given bogies. When withdrawn for preservation (upper view) WCJS 186 was re-fitted with radial type running gear. Before withdrawal, the coach also ran as LMS 3234, later 30384. Note that in its original state (lower view) the side door and pick-up nets were nearer to the centre of the coach.

(Plate 221, the late R. P. Cole's collection)

Plate 222 (right, bottom) Wolverton built a variety of postal vehicles other than TPOs and this picture shows a 32ft parcel sorting van to D417 No 09667 at Willesden just after the grouping. It did not receive an LMS number although four similar vehicles of the twelve built to the design, were given LMS series numbers. It is worthy of note that these parcels vans had centre gangways, thus enabling them to run coupled to conventional gangwayed stock. LNWR D418 was very similar to this type but had two pairs of sliding doors positioned where the second and fifth side windows are located on this view.

(F. W. Shuttleworth's collection)

Horse Boxes

The only livestock vehicles built at Wolverton and included in the passenger diagram book were horseboxes. Some railways also included prize and special cattle wagons in this category but not the LNWR.

Plate 223 This unique double horsebox No 10700 was to D435 and equipped to carry six animals, three at each end, with the groom's compartment in the centre. The vehicle was used for the Royal Train and this picture was taken in 1924. The horse box was renumbered 4020 by the LMS but did not survive long enough to receive its second LMS number.

(F. W. Shuttleworth's collection)

Plates 224 & 225 The standard LNWR horsebox was the extremely well appointed design to D436 of which LNWR 337, later 10337 is depicted here showing both exterior and interior arrangements. Almost seven hundred of these 21ft vehicles are listed in the diagram book and they were probably derived from a shorter 19ft 6in design with straight sides to D438. None of the earlier design seem to have reached the LMS and many of their running numbers were used again by the variety illustrated. Equipped with a separate luggage compartment and a well appointed groom's compartment, the standard LNWR horse box had a long life and many hundreds survived to receive LMS second series numbers both in the 43190-436 series and in the LMS standard number series as well. LNWR 337 became LMS 3492 but did not receive a second LMS number.

Other Covered Vehicles

Covered vehicles of passenger rated type were used for a variety of traffics where quick transit was desirable. Some of the many types are described below.

Plate 226 (above) LNWR 569, later 11569 was one of five scenery trucks built to D442 during the early elliptical roof period. All were 50ft dual braked coaches and were given the full passenger livery. Judging from the picture, they were fitted with older pattern 8ft bogies, possibly second hand. The coach illustrated became LMS 4037, later 37679 and was withdrawn in 1951.

Plate 227 Covered Combination Truck to D444 seen running in Departmental service as a stores van No DM395087 at Horwich during the BR period. This was a numerous design of vehicle, equipped with end doors and a high arched roof, thus allowing the conveyance of fairly tall road vehicles, amongst other items. An example is preserved by the National Railway Museum. The picture shows the type virtually as built with double sliding doors.
(Author's collection)

Plate 228 D444A was a variant of D444 with conventional hinged doors and vehicles to this diagram were probably rebuilt from the sliding door version. Like D444, these trucks proved very popular with various departmental officers and DM 395119 is seen in this picture at Wolverton in 1965, awaiting scrapping. Right down to the late 1970s, vehicles of this type could still occasionally be seen in departmental use.
(R. J. Essery's collection)

Plate 229 Four-wheel Covered Combination Truck to D445A seen running as LMS 36831 in 1939 (ex-LNWR 12145, 1st LMS 4598). This diagram was an arched roof version of D445 and the vehicles built to it were probably rebuilds of the older type. D445 had slightly higher sides and a less pronounced roof curve. The original design dated from c. 1908. *(R. J. Essery's collection)*

Plate 230 Motor Car Truck No 011022 does not appear in the final LNWR Diagram Book but its running gear suggests a conversion from an older type of vehicle, probably D445A *(above)*, which was rated at the same carrying capacity. The running number has been 'cyphered', the second 11022 being allocated to a D444 vehicle such as that shown at *Plate 227*.

Plate 231 This stylish and rather modern looking Motor Car Truck was one of six built to D446. The bold style of lettering is worthy of note and the vehicle is finished in the 'all-chocolate' non-passenger coaching stock livery with relatively restrained lining. The absence of intermediate beading suggests that the vehicle panelling was of steel sheets. LNWR 603, later 11603 became LMS 4605, later 37297.

Plate 232 Six-wheel van No LMS 4296, later 38893, ex-WCJS 671, was built to WCJS D107 as a fish van c. 1909. More than 100 of these vehicles are listed in the diagram book and most of them survived to receive second LMS series numbers. During LMS days, some of these vans were re-classified as Meat Vans, including the example illustrated and received numbers in the 38879-99 series. Those remaining as Fish Vans were renumbered in the LMS 40376-441 series after 1933. Prior to 1933, all were numbered in the first LMS 4220-319 series. For the record, the WCJS numbers were 471, 552 and 595-694.

Open Vehicles

The final group of non-passenger coaching stock vehicles consisted of a variety of open top designs, three of which have been selected for illustration.

Plates 233 & 234 LNWR No 12015 *(above)* was a 45ft open truck with parcel containers to D461A (LMS 4771, later 41061). It was one of two so converted from the open scenery trucks to D462 *(below)*. It will be noted that the containers are lettered 'L & Y and L & NW Joint Rys'. A similar conversion, but with three pairs of containers, involved three more of these vehicles and was to D461B. The containers themselves were rated at 1½ tons carrying capacity each. Although all five converted scenery trucks were modified before grouping, the second LMS numbering series kept them in their original number sequence with the unconverted examples. The picture gives a very clear impression of the early pattern of 8ft LNWR bogie with shallow depth main frames as fitted to early bogie coaches and it seems quite feasible that all these 45ft open trucks may well have utilised frames from withdrawn 45ft passenger carrying coaches. The container carrying vehicles were all dual fitted. The later numbers of LNW 1011 *(below)* are not known but may have been LNWR 12011, 1st LMS 4766.

Plate 235 This open carriage truck No 280 was one of hundreds built to LNWR D466. Its form and function are self explanatory from the picture. Note that the sides hinged down and that the buffers were surmounted by metal 'wheel plates' for loading purposes. This design was a long-lived type. LNWR 280 became 11280 and was renumbered LMS 4987, later 41601. It was not withdrawn until 1953.

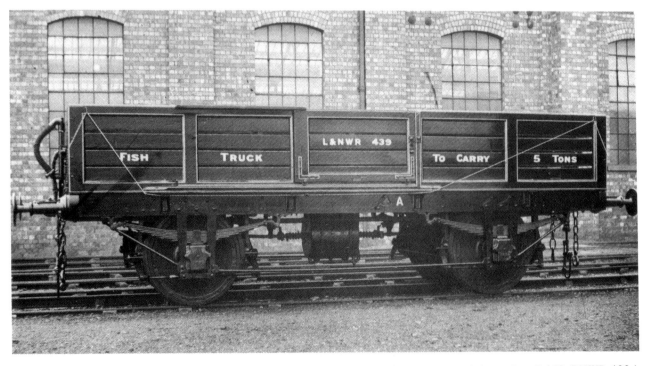

Plate 236 The last design listed in the LNWR Diagram Book is the open fish truck to D468. LNWR 439 is illustrated and was only a little superior to its contemporary goods vehicles. However, the conspicuous brake cylinder clearly indicates its fitness for service in passenger trains and it was finished in the non-passenger coaching stock livery. The subsequent numbering details of this example are not known but, for the record, the later LNWR number series for these trucks included the whole of the 11678-758 block. The LMS number blocks were 5178-384 (in 1923) and 40907-48 (the 1933 survivors).

(The late R. P. Cole's collection)

Notes on the use of Appendices I — III

COLUMN HEADINGS

In amplification of the column headings given in the summary tables and unless otherwise stated, the following assumptions may be made for all vehicles listed:—

Diagram Page All diagram numbers refer to LNWR locomotive hauled stock unless prefaced 'W' (West Coast Joint Stock) or 'M' (Motor fitted stock).

Quantity This column gives the number of vehicles shown in the diagram books. This is generally the same as the number built but, in the case of residual survivors from early batches, e.g. six and eight wheel radial coaches, does not include vehicles withdrawn before the diagram book was raised.

Date Built This information is included where known. A blank entry indicates that information is either not available or is unconfirmed.

Body Length Self explanatory. Length over buffers was usually 4ft more than the figure quoted.

Tare Weight Given to the nearest half ton as listed in the diagram books.

Body Style To save space, these are coded as follows:— SD — Sleeping/Dining car style of body, sub classified into the following categories:
1. 8ft 6in wide clerestory body, narrow vestibules
2. 8ft 6in wide clerestory body, intermediate vestibules
3. 9ft 0in wide clerestory body
4. 9ft 0in wide elliptical roof, recessed entrances
5. 9ft 0in wide elliptical roof, 'full width' entrances

A — Arc Roof body, traditional panelling
C — Cove Roof body, traditional panelling
E — Elliptical Roof body, traditional panelling
T — Elliptical Roof body, 'toplight' type panelling
The last four categories are combined with an indication of width viz:
8 — 8ft 0in wide body (9ft 0in over lookouts where fitted)
8½ — 8ft 6in wide body (9ft 2in over lookouts where fitted)
9 — 9ft 0in wide body (no raised lookouts)
Variations from the above pattern are noted in the remarks column.

Numbering Full first and second series LMS numbers are quoted for all vehicles where this information is known. Full pre-group numbering details are also given where the number of vehicles is ten or less or if the pre-group numbers form a consecutive series. In other cases, only sample numbers are given. No details of the pre-1910 LNWR numbers are given and lack of numbering detail in the LMS columns normally indicates

withdrawal from service before that series was introduced.

Withdrawals Withdrawal dates are only given where confirmed. Blank entries indicate that the information is not known.

GENERAL ASSUMPTIONS

Many general assumptions can be made about LNWR and WCJS coaches which need not be continually repeated in the tables. The main ones are summarised below, exceptions being recorded in the 'remarks' column of the tables.

Brakes All vehicles were fitted with continuous brakes. The type will not be specified unless different from the normal pattern. In this context, 'normal' should be taken to mean dual fitted (i.e. both Westinghouse/Vacuum) in the case of WCJS vehicles and vacuum fitted only for purely LNWR vehicles.

Lighting Coaches should be assumed to be electrically lit unless stated otherwise. The form of lighting (stated or inferred) is as recorded in the diagram book. It should be noted that many gas lit coaches were altered to electric lighting after the diagram books were issued. Confirmed examples are listed in the 'remarks' column but evidence is incomplete.

Interiors Most passenger carrying coaches listed can be cross-referred to the schematic plans or compartment layouts given in the main text of the book and, therefore, details of layout, seating capacity etc, are not quoted in the summary tables.

Underframe &c Various assumptions can be made about the basic chassis characteristics of most vehicles listed and these are outlined below. As usual, exceptions (where known) are given in the 'remarks' column.

28ft vehicles and shorter	4 wheel chassis
30-34ft vehicles *	6 wheel chassis
42ft vehicles *	8 wheel chassis with 8ft bogies at 27ft 6in centres
45ft vehicles	8 wheel chassis with 8ft bogies at 30ft 6in centres
50ft vehicles	8 wheel chassis with 8ft bogies at 35ft 6in centres
52ft 6in vehicles	8 wheel chassis with 8ft bogies at 38ft centres
54ft vehicles	8 wheel chassis with 8ft bogies at 39 ft 6in centres
57ft vehicles	8 wheel chassis with 9ft bogies at 41ft centres
65ft 6in clerestory roof vehicles †	12 wheel chassis with 11ft 6in bogies at 43ft 6in centres
65ft 6in elliptical roof vehicles	12 wheel chassis with 12ft 6in bogies at 43ft centres
68ft vehicles	12 wheel chassis with 12ft 6in bogies at 45ft centres

* Certain vehicles of these lengths had radial axles — this fact is specified where applicable.
†42ft centres for the 8ft 6in wide coaches.

Note: General details of diagram allocations and coach numbering principles will be found on pages (viii) and (ix).

DIAG	QTY	DATE BUILT	BODY LENGTH	TARE WEIGHT	BODY STYLE	NUMBERING PRE-GROUP	1st LMS	2nd LMS	WITHDRAWN FIRST	LAST	REMARKS
											SLEEPING CARS (For plans see Fig. 2, page 27)
20	5	1897-9	65'6"	38T	SD1	5129-30/4-6	10371-5	438-40	12/27	?	First LNWR 65'6" sleeping cars and built with central cross-vestibule. Dual fitted.
W5	7	1897-9	65'6"	41T	SD1	142-6;265;489	10376-82	443	?	12/32	WCJS equivalent of D20. LMS second series numbers 441-2; 444-6 allotted but not carried.
W4	4	1899	65'6"	40T	SD1	148-51	10367-70	447-50	2/33	2/33	The first 'conventional' sleeping cars with corridor on one side only.
19	1	1900?	65'6"	41T	SD2	5115	10366	451		2/33	LNWR version of WCJS D4. Dual fitted. Vestibule entrances believed to be intermediate width.
W3	1	1902	65'6"	42T	SD3	147	10355	452		11/36	First 9ft wide sleeping car.
17	8	1903-4	65'6"	41T	SD3	5001;5100; 5149-52;5231; 5113	10356-64	453-7 474-5 458 476	10/36	12/41	The 'standard' LNWR 9ft clerestory sleeping car. Originally seven cars to this diagram, LNWR 5113 being a later conversion from D18. All dual fitted.
W2	15	1904	65'6"	41T	SD3	101-4;262-4; 266-9;325-8	10340-54	459-73	2/36	3/60	WCJS version of LNWR D17 and the most numerous Wolverton clerestory sleeping car design. One late survivor (LMS 461) until 1960, being used in Royal Train. Most withdrawn in 1936-7 with a few survivors to 1941.
18	3	1905	65'6"	42T	SD3	5113-4;5132			see	notes	LNWR D18 built to layout of WCJS D3. All dual fitted. No 5132 destroyed at Quintinshill; 5113 converted to D17; 5114 altered to D18A for service in Royal Train and became last Wolverton clerestory 12 wheeler to run on BR.
18A	1	1905	65'6"	46T	SD3	5114	10365	477		10/68	
16	6	1907	65'6"	42T	SD4	5036;5088-9; 5112;5116;5180	10334-9	478-83	10/36	11/36?	First elliptical roof sleeping cars and only elliptical roof sleepers to 65'6" length. Dual fitted.
W1	8	1914/ 1917	68'0"	45T	SD5	444-51	10322-9	484-90; 496	7/58	2/59	Identical designs and the final pre-group sleeping cars. LNWR cars all dual fitted. These became basis of LMS standard sleeping car design.
15	4	1916	68'0"	45T	SD5	5029-32	10330-3	491-4			
14c	1	1917	68'0"	48T	SD5	5132	10321	495		10/68	Built as a replacement for Quintinshill accident victim (above) and a variation of D15 for use in Royal Train. Dual fitted. Not clear whether this car ran as D15 before conversion for Royal Train. The last pre-group 12 wheel sleeping car in service.
											SLEEPING COMPOSITES (For plans see Fig. 2, page 27)
W28	6	c.1906	50'0"	29T	see notes	100;117;119-21; 124	8415-20		pre '32	pre'32	Rebuilds from 8'6" brake composites to WCJS D41 with standard 9ft clerestory styling at first class end; conventional panelling with clerestory roof at third class end.
W27	3	c.1907	50'0"	29T	see notes	108;113;118	8421-4		pre '32	pre '32	Elliptical roof version of WCJS D28.
W26	10		50'0"	29T	see notes	27;29;33;36-8; 44;114;205-6	8402-11	790-9	11/36	12/36	'Opposite hand' version of WCJS D27. These were rebuilt from 8'6" composites to WCJS D30. In the early 1930s six were modified to have eight genuine third class berths. This was classified D26A (LMS Cars 790-1/4/67/9).
											DINING CARS (For plans see Fig. 12, page 50)
36	3	1893	45'0"	31T	see notes	5308					Ex-WCJS Nos 530-2 and built for first WCJS corridor train. They had normal LNWR panelling and did not have narrow entrance vestibules at the extreme ends of the coach. Believed to have been divided between CR and LNWR when removed from WCJS list. These were the 'Edinburgh' centre kitchen composites.
41	3	1892	50'6"	36T	SD1	5301					Kitchen-firsts, downgraded to third class; ex-WCJS Nos 483-5. The first clerestory diners to have outside verandah entrances. Only one seems to have reached LNWR; the others may have gone to the CR.
31A	3	1892	47'9"	34T	SD1	5302-4					Kitchen-firsts; but originally open firsts Nos WCJS 486-8. One end verandah only. Converted to kitchen-first on transfer from WCJS lists. Converted to ambulance use in World War I and did not return to book stock.
42	2	1893	47'9"	33T	SD1	5305-6	10497-8				Open thirds with one end verandah only. Ex-WCJS Nos 527-9 and built to match D41; D31A. The only dining cars from the group of pioneer 12 wheelers to reach the LMS.
43	1	1893	47'9"	32T	SD1	5307	10499				
30	3	1895	65'6"	39T	SD1	5196-8	10413-5		1930	1930	Open composites. Rebuilt from pioneer 20 seat kitchen-firsts c.1927. The first of the 65'6" dining cars. Only one (LNW 5196) dual fitted.
W10	15	1897	65'6"	41T	SD1	373-8 561-9	10432-7 10438-46	241-9	pre '32 8/33	pre '32 2/34	Centre kitchen composites. LMS 10436-7 allocated Nos 257-8 in second LMS series but not carried before scrapping.
29	25	1897-1901	65"6"	42T	SD2	Various 5092-5250	10395-412 10465-71	60-77 250-6 see note *	11/32 12/33	13/66 10/36	The 'standard' 8'6" clerestory end kitchen dining cars and derived from unrebuilt D30 (above). Many dual fitted. Some may have had narrow vestibule entrances. Late survivors were LMS 76/77 — see page 57 * These were rebuilt as composites to D35C in 1923 and their numbers as composites are given in the LMS series.
40	10	1901	65'6"	42T	SD2	5251-60	10493-6 10459-64	167-70 259-64 see note *	11/34 1/34	10/36 11/35	Third class version of D29. One only (LNWR 5255) dual fitted. Ex-2nd/3rd class composites. * Reclassified as composite c.1923 and allocated D35B. In 1929, these cars had bottom stepboards removed for Ramsgate services.
35A	20	1903-4	65'6"	43T	SD3	5281-300	10451-8 10481-92	265-72 171-82 see note *	11/33 10/36	12/35 7/38	9ft clerestories originally built as 2nd/3rd composites. * In 1912 eight reclassified 1st/3rd and twelve marked down to all third and re-allocated D39. These were LMS 171-82. In 1938, LMS 178;180-1 became ARP lecture cars. All dual fitted.
W9	12	1905	65'6"	42T	SD3	483-8;527-32	10420-31	273-84	7/37	7/50	9ft version of WCJS D9. Ran with '2 pm' coaches — see p. 179. Seem to have replaced the bulk of the 1893 dining cars in WCJS services, taking their original WCJS numbers. Six (LMS 273-8) later modified to run to Ramsgate in succession to D35B (above).

DIAG	TY	DATE BUILT	BODY LENGTH	TARE WEIGHT	BODY STYLE	NUMBERING PRE-GROUP	1st LMS	2nd LMS	WITHDRAWN FIRST	LAST	REMARKS
35	4	1907	65'6"	43T	SD4	5082-5	10447-50	285-8	9/36	3/40	The first elliptical roof diners. Always composites. Dual fitted.
27	1	1908	65'6"	42T	SD4	5302	10391	78		7/41	A one-off design for Euston-Broad St services. Sometimes used later in Royal Train.
34	4	1910	65'6"	43T	SD4	5086-7;5090-1	10416-9	289-92	11/47	12/60	Elliptical roof derivative of WCJS D9 but built for LNWR and vacuum fitted only.
37	3	1914	65'6"	44T	SD5	5024-6	10475-7	293-5	11/46	1/57	Shown as "all third" but ran most of their life as 1st/3rd composite. The only wide entrance dining cars.
36A	3	1920	68'0"	42T	SD4	5033-5	10472-4	197-9	3/51	3/55	The only 68ft dining cars, probably built in lieu of 3 more D37 cars. Note the reversion to older style of entrance vestibules.

TEA CARS (For plans see Fig. 12, page 50)

DIAG	TY	DATE BUILT	BODY LENGTH	TARE WEIGHT	BODY STYLE	NUMBERING PRE-GROUP	1st LMS	2nd LMS	WITHDRAWN FIRST	LAST	REMARKS
47	8	1906-7	57'0"	32T	C9	245;298;317; 348;442;1195; 1556;1571	4597-604	189-96	10/33	12/36	Conventional cove roof corridor thirds with two compartments replaced by kitchen/pantry. Small clerestory over kitchen area. First four ran on 8ft wheelbase bogies, remainder on 9ft bogies.
48	6	1915	52'6"	?	T9	229-33;237	4655-60	183-8	2/51	3/52	Elliptical roof equivalent of D48 but shorter in length. Like D48, first LMS numbering was in corridor series but second LMS numbers were in dining car series.

CORRIDOR FIRST CLASS COACHES (For plans see Figs. 16, 26, pages 66, 84)

DIAG	TY	DATE BUILT	BODY LENGTH	TARE WEIGHT	BODY STYLE	NUMBERING PRE-GROUP	1st LMS	2nd LMS	WITHDRAWN FIRST	LAST	REMARKS
W15	3	1897	50'0"	26T	A8½	570-2	10060-2	1130-2	1/35	3/35	Gaslit coaches, probably electric later.
97	6	1899	50'0"	24T	A8	4597;4600-1/ 3/5;4613	10054-9	1133-8	3/34	4/35	LNWR version of WCJS D15. LMS 1137 downgraded to third in 1926, eventually becoming 2250.
95	9	1906-7	57'0"	32T	C9	4632-3/8-9; 4651-2/6-7/60	10036-44	1143-51	9/33		In 1936, all but LMS 1148 (withdrawn in 1933 following an accident) downgraded to 3rd, becoming 2241-8 in same order.
94	3	19??	57'0"	32T	E9	4537/51/61	10033-5	1152-4			Elliptical roof version of D95. Became third class in 1937 and numbered 2249;2236-7 in same order.
96	3	1908	57'0"	31T	E8½	4614/42/50	10045-7	1155-7	see notes	10/51	Narrow version of D94 built for 'Sunny South' specials. Nos 1155-6 downgraded in 1937, becoming 2238-9.
W14	2	1913	57'0"	30T	T9	270-1	10048-9	1158-9			Built as part of new coach sets in 1913 for 10 a.m. and other trains.
96A	2	1917	52'6"	30T	T9	4599;4623	10050-1	1139-40	10/58 (1139)	1/59 (1140)	Recessed door coaches for Liverpool-Newcastle sets. Dual fitted.
96B	2	1920	52'6"	29T	T9	4606;4676	10052-3	1141-2	4/57 (1142)	6/59 (1141)	Conventional version of D96A. Dual fitted.

CORRIDOR FIRST CLASS BRAKES (For plans see Figs. 16, 26, pages 66, 84) (See also D210, D210A)

DIAG	TY	DATE BUILT	BODY LENGTH	TARE WEIGHT	BODY STYLE	NUMBERING PRE-GROUP	1st LMS	2nd LMS	WITHDRAWN FIRST	LAST	REMARKS
W19	3	1897	50'0"	25T	A8½	573-5	10079-80	5145-6	1/34 (5146)	8/34 (5145)	WCJS No 574 did not reach LMS. Gaslit coaches. LMS No 5145 became camping coach on withdrawal.
W18	6	1902	50'0"	25T	A8½	256-61	10073-8	5147-52	12/37	9/43	Gaslit coaches and no projecting guard's lookouts.
127	4	1906	57'0"	29T	C9	5602;5624-6	10069-72	5153-6	see notes		LMS 5154-5 given clerestories and altered to first class sleeping brakes (D127A) for Royal Train. Preserved (1978). These two dual fitted on conversion. Normal coaches withdrawn 3/49 (5153) and 12/51 (5156).

CORRIDOR COMPOSITE COACHES (For plans see Figs. 16, 26, pages 66, 84)

DIAG	TY	DATE BUILT	BODY LENGTH	TARE WEIGHT	BODY STYLE	NUMBERING PRE-GROUP	1st LMS	2nd LMS	WITHDRAWN FIRST	LAST	REMARKS
W31	27	1898	45'0"	24T	A8	Various 1-296	8384 8421-39 8441-7	4357 4358-76 4377-82	see notes	7/34	Gaslit coaches. LMS 8447 did not receive 2nd LMS number. LMS 4359;4373 converted to camping coaches 1934. LMS 4360 renumbered 4786 in 1945 and was the last survivor.
138	80	1898-9	50'0"	25T	A8	Various 2513-3701	8230-309	4383-408 4414-58			Gaslit coaches, originally tri-composite. LMS 4402 became camping coach No 46167.
139	16	1898-1901	50'0"	24T	A8	Various 3622-57	8310-25	4487-501			Mostly gaslit. Two only (LNWR 3644;3652/1st LMS 8324-5/2nd LMS 4497;4501) electrically lit and these two dual fitted.
140	22	1898-1901	50'0"	24T	A8	Various 3621-58	8326-46	4409-13 4459-71			All gaslit and ex-D139 with one compartment downgraded to 3rd. One only dual fitted (LNWR 3635) which did not reach LMS.
W29	16	1903	50'0"	27T	A8½	Various 46-136	8347-62	4472-86	1/36	5/53	WCJS No 132 did not reach LMS second renumbering stage (1st LMS 8358). Last survivor was LMS 4486, renumbered 4790 in 1945. LMS 4482 should have become 4789 in 1945 but was withdrawn first.
W30	41	1902-3	50'0"	27T	A8½	Various 2-303	8363-83 8385-401 8440	4502-39	pre '33	1/53	Many late survivors beyond 1945 renumbered into LMS 47xx and 48xx series and one even got four LMS numbers (WCJS 43; LMS 8383-4528-4802-4985; withdrawn 5/52). Some of these coaches converted to sleeping composite (see WCJS D26)
134	9	1907	57'0"	31T	C9	Various: 2670-4030	8145-53	4656-64	6/46	10/58	Originally 1st/2nd composites.
133	32	1907-8	57'0"	30T	E9	Various: 2640-3958	8113-44	4626-55 4665-6			Probably the first elliptical roof corridor coaches. Works drawing shows cove roof profile. Originally tri-composite. LMS 4634 downgraded to all 3rd No. 3061.
136	16	1911	52'6"	29T	E9	Various 2557-2902	7991; 8205-19	4540-55	4/51	4/56	Gaslit when built and originally tri-composite.
137	20	1912-13	52'6"	29T	T8½	Various: 2542-3111	7992-8000 8220-9	4556-64 4565-74	4/51 11/41	10/58 4/56	8ft 6in wide toplight version of D136 but never tri-composite. All dual fitted. LNWR No 2667 did not reach LMS.
135	51	1913-14	52'6"	28T	T9	Various: 2502-3772	8154-204	4575-625			9ft wide equivalent of D137. Many dual fitted and some downgraded to 3rd class c.1950.
W24	2	1913	57'0"	30T	T9	272-3	8109-10	4776-7			Built as part of new sets of coaches in 1913.
W25	2	1913	57'0"	30T	T9	274-5	8111-2	4667-8	4/52 (4667)	9/52 (4668)	Built alongside WCJS D24 for the new 1913 WCJS trains.
131	40	1914-17	57'0"	30T	T9	Various: 2511-2840	8005-44	4669-708			'Standard' 57ft corridor composite and built alongside D132. Many dual fitted.
	26	1917-20				Various: 2958-2999	8083-108	4747-73*			* – Does not include 4760

169

DIAG	QTY	DATE BUILT	BODY LENGTH	TARE WEIGHT	BODY STYLE	PRE-GROUP	1st LMS	2nd LMS	WITHDRAWN FIRST	LAST	REMARKS
132	38	1914-17	57'0"	30T	T9	Various: 2841-2957	8045-9; 8051-82 8001	4709-46*			Identical to D131 except for two per side in first class compartments. * – Does not include 4726.
W23A	1	1917	57'0"		T9	58	8004	4726			WCJS version of D131. Downgraded and renumbered 3070 later.
W23B	1	1922	57'0"	29T	T9	40	8002	4774		9/69	Non-standard coach with layout of D131 but different interior sizes.
131A	1	1922	57'0"	29T	T9	3000	8003	4775		11/57	Identical LNWR version of WCJS D23B. Dual fitted.

CORRIDOR COMPOSITE BRAKES (For plans see Figs. 16, 26, pages 66, 84)

DIAG	QTY	DATE BUILT	BODY LENGTH	TARE WEIGHT	BODY STYLE	PRE-GROUP	1st LMS	2nd LMS	WITHDRAWN FIRST	LAST	REMARKS
W44	3	1893	42'0"	23T	A8½	534-6	9805-7	6957-9	1/34	10/34	Gaslit coaches. Built as part of 1893 sets for pioneer WCJS corridor trains. The only 42ft corridors not dowgraded to all 3rd.
W43	10	1898	45'0"	24T	A8	585-94	9795-804	6960-9	7/34	12/58	Gaslit coaches. Narrower than most WCJS corridor coaches. Note the late date of building for a 45ft design. Many camping coach conversions by LMS in 1934 (LMS 6961-2/6/8). LMS 6965 renumbered 6169 on downgrading to brake third. Some vehicles may have been opposite hand to version shown on sketch plans at Fig. 16.
W41	10	1899	50'0"	26T	A8½	105-7/9/11-2/ 5-6/122-3	9701-10	6984-91	pre '33	10/44	Originally classed as sleeping composite brake. Missing numbers in WCJS series mostly found on WCJS D27/D28 to which many were converted. Originally gaslit. No projecting lookouts.
W42	14	1902	50'0"	27T	A8½	Various: 76-140	9711-24	6970-83	5/36	11/52	Two marked down to all 3rd (6397 ex 6976; 6416 ex-6978). No projecting lookouts.
216	60	1900-1	50'0"	25T	A8	Various: 5703-6029	9735-94	6992-7048			The only arc roof LNWR brake composite. Gaslit when new and many dual fitted.
214	10	1903	50'0"	27T	C9	Various 5715-5885	9725-34	7049-58	10/40	5/53	The first cove roof corridor coaches. One of them (LNWR 5718; LMS 9734-7058) was altered to D215 and had a typing compartment. LMS 7057 later marked down to all third No. 6429.
210A	20	1922*	57'0"	30T	C9	5990;5992-6010	9661-80	7059-78	7/41	7/53	* Converted in 1922 from first class brakes to D126, originally built 1906-7 and numbered 5604-23. LMS 7071-8 ran on 8ft wheelbase bogies. LMS 7070 later marked down to third class as No 6111.
210	2	1922*	57'0"		E9	5988-9	9681-2	7079-80	12/47 (7080)	3/48 (7079)	* Converted in 1922 from first class brakes to D125, originally built 1908 and numbered 5601/3. Elliptical roof version of D210A.
208	40	1906	57'0"	32T	C9	6092/6;6101/4; 6110-45	9575-14	7086-124	12/37	11/56	Double ended brakes, originally tri-composite. One altered to D209 with a typing compartment (LNWR 6132; LMS 9601-7111). All fitted with 8ft wheel-base bogies. LNWR 6113/5 (LMS 9512/4-7093/5) dual fitted. Several marked down to all third later.
213	10	1909	57'0"	32T	E8½	5728;5772/7; 5780/4/6-7; 5791; 5825;5899	9651-60	7202-11	7/43	12/56	Dual fitted coaches of 8ft 6in width for working on restricted loading gauge areas – e.g. 'Sunny South' special trains. Originally first and second class.
207	6	1908	57'0"	32T	E9	6146-51	9569-74	7135-40	7/48	1/56	Elliptical roof version of D208. Originally tri-composite.
205	18	1908-10	57'0"	32T	E9	Various: 6093-6158	9544-61	7125-34 7141-8	11/47	8/53	Very similar to D207 but slightly smaller third class compartments and larger luggage areas. LMS 7142-8 originally gaslit.
241	2	1910	57'0"	32T	E9	6095/8	9629-30	7150-1	1/51 (7150)	8/53 (7151)	'Slip' coach version of D205 but not, apparently, tri-composite when first built. Gaslit when built and fitted with raised roof lookouts. See also D240 (below)
W40	10	1913	57'0"	30T	T9	397-406	9688-97	7152-61	6/52	5/58	Built along with other coaches for new set trains on WCJS routes in 1913. This design used for individual through coach working from provincial cities to Scotland. LMS 7161 downgraded at a later date to all third class No. 6179
W39	4	1913	57'0"	29T	T9	207-10	9683-6	7081-4	10/45	3/57	Again built as part of 1913 sets and originally used in the 'Day North Express' from Lancashire to Scotland. Two of these coaches may have been opposite handed (probably WCJS 209-10)
206	7	1913-14	57'0"	30T	T9	6050-6	9562-8	7172-8	1/48	1/57	Toplight version of D205/D207 but never tri-composite. Dual fitted.
239	3	1914	57'0"	31T	T9	6057-9	9615-7	7179-81	5/51	11/56	'Slip' version of D206 but vacuum fitted only.
240	11	1913*	57'0"	32T	T9 –but see notes *	6040-9; 6094	9618-28	7162-71 7149	11/34	6/56	'Slip' brakes and very similar to D239 but three per side seating in first class area. * LNWR 6094 was built in 1910 and seems to have been put on this diagram because it was electrically lit. It is felt that this coach should have formed the third representation on D241 (above)
212	7	1913	57'0"	30T	T8½	6030-4/6/9	9641-7	7182-8	1/51	4/58	'Narrow' equivalent of D206. All dual fitted
242	3	1913	57'0"	30T	T8½	6035/7-8	9648-50	7189-91	4/51	2/58	'Slip' version of D212 and built at same time. Vacuum fitted only. LNWR 6038 was converted from D212 and all three may have been similar.
211	10	1917	57'0"	30T	T8½	6060-9	9631-40	7192-201	10/51	5/59	Late batch of double-ended brakes; all but identical to D212 but with slightly larger 3rd class compartments. Dual fitted.
W39A	1	1920	57'0"		T9	213	9687	7085		4/58	A late built one-off, all but identical to WCJS D39 but with slightly larger 3rd class compartments.

CORRIDOR THIRD CLASS (For plans see Figs. 16, 26, pages 66, 84)

DIAG	QTY	DATE BUILT	BODY LENGTH	TARE WEIGHT	BODY STYLE	PRE-GROUP	1st LMS	2nd LMS	WITHDRAWN FIRST	LAST	REMARKS
269	3		42'0"	24T	A8	0420;637; 1954	5196		pre '33	pre '33	The first LNWR corridor coach and a very odd design – see plans. From the compartment and lavatory dimensions it looks as if this design may have been an experimental conversion of a standard 42ft, seven compartment non-corridor third. Gaslit
W55	3	1893	42'0"	23½T	A8½	508-9;537	5190-2	2251-3	1/35	2/35	Ex-first class corridor coaches from original WCJS corridor train. Gaslit
W54	18	1893	42'0"	24T	A8½	510-26;533	5172-89	2254-68/71	pre '33	11/38	Ex-composite from original WCJS series. Gaslit.

DIAG	QTY	DATE BUILT	BODY LENGTH	TARE WEIGHT	BODY STYLE	PRE-GROUP	1st LMS	2nd LMS	WITHDRAWN FIRST	LAST	REMARKS
W56	3	1893	42'0"	24T	A8½	506-7;538	5193-5	2269/70/2	2/33	5/35	Genuine corridor thirds from original WCJS series. Gaslit.
W53	19	1896	45'0"	25T	A8½	276-81;301-2;304-14	5153-71	2275-93	1/34	10/42	The only 45ft corridor thirds. Gaslit. Probably originally 20 built, including WCJS No 303. LMS 2276/8/82 to camping coaches in 1934.
W52	6	1897	50'0"	26T	A8½	576-81	4757-62	2315-8	pre '33	9/35	Coaches built as part of 1897 sets. Gaslit.
268	244	1898-1903	50'0"	25T	A8	Various: 96-1441;plus 2260-329; 2336-485	4910-5152	2319-550			Standard LNWR 50ft corridor third. Originally gaslit and many dual fitted. Some variations in detail — see page 67.
W51	23	1902-3	50'0"	27T	A8½	233-55	4736-56	2294-314	1/36	10/45	Two scrapped before grouping (WCJS 234;250). Some later renumberings by LMS viz: 2294-3479; 2297-3480; 2306-3482; 2310-3483;2312-3485.
264	30	1906-7	57'0"	32T	C9	Various: 131-1612	4313-39	2773-99	9/46	11/53	The first 57ft corridor thirds. Three coaches were motor-fitted before grouping and transferred to diagram M75.
263	7	1908	57'0"	32T	E9	721;804/6-7;1469;1636/49	4306-12	2800-6	8/42	4/56	Elliptical roof version of D264.
262	2	1908	57'0"	31T	E9	524;551	4304-5	2826-7	5/51 (2827)	7/52 (2826)	Eight compartment version of D263. The first eight compartment corridor thirds
265	174	1908	57'0"	29T	E8½	Various 15-2214	4422-595	2828-2987			'Narrow' version of D262. One or two dual fitted. Only 160 given LMS second series numbers; bulk of remainder being motor fitted to diagrams M76, M77.
267	68 91	1910-11 1912-13	50'0"	28T	E9 T9	Various 27-1997	4763-821 4822-909	2551-697			Two body styles on one diagram. Toplight coaches originally gaslit. A few dual fitted and some to ambulance service in WWI, not reaching LMS. Some motor-fitted versions (diag M52)
W50	20	1913	57'0"	30T	T9	407-26	4403-21	2807-25	12/49	8/58	WCJS No. 407 withdrawn before grouping. Built along with other WCJS designs for new sets of coaches in 1913.
266	97	1915	52'6"	28T	T9	Various: 7-446	4661-729 5231-5*	2698-766 1207-11			52ft 6in version of D267 but not gaslit. Many dual fitted. Many to ambulance use in WWI and not returned. * These five were ex-ambulance coaches returned after 1922 and rebuilt to original style but given LMS diagram (D1710) and LMS standard series numbering.
266A	6	1917	52'6"	28T	T9	1171-6	4730-5	2767-72			Recessed door version of D266 for Liverpool-Newcastle sets. Dual fitted.
264A W49	60 3	1917-20 1920-2	57'0"	31T	T9	Various: 4-409 407;234;250	4340-99 4400-2	2988-3046 3047-9	11/56	7/60	The final 57ft corridor third. LNWR & WCJS examples were identical and all LNWR vehicles were dual fitted. The WCJS coaches were probably post-war replacements for premature withdrawals from WCJS D50, D51 (above)

CORRIDOR THIRD CLASS BRAKES. For plans see Figs. 16, 26, pages 66, 84

DIAG	QTY	DATE BUILT	BODY LENGTH	TARE WEIGHT	BODY STYLE	PRE-GROUP	1st LMS	2nd LMS	WITHDRAWN FIRST	LAST	REMARKS
W70 W71	1 2	1893 1893	42'0"	21½T	A8½	494 495;501	6879 6880-1	5993 5994	pre '33	11/34 1/33	Two compartment brakes for 1893 corridor trains. Gaslit. There may, originally, have been two of each type.
W68 W69	7 2	1893 1893	42'0"	22T	A8½	496/8;500/2-5 497/9	6870-6 6877-8	5995-6000 6001-2	pre '33 11/33 (6001)	4/37 11/36 (6002)	Three compartment brakes built along with D70/71. All for WCJS trains of 1893. Like D70/71, these diagrams were identical except for the question of 'handing'. Gaslit when built.
W66	3	1897	50'0"	25T	A8½	582-4	6743-5	6003-4; 6056	7/33	3/52	Built for the 1897 sets. Possibly gaslit when new.
316 317	64 36	1898-1903	50'0" 50'0"	24½T 25T	A8 A8	Various: 6768-831 6919-7883	6768-831 6832-67	6059-119 6005-23; 6034-44 6050-5			Originally all D316 – five compartment centre-brake 2nd/3rd class composite. D317 was a conversion with two ex-2nd class compartments removed. Gaslit when new. Some dual fitted.
W67	15	1902-3	50'0"	26T	A8½	62-75;232	6746-60	6024-33 6045-9	3/35	11/52	Similar to WCJS D66 but no projecting lookouts and slightly larger compartments. Gaslit.
310	18	1906-7	57'0"	28T	C9	Various: 7462-7617	6607-24	6124-41	4/40	8/53	Three compartment brakes.
313	12	1906-7	57'0"	29T	C9	6658;6660-70	6675-86	6168-76/ 8-80	10/37	5/55	Four compartment brakes, otherwise as per D310.
312	49	1908	57'0"	29T	E9	Various: 6657-7307	6627-74	6177;6181-227	9/33	9/58	Elliptical roof version of D313. Three coaches seated 24 only (LNWR 7062;7131;7178 later LMS 6640/50/5 – 6193/203/8). LNWR 7236 did not reach LMS. One coach (LNWR 6659; LMS 6628-6177) was confused with D313 at 1932 renumbering.
309	33	1909-10	57'0"	28T	E9	Various: 7161-7670	6587-604	6150-67	9/33	7/55	Elliptical roof version of D310. Fifteen coaches to ambulance use in WWI.
311	2	1908	57'0"	28T	E9	7186;7401	6625-6	6142-3	4/51 (6142)	4/55 (6143)	As per D309 but with smaller compartments
308	25	1907	57'0"	29T	E9	Various: 7047-7595	6562-86	6261-85	2/37	12/55	First elliptical roof corridor brake thirds, derived from cove roof style but five compartments and opposite handed.
315	6	1908	57'0"	29T	E8½	6932;7215/30; 7352/91;7439	6729-34	6144-9	4/51	4/54	8ft 6in three compartment design. Four dual fitted (not LNWR 6932;7439). Some may have been opposite handed.
314	10	1909	57'0"	30T	E8½	6859;7053-4/7; 7411-2/20/ 30-1/4	6719-23 6724-8*	6286-90 6291-5*	4/47 1/51	5/55 5/53	Five compartment 8ft 6in design. All dual fitted. * Altered to D314A by removing projecting lookouts, otherwise no change. (LNWR 7054/7; 7430-1/4)
307	83	1913	57'0"	28T	T9	Various: 6504-7857	6501-61	6318-78			Dual fitted coaches. Many to WWI ambulance use and did not return. Almost identical to WCJS D65 except for square cornered lower panel edges.
W65	4	1913	57'0"	28T	T9	297-300	6497-500	6314-7	12/52	2/57	WCJS version of D307 but with slightly larger compartments and fully rounded panel corners. Built as part of 1913 sets.
306	28	1913-14	57'0"	28T	T9	Various: 6567-7815	6470-96	6296-313; 6379-87	6/41	12/60	Dual fitted coaches. Again similar to WCJS D65 but again slight compartment size differences. Some of this type went to ambulance use and returned in 1924 when they were rebuilt back to original form becoming LMS D1712. Numbered 5216-21; 5200-1 in LMS standard series, 5200-1 having only 3 compartments.

DIAG	QTY	DATE BUILT	BODY LENGTH	TARE WEIGHT	BODY STYLE	PRE-GROUP	1st LMS	2nd LMS	FIRST	LAST	REMARKS
315A	2	1917		28T	T9	7471/7	6735-6	6120-1	2/58	2/58	Recessed door brakes for Liverpool-Newcastle sets.
315B	2	1917	52'6"	28T	T9	7475/80	6737-8	6122-3	2/58 (6123)	11/58 (6122)	Dual fitted. Two diagrams were identical except for handing.
309A	2	1919	57'0"		T9	6690/2	6605-6	6228-9	3/55 (6228)	11/58 (6229)	Converted in 1919 from pharmacy and ward cars from US Ambulance Trains Nos 71/72. Four compartment brakes; dual fitted.
313A	31	1920	57'0"	29T	T9	Various: 6581-791	6687-13/ 15-8	6230-60	3/55	11/57	Similar to D309A but larger compartments. Dual fitted.
318	1	1919	50'0"		C8½	6695	6868	6057		3/56	Ex-Cot Coach No 1 from Naval Ambulance Train No. 6. Dual fitted
319	1	1919	50'0"		C8½	6696	6869	6058		2/58	Ex-Cot Coach No 2 (Naval A.T. No. 6). Opposite handed to D318. Dual fitted.

LAVATORY FIRST CLASS COACHES (For plans see Figs. 32, 34, pages 101, 106)

DIAG	QTY	DATE BUILT	BODY LENGTH	TARE WEIGHT	BODY STYLE	PRE-GROUP	1st LMS	2nd LMS	FIRST	LAST	REMARKS
106	2	c.1892	42'0"	19T	A8	4606;4676					Built for Liverpool-Leeds expresses. Not to LMS stock. 4606 was gaslit. Radial underframe.
104	2	c.1892	42'0"	20T	A8	4599;4623					Not to LMS stock. Similar to D106 but with centre luggage compartment. Radial underframe. Gaslit.
105	11	1893	42'0"	22T	A8	Various: 4519-4695	10093-103	18164-71*	pre '33	9/35	Some dual fitted. * One more (1st LMS 10103) marked down to 3rd (and numbered 18617 after 1932); Re-allocated D293A.
102	10	1905-6	50'0"	29T	C9	4516/41/7/53 /5/62/4604/12 /36/43	10083-92	18172-81	9/46	11/52	One downgraded to 3rd class by LMS (18181-18614)
101	1	1908	50'0"	29T	E9	4616	10082	18182		11/46	Elliptical roof equivalent of D102. n.b. for First Class coaches to D100, see summary table for saloons (Appendix II – page 180)

LAVATORY COMPOSITE COACHES (For plans see Figs. 32, 34, pages 101, 106)

DIAG	QTY	DATE BUILT	BODY LENGTH	TARE WEIGHT	BODY STYLE	PRE-GROUP	1st LMS	2nd LMS	FIRST	LAST	REMARKS
170	51	1891-4	30'1"	12½T	A8	Various: 2509-4028	8792-9	27440-1			Most of these coaches converted to non-lavatory composite D197A before grouping. Only eight genuine D170 coaches received LMS numbers but many survivors as D197A. Gaslit.
169	63	c.1890	32'0"	13T	A8*	Various: 2501-3508	8791				* Actually 7ft 9in wide. Radial six wheelers and by grouping, most were converted to non-lavatory D195A/B. Many more survivors in the latter form. Gaslit.
168	1	c.1884	33'0"	12T	A8	2923	8790			12/27	Six wheel coach of non-standard length. Gaslit. Last survivor of a batch of 65.
165	16	c.1887	42'0"	18½T	A8	Various: 2744-3489	08072; 08079				Radial coaches, some converted to bogies. One (LNWR 3185) was electrically lit. More may have been built and converted later to D161 (below). May have originally been tri-composite.
161	31	c.1889	42'0"	19T	A8	Various: 2503-3469	8747 (ex-LNWR 3372)	19388 (ex-LNWR 3436)		8/37	Radial coaches, later converted to bogies. Probably 40 originally built and very possibly all converted ex-D165. Some dual fitted and all gaslit. Originally tri-composite.
162	26	c.1889	42'0"	19T	A8	Various: 3448-3676	8748-55				Radial coaches; dual fitted and gaslit. Originally tri-composite and WCJS – see Plate 124.
164	17	c.1889	42'0"	19T	A8	Various: 2739-3363	8759-69, plus a few 80xx examples (unconfirmed)	19389-92			Originally radial, later to bogies. A few gaslit but mostly electric.
160	34	1890-1	42'0"	22T	A8	Various: 2520-3844	8712-45	19393-5 19397-9		8/35	All dual fitted and bogie coaches – probably some ex-radials but some built with bogies from new. Tri-composites and gaslit. One to Chicago exhibition in 1893 (a late example)
163	3	c.1891	42'0"	22T	A8	3312/26/36	8756-8	19400		c.1933	Identical layout to D164 but slightly smaller luggage compartment. Gaslit.
167	20	1893	42'0"	22½T	A8	3568-87	8770-89	19401-9	pre '33	10/45	Some dual fitted and bogie coaches from new. Gaslit.
157	29	1894-5	42'0"	20½T	A8	Various: 2510-3487	8653-80	19410; 19419-31			Some dual fitted, all gaslit. Identical in layout to D167 except that in the coupé compartment, the seats in D157 faced the end of the coach (which had windows in it). Highly possible that LMS 8681 (later 19432) was also of this diagram.
159	20	1894	42'0"	22½T	A8	3588-3607	8692-711	19411-8	pre '33	10/41	Gaslit coaches, very similar in layout to D157/ D167 but with extra lavatory.
158	10	1895	42'0"	22T	A8	2579/94; 2609;2797; 3190;3360/4; 3435/8-9	8682-91*	19433-8	pre '33	7/35	* LNWR 2797 not positively confirmed as 1st LMS 8685 but strong probability that it was so renumbered. Gaslit coaches.
154	87	1896-7	45'0"	22½T	A8	Various: 2525-3855	09366 plus 8567-652	19442-99			Some dual fitted, mostly gaslit. Possible that 09366 should have received 1st LMS No. 8566 but not confirmed.
153	4	1905	50'0"	27T	C9	2538;3862/6-7	8562-5	19500-3	10/46	5/52	The only 50ft lavatory composite design.
149	5	c.1906	54'0"	27½T	C9	3870/5-8	8545-9	19504-8	5/45	11/52	Identical coaches except for three extra first class seats in D149
150	5	c.1906	54'0"	28T	C9	3868-9/79-81	8550-4	19509-10 19512-4	5/47	8/52	
148	1	c.1907	54'0"	30T	E9	2562	8544	19511		5/45	Elliptical roof equivalent of D149 – c.f D101 (above)
151	7	1912-13	54'0"	28T	T9	3144-6/9; 3684-6	8555-61	19515-21	5/45	12/56	Unusual design with only one 3rd class compartment. See also D274/D322/D323.
147	10	1907	57'0"	31T	E9	3919-28	8534-43	19522-31	5/45	5/53	Built alongside Lavatory Brake Thirds to D321. probably as set trains.
146	85	1914-9	57'0"	28T	T9	3743-50/2-63; 3774-805; Various: 3812-3973;3975-92	8448-532	19532-616			A large batch of this style of coach to be built at such a late date.

DIAG	QTY	DATE BUILT	BODY LENGTH	TARE WEIGHT	BODY STYLE	NUMBERING PRE-GROUP	1st LMS	2nd LMS	WITHDRAWN FIRST	LAST	REMARKS
											LAVATORY COMPOSITE BRAKES (For plans see Figs. 32, 34, pages 101, 106)
230	20	1891	32'0"	12T	A8	Various: 5702-5932	9897-916	27980-7			Radial six wheelers; gaslit.
229	7	1887	42'0"	18½T	A8	5709/30/39/ 62/70;5815/ 20	9896; 09548	25799		4/37	Radial coaches, only one to bogie form (LNWR 5815; LMS 09548). All gaslit. Coaches had no projecting lookouts and appear to have been converted from D165. LMS 25799 was ex-LNWR 5730 and never received 1st LMS series number.
228	16		42'0"	21T	A8	Various: 5727-5959	9880-95				Radial coaches, all gaslit and mostly dual fitted. One or two examples given bogies later.
227	26	1895	42'0"	21½T	A8	Various: 5708-5987	9854-79	25778-98	pre '33	10/43	Gaslit coaches, many dual fitted. One further example converted to D330 before grouping.
250/222	5	c.1896	45'0"	24T	A8	5936/40/71/ 76-7	9828-32	25818-21	1931	12/35	Originally slip brakes (D250), converted to orthodox form (D222) by removal of slip gear and raised roof lookouts. All gas lit.
251/223	12	c.1896	45'0"	24T	A8	Various: 5736-5974	9827; 9833-43	25800-8; 25815	pre '33	4/39	Virtually identical to D250/D222 but with one first class compartment downgraded to 3rd. Most seem to have started as slip brakes (D251) but were converted to orthodox form (D223). Some may have never been slip brakes. Mostly gaslit.
224/225	3	1897	45'0"	24T	A8	5925;5973/5	9844-6	25822 (ex-9845)	pre '33	5/34	Only difference between coaches was raised lookouts on roof of D224 (LNWR 5973/5; LMS 9844/5) but neither diagram seems to have been a slip brake. Identical to D250/D222 but without projecting side lookouts. All gaslit.
226	7	1896	45'0"	22½T	A8	5721;6081-6	9847-53	25809-13	12/29	12/39	The only 45ft centre brakes. Five were dual fitted (not LNWR 6082/5). All gaslit.
249/221	9	1901	50'0"	24½T	A8	5719/23;5887; 5922/68; 6087-90	9818-26	25823-31	1/34	11/52	Originally slip brakes (D249), converted to orthodox form (D221) before grouping or at that time. All gaslit when new but electric later. The only 50ft lavatory arc roof coaches.
248	5	1906	57'0"	29T	C8	5822/76/9; 5978;6091	9813-7	25835-9	4/51	11/52	Narrow body cove roof slip brakes with raised 'birdcage' roof lookouts. Later to orthodox type but not issued with a new diagram number.
247	3	1913	57'0"	31½T	T9	6076-8	9810-2	25832-4	1/52	12/56	Double brake ended slip coaches with raised roof lookouts. Later to conventional type of roof and usage but no change in diagram page. The only double ended non-corridor brakes.
											LAVATORY THIRD CLASS COACHES (For plans see Figs. 32, 34, pages 101, 106)
279	42		30'1"	13T	A8	Various: 1811-2131	5296-300/ 3/6-10 plus 4389/97; 4455/63; 4577;6023	27414			Six wheel coaches, almost certainly ex-five compartment thirds. Gaslit.
278	5	1891	42'0"	21T	A8	31;61;75-6;92	5291-5	18614-6	pre '33	9/35	Bogie coaches but probably ex-radial. Gaslit.
293A	1	1893	42'0"	21½T	A8	4695	10103	18617		11/34	Downgraded ex-D105.
277	50	1886-7*	42'0"	18T	A8	Various: 910-1800	5281-90; 4606 4597-9; 4641	18618-20	pre group	4/39	Radial coaches, some dual fitted. Converted from 7 compartment thirds. * Date probably refers to original building as 7 compartment coaches. LMS second series numbering suggests that lavatories were c.1893. All gaslit. Originally 2nd/3rd class composite.
276	24	1905-7	50'0"	28T	C9	Various: 33-1969	5259-80	18621-41/ 3	pre group	5/53	Only 22 examples reached the LMS.
275	1	1907	50'0"	28T	E9	1348	5258	18642		5/52	A 'one-off' equivalent of D276 (c.f. D101/D148 – above)
274	7	1912-13	54'0"	28T	T9	1483-6;2182-4	5251-7	18644-50	5/51	3/56	Seem to be 3rd class contemporaries of D151 (above) but not known if used in same sets.
											LAVATORY THIRD CLASS BRAKES (For plans see Figs. 32, 34, pages 101, 106)
330	1	1895	42'0"	21½T	A8	7701	6956	25508		1/33	A rebuild of D227 (above) by removing first class compartment and lavatories. Electric lighting.
329	2		42'0"	18½T	A8	6538/45	6954-5				Radial coaches and gaslit. Seem to be conversions standard 4 compartment 3rd brake with interior p..t corridor leading to lavatories.
327	7	1896	45'0"	22½T	A8	6861;7569/ 74/7-8/82-3	6948-53	25509-13	pre group	3/42	Dual fitted and gaslit.
326	8	1905	50'0"	26½T	C9	6528;6613 /9/33;6913/ 35;7148;7289	6941-7	25515-21	12/44*	10/55	* One premature pre-group withdrawal (LNWR 7148).
325	2	1906	50'0"	25½T	C9	7045;7625	6939-40	25522-3	5/53	6/53	4 compartment version of D326.
324	20	1905-7	54'0"	28T	C9	Various: 6501-7476	6919-38	25524-42	12/29	5/55	1st LMS 6921 (LNWR 6511) was the one coach withdrawn early.
322	4	1912	54'0"	28T	T9	7454;7601/18 /46	6911-14	25543-6	2/51	11/56	Small batches, apparently built with D151 and D274 (above). Not known if used in same sets.
323	4	1912	54'0"	29T	T9	7105;7441/6 /50	6915-8	25547-50	2/51	11/56	Number of brakes built does not relate to number of composites/thirds.
321	20	1907	57'0"	29T	E9	Various: 6863-7127	6891-910	25551-70	10/43	8/53	Numbered (by LMS) at end of the series because although older than D322/D323, they were longer coaches. Probably built to run with composite to D147.
											NON-CORRIDOR FIRST CLASS (For compartment arrangements see Table 3 – page 110)
121	3	c.1894	28'0"	14½T	A8	4505/21;4648	10245-6				LNWR 4521 to composite (D200) before 1923. Four wheel coaches.
120	20	c.1892-1900	28'0"	14½T	A8	Various: 4510-4685	see notes				Identical to D121 except for 4 per side seating. No record of survival in this form to LMS and believed all converted to composite (D176A – below).
116	4	1896	45'0"	21½T	A8	4523/33/52/79	10238-41	10310-2	12/32	7/35	Gaslit coaches. Second LMS 10309 probably allocated to this diagram but coach scrapped in 1932.

DIAG	QTY	DATE BUILT	BODY LENGTH	TARE WEIGHT	BODY STYLE	PRE-GROUP	1st LMS	2nd LMS	FIRST	LAST	REMARKS
						NUMBERING			WITHDRAWN		
112	70	1898-1902	50'0"	24½T	A8	Various: 4502-722	10160-229	10313-42 10353-6 10362-79 10382-95			The standard 50ft first class coach, diagrams differing only in seating capacity. Four of D113 later marked down to third (13592-4) and composite (16930). Many mark downs of D112 to third class viz: 13420;13478;13578-91;13596; 13600-2;13605/7;13618;13640. Except for 13640, all mark downs were after 1933. Two downgraded to composite in 1929 and given D186A (below). Third class mark downs were not allocated to a new diagram.
113	5	1898-1902	50'0"	24½T	A8	4501/89/93/95;4664	10230-4	10398-402	11/34	4/43	
114	1	1898	50'0"	24½T	A8	4540	10235	10397		10/41	
111	17	1900-1	50'0"	24½T	A8	Various: 4607-4716	10143-59	10343-52 10357-61 10380-1	11/33	11/51	These started life as composites as per D187 and after conversion still retained three small sized compartments. LMS numbers interlocked with D112 reflect building dates. LMS 10345 marked down to all third becoming 13576.
115	2	1906	50'0"	24½T	C8	4512/7	10236-7	13642; 10396	3/52	10/53 (13642)	Built for Manchester-Buxton trains. LMS 13642 was marked down to all third before second LMS renumbering. LMS 10396 downgraded to all third later, becoming 13606.
110	24	1903-4	50'0"	27T	C9	Various: 4507-4709	10119-42	10403-26	3/37		The original 9ft wide firsts. Many later mark downs to all third, taking the following numbers: 13419;13423-5;13514;13571-5;13603;13619.
118	3	1911	30'0"	15T	E9	4548/80/83	10242-4	26041-3			Birmingham-Sutton six wheel elliptical roof coaches.
109	7	1914-6	50'0"		T9	4565;4644/89-93	10112-8	10427-32	12/33	2/57	One scrapped before receiving 2nd LMS number (LNW 4565; 1st LMS 10112). LMS 10429 downgraded to 13616.
108	4	1919	54'0"	28T	T9	4723-6	10108-11	10433-6	12/56	10/58	Converted in 1919 from ward cars of USA ambulance trains Nos 71 and 72.
107	4	1919	57'0"	28½T	T9	4525/94; 4610/31	10104-7	10437-40	2/58	6/61	LMS 10439 downgraded to 13617 and the first to be scrapped.
200	1		28'0"	14½T	A8	2535	9480	27128		2/33	**NON-CORRIDOR COMPOSITE (For compartment arrangements see Table 3 — page 110)** Ex-D121 (above). Gaslit coach — probably converted to compo before D121 coaches were given electric lighting
198	13	1894	28'0"	11½T	A8	Various: 2987-4015	9443-55	27100-5	pre '30	4/38	Four wheel coaches.
199	24	1892-1900	28'0"	11½T	A8	Various: 2518-4014	9456-79	27106-26	pre '30	4/38	As per D198 except for 4 per side seating in first class section.
197A	43	1891-4	30'1"	12½T	A8	Various: 2509-4028	9400-42	26246-7 27166/8-80 27442			Converted from D170 at about time of grouping. Centre compartment was slightly smaller than the others. Second LMS 27442 was numbered in lavatory series but there is no evidence that it was converted. It may have been an intended conversion which did not, in fact, take place. Gaslit vehicles. 2nd LMS 26246-7 were downgraded coaches.
197	126	1893 onwards	30'1"	12½T	A8	Various: 2508-4029	9285-399	26245/8-9 27132-65			Identical coaches, the extra first class in D196 being converted from an orthodox third class compartment. Second LMS 26xxx numbers given to downgraded coaches. All gaslit except D196.
196	1		30'1"	12½T	A8	2783	9284			1925	
195A	c.60	c.1890	32'0"	13T	A8*	Various: 2501-3507	9222-74/6-81	27182-91/3-4 26445			Identical coaches, all ex-D169. * Actually 7ft 9in wide. D195B had one extra first class compartment (actually an up-graded ex-third class). Gaslit radial six wheelers. First LMS 9275 (later 21792) was probably this type of coach but not confirmed.
195B	2	1890	32'0"	13T	A8*	3096-7	9282-3	27195		6/34	
195	1		32'0"	12½T	A8*	3894					Gaslit radial six wheeler. * Actually 7ft 9in wide.
194	1		32'0"	14½T	A8*	3217					Gaslit ex-first class radial six wheelers. * Actually 7ft 9in wide.
193	1		32'0"	14½T	A8*	3886					
192	15		32'0"	12T	A8*	Various: 2933-3494	9221	27181			Gaslit ex-tri composite radial six wheelers. * Actually 7ft 9in wide. Diagrams identical except for compartment class (see Table 3). Note: 2nd LMS 27181 was not ex-9221!
191	2		32'0"	12T	A8*	3089;3349					
190	3	1892	42'0"	18T	A8	02504;2545 02754	08077; 9220 08081	16938		3/35	Originally radial, gaslit coaches. One (LNW 2754) converted to bogies and survived to reach LMS, believed ex-3rd class coaches to D292 or D293 (see below)
189	5	1899-1900	50'0"	24T	A8	3708-11; 3714	9215-9	16939-42	pre '33	11/49	Identical eight compartment coaches with small size compartments as D289 (below).
188	5	1899-1902	50'0"	23T	A8	3712-3;3715-6; 3718	9210-4	16953-6	pre '33	6/51	Probably ex-second class coaches — a by-product of abolition of second class. No 16954 later downgraded to all 3rd No 13570.
186A	2	c.1900	50'0"	25T	A8		10204; 10212	16943-4	1/38	3/40 (16944)	Downgraded ex-First Class coaches from D112 (see above).
187	54	1897-1902	50'0"	24½T	A8	Various: 2523-3822	9158-209	16957-17004			The standard 50ft arc roof composite. One (LNW 3175) to Motor fitted (Diagram M36 — see Appendix III) before grouping. One other (probably LNW 2756) did not survive to reach LMS.
186	2	1907	50'0"	26T	C8	2651;2708	9156-7	16945-6	8/50	2/51 (16946)	Identical coaches with 4 large and 3 small compartments. D186 had the large centre compartment downgraded to 3rd class. Curious weight discrepancy. Coaches believed built for Manchester-Buxton services.
185	1	1907	50'0"	24½T	C8	2665	9155	17007		9/49	
181	2	1906	50'0"	27T	C9	3417;4032	9118-9	17005-6	9/45	6/46 (17005)	Cove roof, 9ft wide version of D187. One converted to D286 (below).
182	29	1904-7	50'0"	27T	C9	Various: 2548-3918	9120-44	17008-16 17021-32 17037-40	5/37	3/58	The standard 9ft cove roof composite. Almost certainly 30 originally built. The missing 30th vehicle is probably the coach listed as motor fitted Diagram M24 — Appendix III. Four others (LNW 3864;3882;3914;3918) Motor fitted before 1923 (Diagram M29 — see Appendix III). Several LMS mark-downs of main loco-hauled batch to all-third (Nos: 13418;13549;13560-1/3-4).
183	4	1904	50'0"	28T	C9	3463;3974; 3994;3996	9145-8	17017-20	6/40	5/52	This batch had only one small compartment and probably started life as 6F + 1T. LMS 17018 marked down to all 3rd No 13565.

DIAG	QTY	DATE BUILT	BODY LENGTH	TARE WEIGHT	BODY STYLE	NUMBERING PRE-GROUP	1st LMS	2nd LMS	WITHDRAWN FIRST	LAST	REMARKS
180	19	1907-9	50'0"	27T	E9	Various: 2507-3966	9100-17	17033-6 17041-50 17058-60	11/38	2/57	Two diagrams identical except that D179 had one compartment downgraded (LNW 3036). This coach motor fitted (Diagram M38) before 1923. – see Appendix III. One coach of D180 (LNW 2758) also motor fitted (Diagram M22) before 1923. LMS 9113 downgraded to D286A (below) in 1931.
179	1										
178	8	1908-9	50'0"	26T	E9	2517;2715-6/ 72;2887;2901; 3023/6	9094-9	16947-52	1/51	7/59	Six only received LMS numbers. The other two (LNW 2887;2901) were motor fitted (Diagram M23) before 1923. One coach marked down to all 3rd No 13533.
177	7	1909	50'0"	28T	E9	2598;2627/9/ 50/68 2735/52	9087-93	17051-7	2/45	12/56	Elliptical roof version of D183 (above) and also probably 6F + 1T when new. They seem to have generally run in 3-coach sets with D335 (below).
184	6	1909	50'0"	28T	E8½	2681;2710; 2820/61 3028; 3902	9149-54	17061-6	2/38	9/56	Essentially an 8ft 6in wide version of D180. Ran in 4 coach sets with D287 and D341 (below), the only 8ft 6in elliptical roof non-corridors.
176A	9	1920-1	56'0"	27T	A8	3241/3/5/7/ 9-53	9076-84	17067-75	8/34	12/56	Built from 2 x 28ft four compartment firsts of D120 (above).
176B	2	1921	56'0"	27T	A8	3254-5	9085-6	17076-7	2/34	8/38 (see note)	Also ex-28ft four wheelers, first class end from D120 (above) and opposite end from another source (not verified). In these coaches, the third class compartments were very small (5ft 5in wide) and separated from the firsts by void between partitions. Last to go (17076) was downgraded to all third No 13554 before withdrawal.
176	160	1913-24	57'0"	28T	T9	3731-42;4038 -114 plus others	8900-9059	17078-234			The standard 57ft composite which established the layout of the LMS version. Two were motor fitted in 1927 to Diagram M39. LMS 8901-50 were built after 1922 and, of these, 8927-50 had LMS numbers from new. It is possible that 8901-26 (scheduled LNW Nos:4089-114) also had LMS numbers from new.
175	16	1914-20	57'0"	28T	T9	3764-71; 3861/ 3;3871-4; 3883-4	9060-9075	17235-50	3/52	11/59	Similar styling to D176 but fewer third class compartments. One example (LMS 9063-17238) was motor fitted in 1931 to Diagram M19B.

NON-CORRIDOR COMPOSITE BRAKES (For compartment arrangements see Table 3, page 110)

DIAG	QTY	DATE BUILT	BODY LENGTH	TARE WEIGHT	BODY STYLE	NUMBERING PRE-GROUP	1st LMS	2nd LMS	WITHDRAWN FIRST	LAST	REMARKS
236	19	1891	30'0"	11T	A8	Various: 5701-5962	9922-40	27606 27703-4 27955-9	pre '33	3/36	Gaslit 6-wheel coaches. Note that 27606 and 27703-4 are LMS Brake 3rd series numbers following downgrading.
235	10		42'0"	18T	A8½	5809/12/24/37 /40/51/5/63/5-6					Ex-42ft radials (some scrapped as radials). Some dual fitted and probably ex-WCJS. Many gaslit.
234	4	1896	45'0"	21T	A8	5712/6/90; 5929	9918-21	24718-20	pre '33	4/39	A small batch of 45ft gaslit coaches, originally First/Second class for Manchester and Buxton trains.
233	1	1906	50'0"	24½T	C8	5991	9917	24721		1/54	Originally D346 (below) which had originally started as a Brake Second. All compartments were same size and this coach may have gone direct from Brake Second to First/Third composite.

NON-CORRIDOR THIRD CLASS (For compartment arrangements see Table 3, page 110)

DIAG	QTY	DATE BUILT	BODY LENGTH	TARE WEIGHT	BODY STYLE	NUMBERING PRE-GROUP	1st LMS	2nd LMS	WITHDRAWN FIRST	LAST	REMARKS
300	104	1894-1900	28'0"	12½T	A8	Various: 34- -2222 also 2227 -40/3-7/50-8	6113-72	26108-17 26124-62			Four wheel coaches. Many subsequently converted to D283A, D333B (below), probably the bulk of the pre-group withdrawals.
297	500+	1894-1900	30'1"	13T	A8	Various: 2-2207	Many in 43xx 45xx and 58xx 68xx series	Any or all the series 26250-420			The standard LNWR six-wheel third. The most numerous type of LNWR coach. LMS numbers not confirmed accurately. Some converted to D282 (below). Mostly gaslit but a few electrically lit.
299	6	1911	30'0"	15T	E9	620/8;630/ 9;2241-2	6107-12	26435-40	5/43	7/52	Six wheel elliptical roof coaches for the celebrated Birmingham-Sutton set. LNWR 2241-2 almost certainly ex-second class. Gaslit when new.
296	2		32'0"	11T	A8	339;522 1438					Last survivors of 32ft radial coaches – probably did not reach LMS. D295 had central luggage compartment in place of passenger accommodation.
295	1										
292	30	1892-3	42'0"	20T	A8	Various: 4-1957	5680-90; 4613/9/ 21/33	13626/ 8-32	pre '33		Standard 42ft radial third class. Some later converted to bogies and some dual fitted. Only difference between diagrams is centre luggage compartment in D293. Originally gaslit – most subsequent conversions to electric were D293.
293	24					Various: 24-1095	5691-712	13612-24	pre '33	11/46	
291	4	1896	45'0"	21T	A8	193/6;892;950	5676-9	13633-6	1/34	4/36	45ft equivalent of D292. Possibly ex-second class. Gaslit.
290	3	1897	50'0"	24½T	A8	1796;1805; 1798	5673-5	13637-9	9/36	6/43	Ex-composites (possibly from the first six first class/second class coaches of the pioneer Watford 50ft sets). Exactly the same style as D111 and D187 (above).
289	136	1897-1901	50'0"	24T	A8	Various: 38-2225	5563-672	13644-742			Standard 50ft arc roof third class. Many motor-fitted to Diagrams M62; M63 – see Appendix III. This conversion started before 1923 and continued into LMS period. Three transferred to CLC by LMS (LMS 5573/93/5662) becoming CLC 578/ 580/579 in order.
285	73	1903-6	50'0"	26½T	C9	Various: 30-2223	5491-5554	13743-802 13808-11			Standard cove roof third class. Nine conversions (pre-1923) to motor-fitted (Diagram M57). A few of these coaches may have been built in 1907.
286	1	1906	50'0"	27T	C9	1763	5555	13641		6/46	Almost certainly ex D181 (above). Four large and three small compartments.
288	2	1906	50'0"	24T	C8	820;850	5562 (ex-850)	13826		7/50	The only 8ft wide cove roof third. Contemporary with D185/186 and D115 (above) and D346/348 (below). Probably for Manchester-Buxton sets.
286A	1	1931	50'0"	27T	E9		9113	13643		3/54	Converted from D180 (originally built 1907).
287	6	1909	50'0"	28T	E8½	863;918;952; 997;1028;1208	5556-61	13827-32	11/40	9/57	8ft 6in elliptical roof coaches to run with D184 (above) and D341 (below)

DIAG	QTY	DATE BUILT	BODY LENGTH	TARE WEIGHT	BODY STYLE	PRE-GROUP	1st LMS	2nd LMS	WITHDRAWN FIRST	LAST	REMARKS
284	see remarks	1907-9	50'0"	26½T	E9	Various: 827-1664	5472-90	13803-7 13812-25	5/45	11/59	At least 20 built. One of this batch of 20 definitely converted to motor-fitted style (Diagram M55) before 1923 (became LMS 15838) and generally believed that Motor-fitted diagrams M53-5 all originated as this type — see Appendix III — making a probable figure of 25 originally.
283A	11	1920-1	56'0"	27T	A8	1433-4/6/40/2/ 5-6/8-9/53/9	5461-71	13833-43	1/34	5/45	Built from ex-4 wheelers to D300 (above).
283	93	1913-20	57'0"	28T	T9	Bulk of series 1613-1724	Bulk of 5357-5460 (see also D282)	13844-935			Standard 57ft third class. Several inexplicable gaps in first LMS number series (aside from those used for D282) viz: 5358-60/76/97/403.
282	5	c.1923	60'2"	29T	A8		5381/4/9 406/9	13936-40			Converted from ex-30ft six wheelers to D297 (above).
											NON-CORRIDOR THIRD CLASS BRAKES (For compartment arrangements see Table 3, page 110)
365			28'0"		A8						Four wheelers — all subsequently used for D333B (below).
364	49	1894-1900	28'0"	12T	A8	Various: 6851-7620	7911-59	27509-51			Four wheelers, D363 being ex-second class with slightly larger compartments — otherwise identical. Possible that original quantities were 50 and 10, the missing examples being used for D333B (below) — not confirmed.
363	9	1894	28'0"	12T	A8	Various: 6509-48	7902-10	27502-8			
361	209+	1889-92	30'0"	13T	A8	Various: 6503-7929	7694-899	27564 27571-3 27583-9 27593-605 27607-81 27697/ 9-702 27705-8			Standard 3 compartment six-wheel Brake third, second LMS numbers slightly mixed up with D360/D359 (below). Mostly gaslit.
360	33	1891-4	30'0"	13T	A8	Various: 6907-7859	7667-93	27553-61 27582			As per D361 but one less compartment (removed subsequent to original building?) mostly gaslit.
359	59	1889-91	30'0"	13T	A8	Various: 6854-7487	7612-66	27566-8 27570 27574-81 27590/2 27696/8			Centre brake version of D361. Gaslit. Second LMS 27563 may also have been this type.
362	2	1911	30'0"	15T	E9	6686;7436	7900-1	27689-90	12/43	3/47 (27689)	Birmingham-Sutton Brakes (see D118/D299 — above). Gaslit when new. LNW 6686 originally second class.
358	see remarks		30'0"	13T	A8	7539/41;7551					At least three built. Appear to be conversions ex-D297 (above) but not confirmed. Gaslit.
356	1		32'0"	13T	A8	6858					Residual 32ft radial. Gaslit.
355	1		34'0"	13T	A8*	7099					Residual 34ft radial. Gaslit. * Actually 7ft 9in wide.
354	38	1886-94	42'0"	18T	A8	Various: 6850-7714	6489-90 /2/4 7601-11	22222/4-5 22230/55			Originally 42ft radials but some converted to bogie. Mostly gaslit. Second LMS 22223/31-2 may also have been this type. Many 'cyphered' numbers.
352	46		42'0"	21T	A8	Various: 6543-7693	6506/9;6520 /3-4 6461; 7570-600	22226-9 22233-54 22256			End-brake version of D354. A few still radial but most converted to bogie. A few gaslit. Some converted to corridor (1st LMS 6xxx series)
350	4	1896	45'0"	21T	A8	6952;7000; 7106;7147	7566-9	22258-60	pre '33	12/43	45ft equivalent of D352 but not, of course, radial. Gaslit.
349	7	1899-1900	50'0"	24T	A8	6901/27;7459/ 63;7503/41/58	7559-65	22261-6	pre '33	6/41	Probably eight built originally.
347	83	1898-1902	50'0"	24T	A8	Various: 6516-7822	7472-554	22286-364			First LMS 7474 subsequently motor-fitted becoming 24474 but no motor diagram (apparently) issued.
345	68	1897-1902	50'0"	24T	A8	Various: 6502-7645	7400-66	22493-558			With D347, the standard 50ft arc roof brake third type. This was the original type, later somewhat superseded by D347 which had one less compartment. Possibly reflected an extension of use to outer suburban work — hence the larger van portion on D347.
343	2	1899	50'0"	25T	A8	7650;7653	7396-7	22611		1/35	Identical, save for raised lookouts on D342. D343 probably converted from 8-compartment thirds to D289.
342	3	1899-1902	50'0"	25T	A8	7671;7703 7766	7393-5	22609-10 22612			
348	4	1907	50'0"	26T	C8	6507;6513; 7351;7375	7555-8	22267-70	6/44	8/53	Cove roof version of D349. First two may have been second class — probably all built for Manchester-Buxton services.
346	6	1906	50'0"	24½T	C8	6589/96;6637/ 43;7348-9	7467-71	22476-80			Cove roof version of D347 but originally some ex-second class. One converted to D233 (above).
344	2	1904	50'0"	24T	C8	6879.7019	7398-9	22559-60	7/44	4/50 (22559)	Cove roof version of D345.
336	33	1903-4	50'0"	27T	C9	Various: 6514-7811	7220-52	22561-93	1/39	8/53	
338	82	1904-7	50'0"	27T	C9	Various: 6862-7804	7290-363	22365-429 22441-8 CLC 581			Standard 9ft wide cove roof brake. Nine conversions to motor-fitted (Diagram M71 — Appendix III) before grouping.
340	1	1906	50'0"	26T	C9	7386	7380	22430		5/52	A 'one-off' centre brake design — gaslit.
341	12	1909	50'0"	27T	E8½	Various: 6872-7568	7381-92	22481-92			8ft 6in wide elliptical coaches. Ran in sets with D184 and D287 (above).
339	16	1908-9	50'0"	26T	E9	Various: 6574-7432	7364-79	22271-85	pre '33	10/57	Probably built to run in 3-coach sets with D178 (above).
337	39	1907-9	50'0"	26T	E9	Various: 6853-7424	7253-89	22431-40 22449-75	12/34	10/57	Almost certainly 40 originally built. Two subsequent motor fitted conversions (Diagram M70 — see Appendix III).
335	14	1909	50'0"	28T	E9	Various: 7039-7435	7206-19	22594-607	1/51	6/56	Ran with D177 (above) as 3-coach sets.
334	6	1913	54'0"	26T	T9	7085/94; 7121/54/ 7160/81	7200-5	22613-8	11/46	11/56	The only 54ft brake third and no matching thirds or composite (except lavatory stock).
333	154	1916-22	57'0"	27½T	T9	Various: 6530-7987	7012-110 7121-75	22608 22643-793			Standard 57ft brake third. Two motor-fitted in 1927 to Diagram M78 — see Appendix III.

DIAG	QTY	DATE BUILT	BODY LENGTH	TARE WEIGHT	BODY STYLE	NUMBERING PRE-GROUP	1st LMS	2nd LMS	WITHDRAWN FIRST	LAST	REMARKS
333A	2	1917	57'0"	26T	T9	6689/91	7176-7	22641-2	3/55	10/57 (22641)	Non standard 4 compartment brakes, probably ex-ambulance coaches.
333B	22	1920-1	56'0"	27T	A8	7930-51	7178-99	22619-40	/35	/58	Converted from 4-wheel coaches. Brake ends mostly ex D365 (above) and third class ends were ex-D300 (above). Two coaches made use of former 2-compartment 4-wheel brakes, probably from D363/D364 (above).
333C	51	1923-4	57'0"	27T	T9	6401-30 Various: 6515-7869	6961-7011	22794-843			Post-group version of D333 with two pairs of double doors at van end. Many may not have received allotted LNWR numbers. Quantity built is odd. The 51st coach may have been a replacement for an odd early withdrawal (e.g. D337 – above). One early casualty (1st LMS 6976).
											PASSENGER FULL BRAKES — all gangwayed except D385/D387.
387	2		28'0"	12T	A8	8863-4	3075-6	33834-5			4-wheel coaches, non gangwayed. Possibly conversions from 2 compartment brake thirds (not confirmed).
385	290		30'0"	12T	A8	Various: 8013-8714	2830-3074	Most of the series 33848-930			Standard 6-wheel non-gangwayed brake. At least 290 built but withdrawal was rapid and started before 1923. First LMS series virtually confirmed but second LMS number series may have had additional examples.
384	40		32'0"	13T	C8	8752-91	2791-829	33442-79			Milk traffic brakes. A somewhat late reversion to 32ft length. Note the very tidy numbering series – most unusual. One early pre group casualty (LNW 8755) and one early LMS withdrawal (1st LMS 2827).
W81	27		42'0"	21T	A8	WCJS 86-100; 459-70	2766-90	32020-39			The only arc roof 42ft brakes and always bogie coaches. WCJS Nos 99;464 were early casualties and replaced by one each on Diagrams W79;W82 (below).
383	40	1910-11	42'0"	22T	E8½	Various: 8006-8583	2727-65	32040-63 32076-89			Essentially identical designs but D383 had projecting lookouts. Both roofs had toplights below cantrail. Some may have been built after 1922 (not all of D382 seem to have carried LNWR numbers). One pre-1923 casualty (LNWR 8240-D383 and one early LMS withdrawal (1st LMS 2765).
382	165	1911-23	42'0"	23T	E8½	Various: 8127-8594	2249 2563-726	32064-75 32090-242			
381A	25	1902	45'0"	23T	See notes	8924-9; 8938-55;8961	2521-45	32378-401			Clerestory brakes with sliding doors, 8' 4½" wide. D381A had projecting lookouts at end of coach. D381B had similar lookouts in centre. Both types 9'0" over lookouts. Originally these were parcels vans (D381A) and cycle vans (D381B), afterwards used as ambulances in first world war and converted to full brakes later. Two early casualties: 1st LMS 2543;2547.
381B	17		45'0"	23T	See notes	8930-7; 8956-60; 8975-8	2546-62	32402-8 32370; 32409 32371-2; 32410 32373-6 (in same order)			
381	c.105		45'0"	21T	A8	Various: 8010-8724	2420-520	32254-328 32346-69 32251-3;			Standard 45ft arc roof brakes, diagrams identical. Second LMS numbers reflect order of building and hence combine the two diagrams together. Several early withdrawals, notably WCJS 321, replaced by one of Diagram W82 (below).
W80	35		45'0"	21T	A8	WCJS 152-66 173-82 315-24	2387-400; 3197 2401-10 2411-9	32329-37/ 77/32243-50/32338-45			
380	10	c.1907	50'0"	24T	C9	8742-51	2377-86	32527-36			Cove roof vans with sliding doors and marked for milk traffic.
379	14	c.1908-9	50'0"	24T	E9	Various: 8003-8829	2363-76	32663-75			Elliptical roof version of D380 – also for milk traffic. Contemporary with D375 (below) and second LMS numbers are in middle of this series.
378A	3		50'0"		A8½ E8½	8009;8924 8137	2356/8 2357	32458-9 32662			Two body styles on one diagram and classified 'Postal Brake van'. Arc Roofs came from D378, Elliptical from D375. Eventually allocated TPO number series as follows: 32458–30336;32459–30313;32662–30337. It is possible they never carried the LMS 32xxx numbers.
378B	2	ex-ambulance	50'0"	24T	A8½ C8½	8064 8153	2359 2360	32518			Again two styles. Arc Roof ex-D377, Cove Roof ex-D376 with guard moved to end of coach after conversion from ambulance use.
378	48	ex-ambulance	50'0"	24T	C8½	8871;8898	2361-2	32744-5			Very similar to D378B except for minor changes in door positions.
378C	2		50'0"	23T	A8½	Various: 8009-8730	2312-55	32440-57 32460-85			Standard 50ft arc roof brakes. Two LNWR examples to D378A, two more withdrawn pre-1923 (LNWR 8130;8220). In WCJS batch, No 213 was an early withdrawal, replaced by No 464. WCJS No 213 later allocated to brake composite Diagram W39A. No trace of 1st LMS 2299 ever being used.
W79	21		50'0"	23T	A8½	WCJS 212-31; 464	2291-8 2300-11	32421-39 32583			
377	41		50'0"	23T	A8½	Various: 8001-8513	2248 2250-87	32415-20 32486-517 32526			Identical to D378 except that roof is shown as 2 inches higher. One to D378B before 1923 and one early casualty (LNWR 8192). This number used again on D382 (above).
376	10	1907	50'0"	24T	C8½	8012/6/49/87/ 9;8109/19/46/ 53/77	2239-47	32576-84			Standard cove roof bogie brake. One (LNWR 8153) to ambulance service and back as D378B.
375	175	1907-10	50'0"	24T	E8½	Various: 8011-8736 plus 8792-819 8830-58	2065-238	32537-75 32594-661 32676-716 32723-42 32746-7			Standard 50ft elliptical brake. One to D378 before receiving 1st LMS number. Two to D374A retaining allocated numbers. Two later survivors (LMS 32594;32716) converted to sawdust vans in 1952. Second LMS numbering does not correlate with first series in order.
374A	2	c.1907	50'0"	25T	E8½	8078;8819	2065-6	32746-7			Conversions of D375 with raised lookouts removed. Reason for heavier weight is not known.
W82	3		50'0"	25T	E8½	WCJS 99;321 350	2288-90	32748-50			Essentially a WCJS version of D374A. Seem to have been built as one for one replacements of prematurely withdrawn accident vehicles.

Withdrawal data not available for Full Brake coaches

DIAG	QTY	DATE BUILT	BODY LENGTH	TARE WEIGHT	BODY STYLE	PRE-GROUP	1st LMS	2nd LMS	WITHDRAWN FIRST	LAST	REMARKS
375/	1	1924	50'0"	23½T	E9		2955	31955			Ex-ambulance train pharmacy car. Also listed as LMS Diagram 1780. Coach exhibited LNWR panelling combined with Midland style profile and fittings.
374	2		50'0"	see notes	E9	8073;8086	2063-4	32413-4			Royal Train clerestory brakes. Essentially D377 with added clerestory and extra equipment. Weights: 8073-26T;8086-29T.
373	7	c.1906	50'0"	23T	C9	8025;8296; 8737-41	2056-62	32519-25			9ft wide cove roof design.
372	2		50'0"	23T	E9	8007;8036	2048-9	32592-3			Elliptical roof version of D373.
371	6	1907-8	50'0"	25T	SD4	8820-5	2042-7	32586-91			"American Special" brakes with standard '12 wheel' body style and recessed entrances.
W78	6		50'0"	23T	E9	WCJS 341-6	2050-5	32743 32718-22			Postal brakes with offset gangways. One to Diagram W77 (below). The rest renumbered into GPO series viz:– 30330-2;30340;30338 (in WCJS number order).
W77	1		50'0"		E9	WCJS 341	2050	32743			As W78 but with duckets removed. Eventually became 30339 in GPO series.
370	2		57'0"	28T	E9	8915;8974	2001-2	32779; 32737			All these diagrams are post war conversions from World War I ambulance trains, in particular US Ambulance Trains 71 and 72. One or two subsequent conversions to GPO use viz: 3278 1; 30333 (D406A); 32782-3; 30334-5 (D406). Some of D370E were converted back to brake use after 1922 and given numbers in LMS standard series. These vehicles were identical to LMS ambulance conversions to LMS Diagram 1777.
370A	2		57'0"	27½T	E9	8922-3	2003-4	32780-1			
370B	3		57'0"	28T	E9	8920-1;8973	2005-7	32782-3; 32778			
370C	2		57'0"	28T	E9	8918-9	2008-9	32784-5			
370D	2		57'0"	28T	E9	8916-7	2010-1	32786-7			
370E	30		54'0"	27½T	E9	8899-914 8979-88	2016-31 2032-41 2012-5	32761-76 32751-60 31967-70			In general, the body styling of these vehicles reflected the various stages of rebuilding and other than the elliptical roof profile, generalisation is difficult. A typical example is illustrated at Plate 120

Withdrawal data not available for Full Brake coaches.

178

Appendix II - SUMMARY TABLE OF LNWR/WCJS SALOONS AND SPECIAL STOCK

DIAG	QTY	DATE BUILT	BODY LENGTH	TARE WEIGHT	BODY STYLE	NUMBERING PRE-GROUP	1st LMS	2nd LMS	WITHDRAWN FIRST	WITHDRAWN LAST	REMARKS
											ROYAL, DEPARTMENTAL AND SPECIAL SALOONS (For plans see Fig. 37, page 119).
Not issued	1	1869	60'0"	34T				802	still extant		Queen Victoria's Saloon – Preserved at National Railway Museum.
Not issued	2	1903	65'6"	46T	SD3			800;801	still extant		King Edward VII and Queen Alexandra's saloons – Preserved at National Railway Museum.
1	6	1903	57'0"		SD3	5071-6	10503-8	803-8	7/56	6/68	Semi-Royals, built to match standard 9ft clerestory coach and all dual fitted. Many subsequent detail alterations and eventually all but No 803 modified (internally) to Diagrams 1A-1C. No 806 is privately preserved.
2	1	1914	66'6"	43T	See notes	5318	10500	45002	still extant		Inspection Saloon, twelve wheeled. Modified 'toplight' body style but only 8ft 6in wide. Dual fitted. Privately preserved.
3	1	1897	50'0"	28T	See notes	5201	10391(?)	45001, later 45022			Directors Saloon. Clerestory body, 8ft 6in wide with basically traditional panelling. Never received 1st allocated LMS number as far as known. Became 45022 when converted to Inspection Saloon in 1937. Dual fitted.
4	2		42'0"	27T	*See notes	5131;5153					Designated 'Special Saloons' and designed for Prince of Wales (5131) and Equerries (5153). Dual fitted and originally radial chassis, later to bogies. Bodies had traditional panelling and were 8ft 6in wide. Built with cove roof, they later received clerestories. (n.b. LNWR Diagram 5 is shown as a similar vehicle – LNWR No 2180A – but no other record of its existence has been found).
6	1	1892	42'0"		C8½	5179	10683	45013 45014			Designated Inspection Saloons and probably converted from 42ft sleeping cars. D6 was gaslit.
7	3	1892	42'0"		C8½	5176-8	10684-6	45011-2			
8	1		42'0"		C8½	5121	Scrapped?				Inspection Saloon ex D52 (below). No other details.
9	1		32'0"	14T	A8	2087A	Scrapped?				Inspection Saloon ex D54 (below). No other details.
10	See notes	1897	32'0"	14T	A8	2019A;2120A	10400 10397	45028 ↓			Inspection Saloons, probably ex 32ft sleeping cars. Although only two of these vehicles are listed in the diagram book there were several more broadly identical saloons (e.g. LMS 45025/9) and the official record may be faulty in this case. These saloons had an open end balcony (see also D66 – below).
12	1	1920	57'0"	33T	See notes	5000		45000	still extant (1977)		Chairman's, later LMS President's Inspection Saloon. Modified 'toplight' style, 9ft wide body, dual fitted. Fitted LMS bogies 1933 and used in Royal Train at times. Now fitted with BR bogies and cleared for 100 mph service.
											WCJS "2pm" CORRIDOR STOCK (all dual fitted. For plans see Fig. 41, page 135)
W22	2	1908	65'6"	42T	SD4	383-4	7989-90	4778-9	4/51	10/51 (4779)	Composite for Edinburgh portion, no spare examples.
W23	4	1909	65'6"	42T	SD4	379-82	7985-8	4780-3	4/51	5/53	Composite for Glasgow portion, two normally spare.
W38	3	1909	65'6"	41T	SD4	385-7	9698-9700	7212-4	12/49	6/53	Brake composites for Aberdeen, one normally spare.
W62	5	1908/9	65'6"	40T	SD4	390-4	6461-5	6390-4			Five compartment brake thirds for Glasgow portion, running at south end of train, three normally spare.
W63	2	1908/9	65'6"	40T	SD4	388-9	6468-9	6395-6			Identical to W62 but opposite handed. They ran at north end of train. No spare examples.
W64	2	1908/9	65'6"	39T	SD4	395-6	6466-7	6388-9			Four compartment brake thirds for Edinburgh portion, handed as per W62. No spare examples.
											"AMERICAN SPECIAL" STOCK (For plans see Fig. 41, page 135)
28	3	1907-8	65'6"	40T	SD4	5309-11	10392-4	7556-8	9/36	?	Open first class coaches for dining. No 7556 later became 26995.
38	3	1907-8	65'6"	39T	SD4	5312-4	10478-80	9584-6	11/41	5/51	Open composites (second/third class) for dining. Later all third class.
45	3	1907-8	50'0"	31½T	SD4	5315-7	3202-4	30197-9			Kitchen cars (four wheel bogies but matching body style). Always used gas for both cooking & lighting.
91	9	1907-8 &1913	65'6"	42T	SD4	4504/29-30/75/86/8;4602/55/63	10021-9	1167-8; 816;1169-70;1161; 1171; 1162-3	2/37	4/56	Corridor firsts with one five seat and five four seat saloons, all fitted with individual chairs/settees. Three were built at first; followed by six more in 1913. LMS 10023/8 became Club Saloons. (Diagram 68/69 – below).
92	3	1907-8	65'6"	42T	SD4	4629;4659; 4681	10030-2	1164-6	9/47	?	Corridor Firsts, similar to D91 but only one four seat saloon. Remaining four seat compartments were conventional.
261	3	1907-8	65'6"	43T	SD4	1129-30;2144	4301-3	3050-2	9/47	4/51	Corridor composites (second/third class), later corridor thirds.
371	6	1907-8	50'0"	25T	SD4	8820-5	2042-7	32586-91	?	?	Full brakes (four wheel bogies but matching body style).
											DAY, INVALID AND FAMILY SALOONS (For plans see Fig. 43, page 139)
52	4		42'0"	24T	C8½	5121-4					Day saloons, 5121/3 dual fitted. 5121 converted to D8 (above) but no other details known. Gaslit.
53	4		42'0"	24T	C8½	5125-8					Day saloons, 5125/6 dual fitted. All gaslit and built as twins with D52 and shown as gangwayed only between the individual halves of the pair. Scrapped before grouping and some of them probably used on American Boat trains in early days (see Plate 182).
54	3		32'0"	13T	A8	2082A;2084A 2087A					Day saloons. Two scrapped by 1917, one to D9 (above). They contained seats which drew out to form beds and could have originally started life as sleeping cars. All gaslit and 2082A dual fitted.

DIAG	QTY	DATE BUILT	BODY LENGTH	TARE WEIGHT	BODY STYLE	PRE-GROUP	1st LMS	2nd LMS	WITHDRAWN FIRST	WITHDRAWN LAST	REMARKS
						NUMBERING					
55	1	See notes	50'0"	27T	C8½	5320	10681	812		7/52	Invalid Saloon. Converted from Guard, Medical Officers and Nurses car of Ambulance Train No 19. Dual fitted.
56	2	1907	50'0"	27T	E9	5023/7	4619;10509	810-11	10/51	3/53 (811)	Invalid Saloons, dual fitted.
57	1		32'0"	13T	A8	5028					Invalid Saloons, dual fitted. In D57, luggage compartment had internal access to rest of coach.
58	1		32'0"	12½T	A8	5037					Slight variations in window design between the two types. Both gaslit. See Fig. 42.
59	1		28'0"	12T	A8	2023A					Invalid Saloon, dual fitted. Four wheel version of D58. Gaslit.
62	6	1894	45'0"	24½T	C8½	5003/6-7/10/6/81	10510-5	to D78A (below)			Family Saloon, dual fitted and gaslit. These had "12 wheel" style exterior panelling. All converted to picnic saloons.
63	32	1898-1901	45'0"	24-25T	See notes	Various: 5017-5069	10516-47 (not 10521)	876-901 976-7	Most survivors to D78 – see remarks alongside.		Clerestory family saloons with traditional exterior panelling, all dual fitted and mostly gaslit. Most were converted to picnic saloons (D78) in 1926-8.
W13	20	1898-1901	45'0"	24-25T	See notes	WCJS 353-372	10548-67	903;910-12/978-89 3400 45031-3			Two of LNWR batch to Royal Train use (LNWR 5050/6 – LMS 10543-4, later 976-7). LNWR 5058 to D71A (Club Saloon) and then to picnic saloon (D71A2). WCJS series also variable. One to motor fitted (No 3400 – Diagram M73B) and three more (WCJS 353-4/6; LMS 10548-9/51) to Engineers Saloons 45031-3 but not allocated a new diagram. 1st LMS number 10521 does not seem to have been used.
64	5	1896	42'0"	23½T	C8?	5008-9/11-12 5133	10568-72	to D72 in 1928			Family Saloons, dual fitted and gaslit. Diagram suggests cove roof but not confirmed. To picnic saloons in 1928.
65	1		32'0"	12½T	A8	2036A					Family saloon, dual fitted and gaslit.
66	2		32'0"	13T	A8	2078A;2088A					Family Saloons, dual fitted and gaslit. Window/door arrangement exactly as for D10 (above), except for verandah. They may share a common origin and these vehicles may account for some of the extra inspection saloons noted with D10.
67	1		27'0"	13T	See notes	2004A				3/20	Family Saloon, dual fitted. Arc roof with clerestory and of unusual length. Gaslit.
											FIRST CLASS AND CLUB SALOONS (For plans see Fig. 46, page 144).
68	1	1928	65'6"		SD4		10028	1162			Ex-American Special (D91) becoming Manchester and North Wales Travelling Club No. 2.
69	1	1925	65'6"	41½T	SD4		10023	816			Ex-American Special (D91) becoming Manchester and North Wales Travelling Club No. 1.
70	1	1905	54'0"	30T	C9	5068	10573	813		4/63	Gangway at attendant's end only. Probably built for Liverpool-Llandudno service.
71	2	1908	57'0"	30T	E9	5234-5	10574-5	814-5	5/57	5/57	Built as a pair and gangwayed with attendants compartments adjoining. Somewhat similar to D70.
71B	1	1913	42'0"	23T	A8	5238	10577				Third class club ex-D77 (Picnic Saloon) in 1913. Dual fitted and originally built as D77 in 1900.
71A	1		45'0"	24½T	See notes	5058	10576	902	to D71A2 in 1928		Ex-45ft family saloon (D63). Probably became a club saloon before 1923. Dual fitted.
100A	1	1905	54'0"	28T	C9	4646	10081	18183		5/46	In 1924, altered to D100B by making centre area into large saloon for Manchester-Windermere Club Trains.
103	3	1900	50'0"		A8		10063-5	913-5			Essentially centre gangway open firsts. Only slight differences between the two diagrams (see page 143). Both gaslit.
103A	3	1900	50'0"		A8		10066-8	916;1128-9			
											PICNIC SALOONS (For plans see Fig. 48, page 146).
71A2	1	1928	45'0"	25T	See notes		10576	902			Ex-first class club (D71A) and originally D63. Dual fitted.
72	5	1928	42'0"	24T	C8		10568-72	871-5	10/36	6/41	Fairly simple conversion of D64. Dual fitted and mostly gaslit. n.b. Diagrams 73-5 are motor fitted saloons – see Appendix III.
76	10		42'0"	22T	C8½	5080;5154-7; 2113A-4A; 2130A/34A/35A					Dimensions, doors and lavatory arrangements suggest that these were conversions from sleeping cars. All dual fitted and gaslit. All to ambulance service in World War I. No other details.
77	55	1898-1900	42'0"	23T	A8	Various: 5068-5280	10581-631 (51 renumbered)	826-70 (46 renumbered)	pre '23	9/46	Standard arc roof picnic saloon. Some early withdrawals viz 5068 (replaced by D70 – above); 5069;5077;5238 (to D71B – above). All dual fitted and gaslit. Early LMS withdrawals: 10583/94/604/6/15.
78	33	1926-8	45'0"	24T	See notes		10516-20 10522-42 10545-7 10553-4 10557/62	876-901 (not in same order) plus 903; 910-11;912	pre '32	11/46	Ex D63/WCJS D13 (above). Precise number converted is not certain but 33 shown with first LMS series numbers, all dual fitted and over half gaslit.
78A	6	1928	45'0"	24T	C8½		10510-5	904-9	9/35	12/38	Ex D62, all dual fitted and all but one (904) gaslit.
Old p.78	2	1881	34'0"	21T	A8	2149A;2150A			pre '23	pre '23	Amongst the last surviving 34ft radials – see page 3. Dual fitted and gaslit.
79	6		32'0"	13½T	A8	5143-8			pre '23	pre '23	Dual fitted, radial chassis, gaslit.
80	16	1896-7	32'0"	13T	See notes	Various: 5004-5142	10632-47	943-5	pre '32	2/35	These coaches started life as six wheel clerestory family saloons with standard panelling. Conversion to picnic c. 1908-10 losing all interior partitions (except lavatories). Originally windows retained. Gaslit and dual fitted
81	11		32'0"	13T	A8	Various: 05024-05110 plus 2090A 2091A			pre '23	pre '23	Dual fitted and clearly conversions of older coach types (possibly family or sleeping saloons). Gaslit.
82	1		32'0"	14T	A8	2001A			pre '23	pre '23	Totally open saloon, no lavatories. Dual fitted and gaslit.
83	4		32'0"	13T	A8	5096-9			pre '23	pre '23	Dual fitted and gaslit.
84	16	1892	30'0"	13½T	A8	Various: 5002-5175	10648-62	942		1955?	30ft version of D79, dual fitted and gaslit.
85	15	1893	30'0"	13½T	A8	5181-95	10663-7		pre '23	pre '32	As D84 but with folding table in luggage compartment. Dual fitted and gaslit.
86	2		30'0"	16½T	A8	5199;5319	10678-9			pre '32	Dual fitted and gaslit.

DIAG	QTY	DATE BUILT	BODY LENGTH	TARE WEIGHT	BODY STYLE	PRE-GROUP	1st LMS	2nd LMS	FIRST	LAST	REMARKS
						NUMBERING			WITHDRAWN		
											SALOONS AND STEAM RAILMOTORS (For plans see Fig. 50, page 149).
M1	1		42'0"	25T	C8½	5078	10578				Redwharf Bay Saloon ex-D73. Believed converted from 42ft sleeping car.
M2	1		42'0"	25T	C8½	5079	10579				Driving end of Redwharf Bay saloon pair (ex-D74).
M3	2	1898	42'0"	22T	A8½	2129A 2136A	10581 10582	975		2/35	Holywell Town driving saloon. Formerly picnic saloons (D77).
M6	1	1910	60'0"	44T	T9	5507	10700		1928		Steam railmotors. Body style quite distinctive but nearer to toplight style than standard style.
M7	6	1905/6	57'0"	44T	T9	5501-6	10694-9	29988(ex-10697)	11/27	10/48	Diagram M7 built in two lots of 3 vehicles (1905 & 1906). All except 29988 withdrawn by 1930. The latter worked the Moffat branch from 1931.
											OPEN COMPOSITE (For plans see Fig. 50, page 149).
M11	1	1914	57'0"	27T	See notes	3726	9522	3427		8/55	Gangwayed trailer with intermediate height roof. Deep set entrance doors below a full width roof. Ran on Delph branch in later years, downgraded to all 3rd.
M12	1	1916	57'0"	?	see notes	3727	9523	3425		9/56	Similar profile to M11 but doors only slightly set back. Ran as all 3rd on Delph Branch.
M13	1	1913	57'0"	27½T	see notes	3751	9526	3426		7/53	"Cross-bred" style. Deep entrances at 1st class end but only slightly set back at 3rd class. Ran as all 3rd on Delph branch later.
M14	1	1912	57'0"	29T	E9	3102	9514	3422		7/33	Gangwayed trailer, eventually downgraded to all 3rd. Destroyed at Wolverton by fire.
M15	1	1911	57'0"	28T	E9	3722	9518	15846		6/58	Driving trailer similar to M14. To Delph branch 1954; St. Albans 1956. Gangwayed.
M16	1	1911	57'0"	28½T	E9	3723	9519	15847		5/51	Driving trailer (gangwayed). Probably similar to M15.
M17	1	1911	57'0"	28½T	E9	3724	9520	3421		7/53	Driving trailer similar to M15 and M16. To Delph branch 1951.
M18	1	1913	57'0"	29T	E9	3725	9521	3424		5/58	Driving trailer similar to M17 but shorter first class section. To Delph branch 1951.
											OPEN THIRD (For plans see Fig. 50, page 149)
M44	1	1910	60'0"	31T	T9	1777	5197	15851		6/56	Driving trailer (gangwayed), contemporary with and same length as steam railmotor Diagram M6.
M45	4	1913	57'0"	28½T	T9	132-5	5198-201	3417-20	1/51	10/58	Driving trailer (gangwayed). Known workings:— 3417 – Bletchley and Bedford (1956);3418 – St. Helens (1951);3419 – Delph (1954).
M46	1	1911	57'0"	28½T	E9	2488	5202	15844		1/53	Driving trailer similar to M45 but slight dimension differences inside the coach.
M47	1	1913	57'0"	27½T	See notes	500	5203	3423		7/55	Deeply recessed doors (c.f. M11 – above) but high roof. Gangwayed trailer. To Delph branch in 1951.
M48	1	1912	57'0"	29½T	T9	1468	5204	15845		3/57	Driving trailer (gangwayed). Bletchley and Bedford (1954).
M49	6	1911/12	57'0"	29T	E9	1540-3 2490-1	5205-8 5209-10	3413-6 3411-2	11/51	12/58	Driving trailers (gangwayed)
M50	3	1912/3	57'0"	28T	See notes	1500;1503; 1544	5315-7	15841/3/2	2/58	See notes	The celebrated observation cars. No 15843 sold to Bluebell railway in 1962 for preservation. Elliptical roof.
M58	6	1900	50'0"	24-25T	A8	2330-5	5215-20	3401-6	11/37	9/58	Driving trailer and open type interior. Out of sequence diagram in middle of compartment 3rds.
M73A	1	1914	41'7"	20T	See notes	5508	5314	15800		10/41	Driving trailer classified as brake third. Open saloon interior and converted from petrol electric railcar in 1926.
M73B	1	1900	45'0"	25½T	See notes	WCJS 365	10560	3400		8/38	Driving trailer with saloon interior and classified as brake third. Ex-45ft clerestory family saloon (Diag W13); converted in 1930.
											COMPARTMENT COMPOSITE (For compartment arrangements see page 152).
M19	2	1914	57'0"	28T	T9	3728-9	9524-5	17991-2	3/52	6/55	Built new with M51 (below) and no precise loco hauled equivalent. The only compartment type motor fitted coaches built as such by the LNWR. No 17991 worked Brynammon branch (1948); Swansea Victoria (1951).
M19B	1	1914	57'0"	27½T	T9	3767	9063	17945		3/55	Ex-D175. On conversion from 5F + 3T, two first class compartments downgraded but no reduction in compartment size. Rostered to work with Diagram M70 (below) on Leighton Buzzard-Dunstable service. Converted in 1931.
M20	1	1909	50'0"	29T	E9	2741	9504	17975		10/51	Driving trailer. All compartments same size. Probably converted from D284 but not confirmed.
M21	1	1909	50'0"	29T	E9	2781	9507	17969		5/53	Driving Trailer with seven equal sized compartments (Driving cab equivalent to eighth compartment). Probably ex-D284 but not confirmed.
M22	1	1909	50'0"	27½T	E9	2758	9505	17990		7/53	Ex-D180. Pre-conversion layout 5F + 2T and no change in compartment size on conversion. Worked Swansea-Brynammon in 1951.
M23	2	1909	50'0"	26T	E9	2887;2901	9509-10	17979-80	7/51	8/53	Ex-D178 with no change to compartment layout.
M24	1	1904	50'0"	28T	C9	3660	9517	17981		7/51	Driving Trailer. Driver's cab converted from first class compartment. Suspect conversion from D182 but not confirmed – see also M29.
M25	4	1903-4	50'0"	29T	C9	4016-7/9 4027	9532-4 9538	17963-4 17966-7	5/51	3/56	Driving Trailers. Virtually cove roof equivalent of M20, M21 apart from compartment classification. All compartments same size and probably ex-D285 but not confirmed.
M26	1	1903	50'0"	29T	C9	4022	9536	17965		3/51	Driving Trailer. Virtually identical to M25 except for reversed position of double and single van doors.
M27	1	1903	50'0"	29T	C9	4020	9535	17968		9/47	Driving Trailer. Yet another probable conversion of D285 but lacking confirmation.
M28	2	1903	50'0"	29T	C9	4023-4	9537	17960		2/43	Driving Trailers. As M27 but with an extra third class compartment. LNWR 4023 to M64 (below).

DIAG	QTY	DATE BUILT	BODY LENGTH	TARE WEIGHT	BODY STYLE	PRE-GROUP	1st LMS	2nd LMS	WITHDRAWN FIRST	WITHDRAWN LAST	REMARKS
M29	4	1906	50'0"	26T	C9	3864;3882; 3914;3918	9527-30	17986-9	12/51	10/53	All ex-D182. Some variations in compartment layouts in LMS days viz: 17988 to 3331133; 17989 to 1113333. This would normally involve issuing a new diagram but not in this case.
M30	1	1903	50'0"	27½T	C9	3972	9531	17983		4/51	Almost certainly ex-D110 (all-first) but not confirmed. At Swansea Victoria in 1949.
M31	2	1898/9	50'0"	26T	A8	4036-7	9541-2	17978; 17977	10/38	7/43	Driving Trailers. Basically a standard 8-compartment coach with one compartment for driver. Probably ex-D289 but not confirmed.
M32	4	1899	50'0"	26T	A8	2558;2655; 2664;3437	9501-3 9516	17970-1; 17974	1932	3/51	Driving Trailers. Basically the standard 4F + 3T arc roof composite (D187) but confirmation of conversion lacking. Driver's cab was equal in size to one first class compartment.
M33	2	1899	50'0"	26T	A8	2938;2947	9511-2	17972-3	3/37	4/44	Driving Trailers. Again probably ex-D187 but this time with a third class compartment for the driver and one first class compartment downgraded — a somewhat illogical conversion compared with M32.
M34	2	1898	50'0"	26T	A8	4034-5	9539-40	17961-2	5/35	5/38	Driving Trailers. Probably ex-D289 but not confirmed.
M35	2	1898	50'0"	26T	A8	2842 3017	9508 9513	17958 17959		12/33	Driving Trailers. Yet another variation of D187. Converted to dormitory coaches in 1933 at St. Rollox. The original diagram shows LNWR 2842 as having luggage only and no driving gear.
M36	2	1899	50'0"	24½T	A8	3175;3409	9515; 9190	17985; 17982	12/44	3/56	The genuine 4F + 3T, unaltered in form. Almost certainly ex D187.
M37	1	1898	50'0"	24½T	A8	2766	9506	17976		11/46	As M36 but centre compartment downgraded. Sold to Ashington Coal Company in 1947.
M38	1	1908	50'0"	27½T	E9	3036	9543	17984		8/53	Ex-D180 via D179 (See Appendix I). In Western Region stock when withdrawn. Converted 1920.
M39	2	1922	57'0"	28T	T9	4080;4087	9051; 9058	17993-4	2/59	11/59	Ex-D176, converted by LMS with no change in configuration. Converted with M78 (below).

COMPARTMENT AND CORRIDOR THIRD (For compartment arrangements see Table 5, page 152).

DIAG	QTY	DATE BUILT	BODY LENGTH	TARE WEIGHT	BODY STYLE	PRE-GROUP	1st LMS	2nd LMS	WITHDRAWN FIRST	WITHDRAWN LAST	REMARKS
M51	2	1914	57'0"	27½T	T9	243-4	5318-9	15848-9	10/60	3/62	Driving Trailers, built new with M19 (above) and always motor fitted. No 15848 Swansea-Brynammon in 1949.
M52	4	1913	50'0"	27½T	T9	492;506;514 533	5211-4	3407-10	2/52	10/58	Driving Trailers. Orthodox side corridor thirds, shown on diagram with interior doors from corridor to compartment removed. Gangways at both ends except for 3410 (passenger end only). Possibly ex-D267 but not confirmed. Nos. 3408/ 10 to Delph branch in 1951.
M53	1	1909	50'0"	29½T	E9	1002	5320	15807		2/57	Driving Trailer. Probably converted from D284, utilising two compartments for driver/luggage.
M54	1	1909	50'0"	29T	E9	980	5321	15808		7/51	Driving Trailer. Identical to M53 in fact, although diagram shows a difference in position of luggage doors.
M55	4	1909	50'0"	29T	E9	213;899;941; 981	5322-5	15837-40	7/50	11/58	Identical to D284 and almost certainly converted from this diagram.
M56	3	1903	50'0"	29T	C9	537;1000-1	5326-8	15804-6	9/49	5/53	Driving Trailers. Cove roof version of M54 and probably ex-D285.
M57	9	1903-6	50'0"	26-7T	C9	928;1168/85; 1235/84; 1437;1789; 1819;1098	5329-37	15828-36	6/42	7/53	All ex D285 without change in configuration.
M59	3	1899-1901	50'0"	24T	A8	181;1815; 2259	5338-40	15802-3; 15801	3/40	3/50	Driving Trailers. All ex-D289.
M60	1	1899	50'0"	26T	A8	1586	5341	15810		1/51	Driving Trailer. Seven compartment version of M59 and probably ex-D289 (see also M72 – below).
M61	1	1897	50'0"	24½T	A8	1782	5342	15809		4/40	Ex composite to D187.
M62/63	17	1897-1902	50'0"	24-7T	A8	Various: 103-1757	5343-55 5580;5590 5602;5634	15812-27 (not in same order)	12/30	7/55	Standard eight compartment coaches, many (probably all) ex-D289. No apparent difference between the diagrams. Some post-1923 conversions (First LMS 55xx;56xx series).
M64	1	1903	50'0"	29½T	C9	1439	5356	15811		6/53	Driving Trailer. Ex-LNWR 4023 (M28).
M70	2	1909	50'0"	27T	E9	6903;7321	7972-3	24483-4	5/53	6/56	Driving Trailers. Classified brake third and Ex-D337.
M71	9	1906	50'0"	27T	C9	6942;7088/ 7111/25;7224; 7335/7;7465; 7510	7296; 7974-81	24461; 24475-82	4/44	5/55 3/55	Driving Trailers. Classified brake third and cove roof version of M70. LNWR 6942 originally and wrongly inserted on M70, hence out of sequence numbers. It ran for a time as 22407 before becoming 24461. There were some detail variations in body work in this batch of coaches.
M72	2	1899	50'0"	24-5T	A8	7437;7678	7982-3	24487-8	2/39	5/40	Driving Trailers. Classified as brake third and probably ex-D289. No apparent difference to M60 (above). It is not clear whether 7767 ran as M72 before further conversion.
	1	1899	50'0"	25½T	A8	7767	to M73				
M73	2	1899/1902	50'0"	25T	A8	7683;7767	7984; 7599	24485-6	4/47	1/39	Driving Trailers. Classified as brake third and again ex-D289. Six compartment version of M72 and very similar to M59.
M74	1	1915	57'0"	28T	T9	1628	5357	15850		8/54	Ex-D283 and out of sequence in motor fitted diagram book.
M75	3	1906	57'0"	31-3T	C9	131;143;361	5221-3	3428-30	2/44	5/58	Cove roof corridor thirds ex-D264. LMS 3430 had 8ft bogies.
M76	6	1908-10	57'0"	29T	E8½	Various: 392-2171	4488;4502/ 15/31/3/85	to 76A			All corridor thirds ex-D265. Two conversion stages — see page 154. Some evidence that first conversion may have been post grouping. On original conversion, Diagram M76 had one lavatory /one luggage compartment, M77 had two lavatories.
M77	6						4435/7/47/ 50/89; 4556	to 76A			
M76A	13	1908-10	57'0"	29T	E8½		As above plus 4516	3431-43	1/51	6/56	
M78	2	1922	57'0"	27T	T9	7983;7986	7171/4	24489-90	9/61	3/62	Driving Trailers. Classified brake third and ex-D333. No 24489 to WR stock; 24490 to Dumfries 1949 (for Lockerbie service) and to Skipton in 1962.

Appendix IV — Aspects of LNWR Carriage Working c.1910–12

INTRODUCTION

Just as this book was going to press, I was very fortunate to be given sight of some fascinating documents relating to LNWR carriage working just before the first world war. It would have been too costly and time consuming to try and integrate the information with the main text but since it was largely self-contained, it did seem worthwhile adding some of the information in the form of a fourth Appendix to the book. For the source of the information I am very grateful to Mr. D.J. Clarke of the LNWR Society while the accompanying notes, maps and diagrams are the work of my good friend Don Rowland—who also unravelled most of the ramifications of the workings. The notes are given first, followed by the basic data and analyses on which they are based.

Notes on LNWR carriage working 1910 – 1912
D.P. Rowland

To the contemporary observer with any knowledge of railway history it is easy to see that the West Coast Main Line scene is a far cry from that in London & North Western Railway days. Not only has motive power changed dramatically with 'Georges', 'Princes' and 'Claughtons' giving way to sleek electric locomotives but trains of constant profile coaches, each train virtually a standard set, have replaced the infinite variety of coaching stock that was an LNWR express. What is less easy to appreciate is that the whole pattern of operation has changed along with the rolling stock.

Services today are based on speed and frequency with station stops cut down to a minimum and time-consuming tasks, such as parcels loading, eliminated. Furthermore, today's traveller is not accompanied by the amounts of luggage which his Edwardian counterpart found so necessary. All this has meant that the through coach, so much a feature of the pre-group railway scene, has now largely disappeared. With it the frequent and lengthy re-marshallings have also gone, although Preston and Carstairs do their best to keep the tradition alive. Thus we find that at Crewe in 1978 two minutes is a normal stop for an Inter-City train. In 1910 station duties often occupied ten minutes or more.

The through coach or through portion was a feature of virtually every LNWR express in 1910. On a very few trains, standard sets of coaches were beginning to appear (principally on the Euston and Birmingham services) but even these would be strengthened with extra vehicles on Mondays and Fridays. Apart from these few, almost every train out

of Euston conveyed coaches for a variety of destinations and the same applied to Up trains. Whilst the 50ft coach was the most common standard, 42, 45, 57 and 65ft vehicles were also in use to add variety to the scene.

Other features of the LNWR were its highly lucrative passenger train parcels business plus extensive letter post and parcels post traffic. Consequently, vans were frequently found on expresses, sometimes in profusion, and the company even ran corridor parcels trains with sorting en route. Add to this private party traffic in saloons, horse and carriage traffic and extra vehicles added at will to meet demand and one can begin to get some idea of the diversity of North Western passenger services. The next few pages give some examples of typical main line trains and show how the Premier Line used the vehicles described in the preceding pages. They have been taken from the L&NWR Carriage Marshalling Diagrams for July 1910. Reading the examples, some of the apparently hotch-potch collections of carriages seen behind 'George' in old railway photographs now begin to make sense. By way of added interest, an extended analysis of the carriage workings in connection with one such train (the 8.00 p.m. Hereford–Crewe) has been made.

These diagrams cover main line trains only and, again looking at the LNWR through contemporary 1978 eyes, it is easy to forget that the local passenger train, if less prestigious, was just as important as the express. Fewer details of local carriage workings have survived and those which have are less detailed than their main-line counterparts. However, analysis has been made of the diagrams for the Swansea and Central Wales lines in 1912 and the following notes (based on the diagrams) seem valid generalisations.

It is quite obvious that whilst the 50ft coach was common for main-line trains, local passengers were less lucky. It seems likely that the 28ft four-wheeler was in general use, at least in the Swansea District, and the appended drawing suggests probable formations. Nevertheless, all except one of the regular sets were equipped with electric lighting and the remaining set saw service only two days per week. The other feature of local services was the marked increase in traffic on market days and Saturdays. Thus, whilst the 9.20 p.m. train from Swansea to Pontardulais consisted of five (assumed) four wheelers, its Saturday equivalent, the 10.00 p.m. ex Swansea, loaded to eleven vehicles. Again, a study of the diagram gives a valuable insight into L&NWR operating methods.

Notes of Composition of Local Passenger Sets

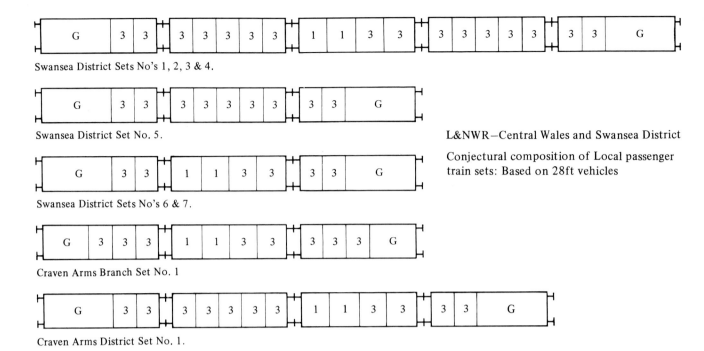

Swansea District Sets No's 1, 2, 3 & 4.

Swansea District Set No. 5.

Swansea District Sets No's 6 & 7.

Craven Arms Branch Set No. 1

Craven Arms District Set No. 1.

L&NWR—Central Wales and Swansea District

Conjectural composition of Local passenger train sets: Based on 28ft vehicles

Notes for diagram

Details of trains (All are L&NW Trains unless otherwise stated).

A	16.10 Cardiff (R.R.) to Merthyr. (Rhymney Rly. train).	
B	17.10 Merthyr to Hereford.	
C	20.00 Hereford to Crewe.	
D	17.35 Brecon to Moat Lane Jcn.	(Cambrian Rlys. train; it is assumed this joins with train E at Moat Lane Jcn. but this cannot be confirmed).
E	18.25 Aberystwyth to Shrewsbury	(Cambrian Rlys. train; through coaches to Tamworth and may also convey through vehicles to Whitchurch).
F	21.05 Welshpool to Shrewsbury	(Train E after re-marshalling).
G	21.00 Welshpool to Whitchurch	(Cambrian Rlys. train; see note to train E. In fact, this is probably a continuation of train E).
H	22.05 Shrewsbury to Crewe	(Train C after re-marshalling).
J	22.39 Whitchurch to Crewe	(Train H after re-marshalling).
K	22.50 Corridor Parcels Train Liverpool to Euston (24.00 ex Crewe).	
L	22.08 Shrewsbury to Tamworth	
M	23.01 Stafford to Tamworth	(Train L after re-marshalling).
N	??.?? Stafford to Euston	(Train K after re-marshalling).

Details of vehicles (All are L&NW unless otherwise stated).

1. Brake Van, Cardiff (R.R.) to Crewe. (Must be fitted with Westinghouse brake).
2. Sorting Van (corridor) Merthyr to Euston.
3. Composite, Hereford to Crewe.
4. Third, Hereford to Crewe.
5. Post Office, Hereford to Tamworth.
6. Brake Van, Hereford to Crewe.
7. Van (Cambrian Rlys.), Brecon to Crewe.
8. Tri-compo. (Cambrian Rlys.), Aberystwyth to Tamworth.
9. Brake Van (Cambrian Rlys.), Aberystwyth to Tamworth.
10. Parcels Van, Newtown to Euston. (Conveys Pryce Jones traffic; attached to train E at Newtown).
11. Tri-compo., Welshpool to Tamworth.
12. Brake Van (42ft.), Welshpool to Birmingham. (Detached at Stafford, whence forward at 01.00).
13. Van, Aberystwyth to Manchester.
14. Sorting Van, Windermere to Euston. (Via Liverpool, 18.30 ex W'mere).
15. Sorting Van, (Small) Liverpool to Euston—corridor vehicle.
16. Brake Van, Liverpool to Euston—corridor vehicle.
17. Sorting Van, Holyhead to Euston—corridor vehicle.
18. Brake Van, Leeds to Euston—corridor vehicle.
19. Sorting Van (Small), Rochdale to Poplar—corridor vehicle.
20. Brake Van, Manchester (L & Y) to Victoria (L B & S C).—corridor vehicle.
21. Brake Van, Manchester (L Rd.) to Waterloo (L & S W).—corridor vehicle.
22. Sorting Van, Manchester (L Rd.) to Birmingham—corridor vehicle.
23. Post Office (Cambrian Rlys.), Aberystwyth to Shrewsbury.
24. Brake Van, Stafford to Tamworth.

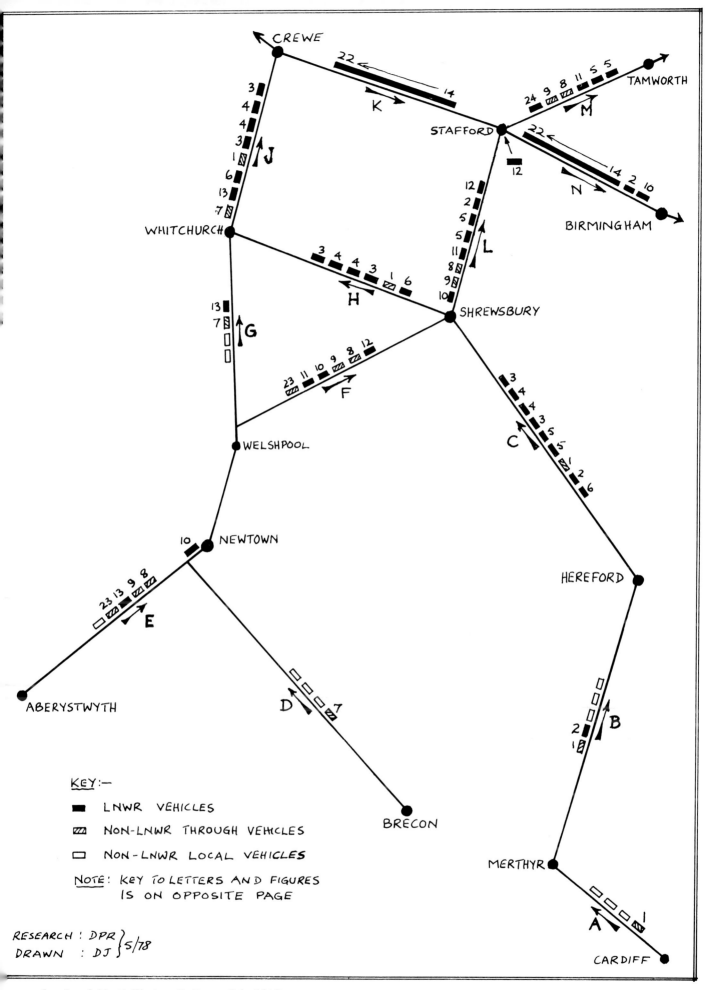

London & North Western Railway—July 1910
Diagrammatic Map (not to scale) showing carriage workings
in connection with the 8.00 p.m. Hereford—Crewe train.

Composition of Coupled Trains allocated to Central Wales and Swansea District.

Author's notes

How lettered.		No. of Vehicles	No. of compartments in each train		How lighted	REMARKS.
			First	Third		
Swansea District	No. 1 ..	5—5	2	16	Electric Light	
,, ,,	No. 2 ..	5—5	2	16	,,	
,, ,,	No. 3 ..	5—5	2	16	,,	
,, ,,	No. 4 ..	5—5	2	16	,,	
,,	No. 5 ..	3—3	..	9	,,	*Circuits 10 & 11.*
,, ,,	No. 6 ..	3—3	2	6	,,	Nos. 6 and 7 strengthened by additional five-bodied Third in Summer.
,, LLANDOVERY No. 7 ..		3—3	2	6	,,	*see Main Availability table.*
Craven Arms Branch No. 1 ..		3—3	2	8	,,	*Circuit Nº 13*
Craven Arms District No. 1 ..		4—4	2	11	Gas.	*Circuit 14.*

For conjectural composition of these sets—see overleaf.

2.
Twin Train 5—5

Swansea.   Pontardulais.

```
          am                                  am
   C  10 48 < ——————————————————— 10 10
          pm                                  pm
      ┌ 3 50 ——————————————————— > 4 30
      │ 5 33 < ——————————————————— 4 55
   A ─┤ 5 50 ——————————————————— > 6 26
      └ 7 42 < ——————————————————— 7  0
   B  9 20 ——————————————————— > 9 56
```

Saturdays Excepted.

A—An additional Third Class to be attached in front of 3-50 pm to work on these 4 trains (Fridays excepted), and detached on arrival at Swansea at 7-42 pm. On Fridays a Set of 3 Third Class Coaches, together with a Break Carriage, to be attached in rear of the 3-50 pm ex Swansea so that it can be detached at Gowerton off the 5-50 pm from Swansea for use on No. 5 Circuit Saturdays.

B—On Fridays this train to be strengthened with chained set of 3 Third Class Coaches for use on No. 8 Circuit Saturdays.

C—Break Van from Brynamman works daily on this train (L. & N.W. and G.W. Vans, alternate days).

Typical circuits worked by Swansea District sets.

6.

Twin Train 5—5 Strengthened by Swansea extra Set No. 3—3

[Duplicates Circuit Nº 1.]

Swansea.   Pontardulais.

```
   am                                  am
   7 35 ——————————————————— > 8 11
```

As above and Strengthened by G.W. Break Third.

```
   9 30 < ——————————————————— 8 50
```

Twin Train 5—5 and Swansea extra Set No. 3—3

```
   am                                  am
   10 10 Goods———————— attached ———— > 10 50
   pm                                  noon
   12 57 < ——————————————————— 12 12
```

Twin Train 5—5 together with Swansea extra Sets Nos. 1 & 3—6

```
   pm                                  pm
   10  0 ——————————————————— > 10 42
   11 30 < ——————————————————— 11  0
```

SATURDAYS ONLY.

13

Twin Train 3—3

Craven Arms.   Knighton.   Builth Road.

```
                        am              am
                        9 40 < —attached— 8 41
          pm            pm
   A—1  5 < ——————— 12 35
   A—3 15 ——————— > 3 45
     5 35 < ——————— 5  5
                                              pm
     7 10 ——————————————————— > 8 37
```

A—Thursdays excepted.

Worked by Craven Arms Branch set No. 1.

14

Twin Set of Four strengthened as required.

Swansea   Llandrindod Wells

```
   am                                  am
   9  0 ——————————————————— > 11 36
   pm                                  pm
   10 30 < ——————————————————— 7 20
```

Thursdays and Saturdays only.

Commencing June 13th.

Worked by Craven Arms District set No. 1.

8.30 p.m. from Euston.
(Postal Train.)

			Balanced at
Break Van	(50 ft.)	}	3 40 p.m.
Parcel Van A	(42 ft.)	} Aberdeen	3 40 ,,
Parcel Van B	(42 ft.)	}	3 40 ,,
Sorting Carriage	(42 ft.)		1 10 ,,
Sorting Carriage	(50 ft.)	} Glasgow	5 55 ,,
Letter Tender	(42 ft.)	}—Edinburgh	7 0 ,,
Parcel Van	(42 ft.)	} Glasgow	6 55 ,,
Break Van	(50 ft.)	}	
5-Bodied Parcel Van		{ Liverpool (via Preston)	10│50 ,,
5-Bodied Parcel Van		}—Manchester	10 45 ,,

Crewe to detach the Manchester Parcel Van, and send forward at 12.20 a.m.
Preston to detach the Liverpool Parcel Van, and send to Liverpool by the 1.7 a.m. train.
Carlisle to attach Break Van for Glasgow off 8.0 p.m. from Euston.

A Saturdays excepted.
B On Saturday nights this vehicle only goes to Perth, and returns thence at 4.6 p.m. on Sundays.
C On Saturdays only, via Warrington, and the 11.31 p.m. thence.

8.45 p.m. from Euston.

			Balanced at
Sorting Van	(X)		8 5 a.m.
Two Post Offices			12 22 ,,
Parcel Van	(65 ft.) (X)	} Holyhead	12 22 ,,
Sleeping Saloon	(57 ft.) (X)	}	12 22 ,,
Break Third	(57 ft.) (X)	}	5 30 p.m.
Second Class	(57 ft.) (X)	}	5 30 ,,
First Class	(57 ft.)		5 30 ,,
Break Van	(50 ft.)	}—Manchester	5 30 ,,
§Break Van (News)			5 30 ,,

On Wednesdays an extra Van to be attached for American Mails.
On Saturdays an extra Break Van (42 ft.) to be attached for Holyhead for parcel post.
Luggage for the Irish Mail steamer must be loaded in the front part of the train, and luggage for North Wall in the Break Van.

§ Saturdays only. Goes forward from Crewe by 12.20 a.m.

12.20 a.m. from Crewe.
(Mondays excepted.)

Break Van	(45 ft.)	(X) } Plymouth to Manchester
G. W. Tri Composite		(X) }
G. W. Third Class		(X) { London to Manchester
Parcel Van		{ Holyhead to Manchester
Trucks, &c.		}—Manchester
Parcel Van		{ Aberystwyth to Manchester
Break Van (C.m.)		{ Pembroke Dock to Manchester
ABreak Van	(X)	}

A Sunday mornings excepted.

10.45 p.m. from Liverpool.
(York Mail.)

			Balanced at
Break Carriage(2&3)		{ Manchester (L. Rd.), via Stockport	9│D25 a.m.
Break (Post Office)		}—Huddersfield	11│A12 p.m.
CThird Class		} York	9│A35 ,,
Tri Composite		}	
Break Van		}—Warrington	
CParcel Van (Mails)			B

A Via Wigan.
B Saturdays only.
C Works forward to London by Up Limited Mail at 11.31 p.m., returning to Liverpool at 8.30 p.m.
D To Crewe, and 2.15 p.m. thence.

Vehicles for the North Eastern Line for beyond Leeds must be fitted with the Dual Break complete.

12.40 a.m. from Crewe.
(Down York Mail.)
(Including Sundays—not Mondays.)

			Balanced at
ABreak Van	(50 ft.)—Crewe to Newcastle		12 22 ,,
*G.W. B'k Compo. (1 & 3)		{ Cardiff to Newcastle	
Post Office		{ Cardiff to York	
Post Office		{ Shrewsbury to York	
P.O.P. Sorting Van		} York	
Tri Composite	(42 ft.) (X)	{ Swansea to York	
Break Van		}—Tipton to Leeds	
Sausage Van		{ Leeds and Yorkshire	
Break Van		{ Holyhead to Leeds	

A Huddersfield to attach York vehicles off 10.45 p.m. from Lime Street. Works forward from Crewe to Euston by 11.38 a.m. from Carlisle, and returns from Euston 1.30 p.m. Crewe by 5.35 a.m. train. Must be fitted with Westinghouse break complete.

Vehicles for the North Eastern Line for beyond Leeds must be fitted with the Dual Break complete.

11.0 p.m. from Birmingham.

			Balanced at
Break Van	(X)—Holyhead		2 0 a.m.
Sorting Van	(X)—Manchester		11 55 p.m.
Sorting Van	(X)—Liverpool		2 35 a.m.
Break Composite	(42 ft.) (X)	}	
Third Class	(X)	} Stafford	5A35 p.m.
Two Tri Compo.	(42 ft.) (X)	}	
Break Van	(X)	}	

A From London.

8.50 p.m. from Euston.
(Saturdays excepted.)

			Balanced at
Break Van(L&N W)	(42 ft.)—Carlisle		1│C40 p.m.
Composite		{ Glasgow	5 55 ,,
Break Van (Parcels)		}	
Third Class		{ London to Perth	8 12 ,,
		{ London to Aberdeen	1 10 ,,
Composite		{ London to Edinburgh	9 5 ,,
Break Van		}	
Composite		{ London to Holyhead	2 30 a.m.
Break Van		}	
Parcel Sorting Van		}—Holyhead	6 0 p.m.

Crewe to detach Holyhead van and send forward by the 10.15 a.m. from Euston, and attach in rear a Break Composite for Edinburgh from July 1st to 22nd and Sept. 1st to 30th, and the Edinburgh coach (July 24th to September 1st) off the 7.40 p.m. from Bristol.

C To Liverpool, and 8.0 a.m. thence to Stafford; 7.10 p.m. Stafford to London.

4.10 p.m. from Euston.
(Corridor Train.)

			Balanced at
Break Van		—Fleetwood	
Break Van			
Break Second	(57 ft.)		10│50 p.m.
Third Class	(57 ft.)	}—Huddersfield	9 45 a.m.
2nd & 3rd Dining Car	(65 ft.)	} Liverpool	11│15 ,,
1st Dining Car	(65 ft.)		11│15 ,,
Break First	(57 ft.)		9 45 ,,
†Break TriCompo.	(57 ft.)	—Blackp'l(Cen)	7 50 ,,
‡Break Tri Composite	(57 ft.)	—Llandudno	8 55 ,,

Rugby to attach Slip Carriage for Nuneaton.
The Llandudno carriage to go forward from Crewe in rear of the 8.0 p.m. train.
The Fleetwood van and Blackpool coach to go forward in front and rear respectively of the 7.55 p.m. train.
On Saturdays the Train to be marshalled as under:—

Liverpool portion	
Fleetwood Van	
Parcel Van	
P. O. Tender	}—Holyhead
P. O. Carriage	
Bk.TriCompo.(50 ft.)(X)	}
Blackpool portion	
Llandudno portion	

When this Train is divided on Saturdays the Llandudno coach will be marshalled next in rear of the Holyhead Mail portion.
Crewe to despatch the Holyhead portion on Saturdays at 7.47 p.m.
Chester to attach Parcel Van with Mails from Liverpool to 7.47 p.m. from Crewe on Saturdays.

A From Warwick.
B Sundays.
C To Cambridge.
D From Stafford.

4.10 p.m. from Bristol.

			Balanced at
(12.11 p.m. from Plymouth.)			2 0 a.m.
(12.32 p.m. from Plymouth.)			11 55 p.m.
(3.8 p.m. from Taunton.)			2 35 a.m.
(4.15 p.m. from Cardiff.)			
(3.5 p.m. from Swansea.)			
†G. W. Break Compo. (1 & 3)		{ Cardiff to Manchester	5A35 p.m.
†G. W. Break Compo. (1 & 3)		{ Kingswear to Manchester	
†G. W. Break Third	(X)	{ Plymouth to Manchester	
*G.W Break Compo	(X)(1&3)	{ Plymouth to Leeds	
†G.W.Break Compo	(X)(1&3)	{ Plymouth to Liverpool	
G. W. Dining Car		{ Penzance to Liverpool	
*G. W. Break Third	(X)	{	

Shrewsbury to attach in front the following vehicles off 5.12 p.m. from Hereford:—

‡Break Tri Composite		{ Swansea to Liverpool
Tri Composite	(57 ft.) (X)	{ Swansea to Manchester
Break Van		{ Swansea to Manchester
Break Composite (1 & 3)	(45 ft.)	{ Pembroke Dock to Manchester

4.30 p.m. from Euston.

			Balanced at
Break Van	(X)	}	
Third Class	(X)	} Birmingham	11│A10 a.m.
Tri Composite	(57 ft.) (X)	}	
Tri Composite	(57 ft.) (X)	}	
Break Carriage	(65 ft.) (X)	}	9│B 0 ,,
Tri Composite	(65 ft.) (X)	}	
Break Van	(57 ft.) (X)	{ Melton Mowbray	

An extra Tri Composite for Melton Mowbray to be run on Fridays.

A Work locally to Dudley at 10.45 p.m. and return as shown.
B From Nottingham.

} 3 10 p.m. — Shrewsbury

4.45 p.m. from Euston.

			Balanced at
Break Third	(57 ft.) (X)	}	11│C20 a.m.
Third Class	(57 ft.) (X)	} Shrewsbury	8│A 5 ,,
Double Composite	(X)	}	11 20 ,,
Break First	(57 ft.) (X)	}	8 45 ,,
Composite Tea Car	(65 ft.)	—Wolverhampton	
Break Tri Compo.	(50 ft.)(X)	—Dudley	
Break Tri Composite	(X)	—Walsall	
Slip Carriage		{ Rugby (for Warwick)	

The Warwick slip carriage to go forward from Rugby at 6.16 p.m.
Euston to attach an extra Tri Composite (X) for Dudley on Fridays.

A Wolverhampton.
B Fitted with Typewriting Room.
C From Walsall.

5.30 p.m. from Euston.
(Corridor Train.)

			Balanced at
†Break Tri Composite	(57 ft.) (X)	} Birkenhead	9 5 a.m.
‡Tri Compo. Dining Car	(65 ft.) (X)	}	10│B28 ,,
‡Break Tri Composite	(57 ft.)	}	3C38 p.m.
Break Van	(45 ft.)	}	
Tri Composite	(57 ft.)	}—Fleetwood	6│A 5 a.m.
Tri Compo. Dining Car	(57 ft.)	}	
Break Third	(57 ft.)	}	
Slip Carriage		—Nuneaton (for Buxton)	7 50 ,,

Crewe to send the Birkenhead coaches forward at 8.36 p.m. with a Break Third (57 ft.) (X), Tri Composite (X), and Break Carriage (X) for Llandudno in rear, and despatch the Fleetwood train at 8.30 p.m.

A Not Mondays. Return 8.5 a.m. Sundays.
B To Crewe, and forward at 5.33 p.m.
C To Liverpool. Works 10.15 a.m., Llandudno to Liverpool.
D From Liverpool.
H From Chester.

5.25 p.m. from Broad Street.
(Saturdays excepted.)
(Corridor Train.)

			Balanced at
ABreak Compo. (1 & 2)	(57 ft.)	}	10 30 a.m.
Tri Composite Dining Car	(65 ft.) (X)	}—Wolverhampton	
Tri Composite	(57 ft.)	}	2 45 p.m.
Break Third	(X)	}	

A Fitted with Typewriting Room.

7.55 p.m. from Birmingham.

			Balanced at
Break Tri Composite	(X)	} Manchester	4│B10 p.m.
Third Class	(X)	}	1│B32 ,,
Composite	(X)	{ Liverpool	5│C30 ,,
Tri Composite	(X)	—Wolverhampton	2 35 a.m.
Local portion			8 5 ,,

Empty stock must not be attached to this train.

A Fridays only.
B From Leeds.
C Saturdays only.
§ Saturdays excepted.

Crewe to despatch the Manchester train with leader at 8.10 p.m., and the Liverpool train at 8.15 p.m.

Two typical pages of "down" trains—LNWR 1910

7.15 a.m. from Liverpool.

*G. W. Break Composite ... Crewe
*G. W. Break Third
Third Class
Tri Composite (42 ft.) } London
Tri Composite (42 ft.)
BParcel Sorting Van (small) (X)
Break Van (X) } Crewe to attach a Break Third for Stafford received off the 9.30 p.m. from Manchester.

A From Bristol. Works the 3.65 p.m. Crewe to Weston.
B Mondays excepted. From Newton-le-Willows with Stationery.
{ From Cardiff. Works 3.55 p.m. Crewe to Cardiff.

8.30 a.m. from Manchester (= 14¼).

	Balanced at
	(Via Colwich.)
Break First (57 ft.) (X) } London	12E40 p.m.
First Class (67 ft.) (X)	12A45 ,,
Second Class (57 ft.) (X)	7 10 a.m.
Third Class	10 0 p.m.
SComposite	—
SThird Class	10 0 ,,
Parcel Van	3 0 a.m.
Fish Vans (3)	—N.S. Line
Manchester to attach an extra Third Class (X) for London on Mondays.	4 5 p.m.
Nuneaton to attach in rear Break Tri Composite from Buxton to London.	

A From London.
B Slip Carriage.
S Saturdays only.

8.0 a.m. from Liverpool.
(Corridor Train.)

Break Van	12S10 a.m.
Third Class	12S10 ,,
Tri Composite } London	12S10 ,,
Tri Composite	10 0 ,,
Composite (1 & 3)	5 35 ,,
Break Carriage	5 35 ,,
1st Breakfast Car (65 ft.) } Stafford	A
2nd & 3rd B'fast Car (65 ft.)	—
Break Van	7010 a.m.
Liverpool to attach extra Break Tri Composite (X) on Mondays.	12B 0 night
Bletchley to attach Break Tri Composite (57 ft.) from Banbury in rear.	4C 5 p.m.

A The Breakfast Carriages attached at Stafford to London, and return at
9.45 a.m. from Liverpool to London by 10.49 a.m. train from Crewe.
D Works 7.10 p.m., Stafford to London, and 7.10 to Crewe, and thence locally to Liverpool.
S Leaves at 12.0 night on Saturdays.

8.15 a.m. from Liverpool.

Post Office	—
ABreak Van } Crewe	4 35 a.m.
APost Office	11B40 ,,
Tri Composite (12 ft.) } Shrewsbury	4 55 ,,
Tri Composite (42 ft.)	11C25 ,,
Break Van	11C25 ,,
} Aberystwyth	9 5 ,,

8.25 a.m. from Manchester.

G. W. Vehicles —G. W. Line	12 30 p.m.
ABreak Van } Swansea	11B40 ,,
Break Van } Aberystwyth	2 30 ,,
Tri Composite (42 ft.) } Aberystwyth	6 40 a.m.
Third Class	—
Break Van (Fish) (X) } Crewe	9 5 a.m.
An extra Third Class for Aberystwyth to be run on Saturday and Mondays.	

9.30 a.m. from Crewe.

Third Class } Liverpool to Shrewsbury	—
BThird Class	—
Tri Composite (42 ft.) } Manchester to Swansea	—
Break Van	—
Break Van } Manchester to London	—
Tri Composite (42 ft.)	—
BThird Class } Manchester to Aberystwyth	—
Third Class	—
Tri Composite (42 ft.) } Liverpool to Aberystwyth	—
Break Van	—

Whitchurch to detach the Aberystwyth vehicles and despatch at 10.5 a.m.
Shrewsbury to detach the Manchester to Swansea vehicles and send forward at 10.30 a.m.
B Saturdays and Mondays.

9.30 a.m. from Wolverhampton.
(10.5 a.m. from Birmingham.)

Break First (57 ft.) (X)	—
Double Composite (67 ft.) (X) } London	—
Third Class (57 ft.) (X)	—
Break Third (X)	—
BThird Class (57 ft.)	—
BBreak Composite (1 & 3) (X) } Yarmouth	5B30 p.m.
Local portion } Rugby	4 1 p.m.

An extra Third Class for Euston to be run on Mondays, and an extra Third Class for Yarmouth on Fridays.
Northampton to attach Tri Composite, with an extra Tri Composite on Mondays only, (X) and Break Van (X), Melton Mowbray to London, and Slip coach for Bletchley.
Rugby to detach the Yarmouth vehicle, and attach to 11.15 a.m. to Peterboro'.

10.50 a.m. from Wolverhampton.
(11.25 a.m. from Birmingham.)
(Corridor Train.)

Break First (57 ft.)	—
Double Composite (67 ft.) } London	—
1st Luncheon Car	—
2nd & 3rd Luncheon Car (65 ft.)	—
Third Class	—
Break Third	—
BTri Composite	—

An additional Third Class (X) and 2nd and 3rd Luncheon Car to be run on Mondays from Wolverhampton.
A Saturdays.
B To London on Sundays.

9.10 a.m. from Liverpool.

†G. W. Break Third (X)	12 32 p.m.
*G. W. Dining Car } Plymouth	—
*G. W. Break Compo. (X) (1 & 3)	—

9.25 a.m. from Manchester.

Break Carriage (2 & 3) —Crewe	10B45 p.m.
†G. W. Break Compo. (X) (1&3) } Manchester to Plymouth	7 A0 a.m.
*G. W. Break Third (X)	—
*G. W. Break Composite (1&3) } Cardiff	4 15 a.m.
MBreak Third	—

A From Penzance to Manchester.
M Mondays only. Works 2.15 p.m., Crewe to Liverpool.
Crewe to attach the Liverpool train in front and despatch at 10.17 a.m.

11.38 p.m. from Carlisle.
(9.5 p.m. from Glasgow.)
(9.5 p.m. from Edinburgh.)

	Balanced at
Break Van } Glasgow to Birmingham	8 C0 p.m.
Composite (50 ft.) } Gourock to London	9A50 a.m.
Break Van (X)	9 B30 p.m.
DComposite } Glasgow to London	9 0 ,,
Sleeping Saloon (65 ft.)	9 0 ,,
Third Class } Edinburgh to London	8 50 ,,
Composite (42 ft.)	9 0 ,,
Break Van } Glasgow to London	9 0 ,,
Break Van (50 ft.)	

Crewe to attach Break Van from Newcastle to London, received off the 12.18 a.m. from Stockport.
Stafford to detach the Birmingham vehicles.

A From Liverpool to Glasgow. Works 7.20 a.m. to Glasgow.
B To Gourock, and returns at 12.5 p.m., Birmingham to London.
C From Glasgow on Saturdays only.
D From Glasgow on Saturdays only.

12.15 a.m. from Carlisle.
(Including Sundays—not Mondays.)
(5.45 p.m. from Perth.)
(8.12 p.m. from Aberdeen.)

SFish Van } Aberdeen to Carnforth	Stock
Break Van } Aberdeen to Liverpool	10K10 p.m.
Post Office	B
ESleeping Composite } Perth to Liverpool	10 10 ,,
Break (45 ft.) } Aberdeen to London	11C35 ,,
Break Van	8 50 ,,
Third Class } Perth to London	11 35 ,,
Sleeping Saloon (65 ft.) } Aberdeen to London	
Composite	
Break Van } Aberdeen to Manchester	10K15 ,,

Wigan to detach the Liverpool and Manchester vehicles.

B Works from Liverpool to London by 12.0 noon Mail, returning by 7.10 a.m., Euston to Carlisle, and thence by 8.42 a.m. Carlisle to Aberdeen, on Sunday mornings; it works to Wigan, and is returned to Carlisle per 2.18 p.m. train from Aberdeen.
C To Perth, and forward to Aberdeen at 12.15 p.m. Leaves Aberdeen 3.60 p.m.
E Will run from July 25th to August 12th only.
K July 25th to August 12th only. Except during the period named, the Vans return to Wigan by 6.0 a.m. and 7.50 a.m. trains from Manchester and Liverpool respectively, to go forward by down stock train.
S Saturdays from Scotland excepted.

2.35 a.m. from Liverpool.
(4.30 a.m., Crewe to Birmingham.)
(Including Sundays—not Mondays.)

	Balanced at
Break Van } Crewe to Birmingham	11 0 p.m.
Sorting Van (45 ft.)	8 30 ,,
Break Van (50 ft.)	8 30 ,,
First Class (57 ft.)	10 15 p.m.
Sleeping Saloon (65 ft.) } London	8 30 a.m.
Second Class (57 ft.)	8 30 p.m.
Third Class (57 ft.)	10 15 ,,
Break Third (57 ft.)	8 30 a.m.
†Break Tri Composite (57 ft.)—Birmingham	2 55 p.m.

Crewe to detach the Birmingham vehicles and send forward at 4.30 a.m.

1.0 a.m. from Carlisle.
(Including Sundays.)
(10.45 p.m. from Glasgow.)
(10.50 p.m. from Edinburgh.)

	Balanced at
Break Third	
Third Class } Glasgow to London	11 55 p.m.
Sleeping Saloon (65 ft.)	
BSleeping Saloon (65 ft.)	
Composite	11 35 ,,
Break Van (50 ft.)	
Third Class } Edinburgh to London	
Sleeping Saloon (65ft.)	
Break Composite	Stock.
ABreak Third (C.R.) } Glasgow to Southampton	

A Fridays only.
B Saturdays from Glasgow excepted.

2.0 a.m. from Holyhead.
(Including Sundays—not Mondays.)
(Corridor Train.)

} Birmingham	
Break Van (45 ft.)	11 0 p.m.
Sorting Van (50 ft.)	8 30 ,,
Break Van (57 ft.)	8 30 ,,
Sleeping Saloon (65 ft.)	10 15 p.m.
Second Class (57 ft.) } London	8 30 ,,
Third Class (57 ft.)	8 30 ,,
Break Third (57 ft.)	10 15 ,,
†Break Tri Composite (57 ft.)—Birmingham	2 55 p.m.

Crewe to attach in front Break Van and Break Tri Composite (X) off 2.0 a.m. from Holyhead for Birmingham.
A Holyhead.
B To Crewe.
C From Carlisle.

1.20 a.m. from Carlisle.

Will run through to London daily, commencing August 2nd, until then will be attached to the 1.50 a.m. from Carlisle whenever possible.
(Including Sundays—not Mondays.)
(5.0 p.m., July and August only, 5.15 p.m., September only, from Perth.)
(9.40 p.m. from Perth.)
(7 0 p.m. from Oban.)

} Inverness to Carlisle A	9 0 p.m.
CSleeping Composite (50 ft.) } Perth to London	8 50 ,,
CComposite	1 0 a.m.
Sleeping Saloon } Inverness to London	A
Third Class	
Composite } Edinburgh to London	
Sleeping Saloon (65 ft.) } Oban to London	12 45 a.m.
Composite	
Sleeping Composite Break } Glasgow to Manchester	
Post Office (45 ft.)—Carlisle to London	
Sleeping Composite Break } Glasgow to Liverpool	

Crewe to attach Third Class for London.
Carlisle to attach the London Vehicles (with the exception of those marked C) to the 1.50 a.m. whenever possible up till August 2nd.
A Will run through to Euston from August 2nd.
B To Aberdeen. Returns 8.40 a.m. locally to Perth. These vehicles to work up by Stock train until August 2nd.

	Balanced at
} Inverness to Carlisle	7 45 p.m.
} Perth to London	8 B 0 ,,
} Inverness to London	7 45 ,,
} Oban to London	8 0 ,,

Two typical pages of "up" trains—LNWR 1910

References

To provide a conventional bibliography is difficult since there are few books which make much more than brief reference to LNWR coaches – and some of these contain considerable inaccuracies. However, there follows a list of articles (not exhaustive), known to the author, together with a few published book titles, which should be available through a good reference library should the reader feel so inclined. Attention is particularly drawn to the fine series of comprehensive contemporary articles in the Railway Engineer which go a long way to cover many of the technical aspects of the subject which lack of space has prevented from inclusion here.

Railway Engineer:

March 1893	WCJS Dining Cars
May 1893	WCJS and LNWR Dining Cars
	Leeds-Liverpool 42ft stock
November 1893	First WCJS Corridor Trains
September 1894	LNWR Carriage Brake (p291)
December 1895	WCJS 42ft Sleeping Saloons
May 1896	First 65ft 6in Dining Cars
January 1898	50ft arc roof corridor dining carriages
February 1899	65ft 6in clerestory Sleeping Saloons
	42ft Picnic Saloons
March 1899	65ft 6in clerestory Sleeping Saloon with transverse centre vestibules
	45ft Family Saloon
July 1901	65ft 6in composite Dining Cars
October 1901	Twelve wheel underframe details
October 1902	32ft Invalid Carriage
April 1903	The Royal Saloons
February 1904	The Semi-Royal Saloons
July 1904	WCJS 9ft wide clerestory Sleeping Saloons
October 1905	Steam Railmotor No. 1 (also December 1905)
February 1906	WCJS 9ft wide composite Dining Cars
July 1906	LNWR Motor Car Trucks (p203)
July 1907	50ft Invalid Saloons
October 1907	American Special Trains
January 1912	50ft Corridor Thirds
	Carriage Heating apparatus (p5)
April 1912	Kitchens and Pantries of LNWR (and other companies)
	Dining Cars
November 1913	New WCJS corridor trains (57ft toplight series)
December 1913	WCJS corridor trains (continued)
August 1914	WCJS 68ft elliptical roof Sleeping Saloons, including underframes.

Note: Several references to LNWR carriages can be found in the many issues of 'The LNWR Society Journal', published at regular intervals since 1973

Railways of England. W.M. Ackworth, John Murray, 1900
Our Home Railways Volume Two. W.J. Gordon. Warne & Co., 1910
Railway Carriages 1839-1939. G.M. Kichenside. Ian Allan 1964
Railway Carriages in the British Isles. C. Hamilton Ellis. Allen & Unwin, 1965
Railway Carriage Album. G.M. Kichenside. Ian Allan 1966
LNWR Portrayed. Jack Nelson. Peco Publications 1975
LNWR Miscellany Volumes 1 and 2. E. Talbot. Oxford Publishing Co. 1978 and 1980
A Register of West Coast Joint Stock. R.M. Casserley and P.A. Millard. Historical Model Railway Society 1980
The Trainmakers – the story of Wolverton Works. Bill West. Barracuda Books 1982
LNWR Liveries. Talbot, Millard, Dow and Davies. Historical Model Railway Society 1985 (reissued in conjunction with Pendragon, 1993)
The Railwaymen – Wolverton. Bill West. Barracuda Books 1987
The London & Birmingham – a railway of consequence. David Jenkinson. Capital Transport 1988
The Moving Force – the men of Wolverton. Bill West. Barracuda Books 1988
British Railway Carriages of the 20th Century, Volumes 1 and 2. David Jenkinson, Patrick Stephens Ltd 1988 and 1990
LNWR Great War Ambulance Trains. Philip A. Millard. LNWR Society 1993
Ambulance Trains – LNWR Gazette 1914
New Electric Rolling Stock – LNWR Gazette 1914
New Ambulance Trains – LNWR Gazette 1915
The Dining Saloon Depot, Euston – LNWR Gazette 1916
The Travelling Post Office – LNWR Gazette 1916
United States Ambulance Train – LNWR Gazette 1918
Wolverton Carriage Works – Railway Magazine (1914)
Dinner is Served (featuring LNWR Dining Cars) – Railway World 1969
Wolverton and the Royal Connection. David Jenkinson. Railways South East Vol. 1 No. 3. Capital Transport 1988

Index